To C/E. Robert Mueller—
Many thanks from
coming aboard today—
Smooth sailing — calm seas

Walter *signature*
6/6/0*?*

signature

SS *Jeremiah O'Brien*

The History of a Liberty Ship
from
The Battle of the Atlantic
to the 21st Century

Capt. Walter W. Jaffee

The Glencannon Press

Palo Alto
2004

Published by The Glencannon Press
P.O. Box 341, Palo Alto, CA 94302
Tel. 800-711-8985, Fax. 707-747-0311
www.glencannon.com

First Edition, first printing.

Library of Congress Cataloging-in-Publication Data available on request.

Publisher's note: Every effort is made to obtain and reproduce the best quality photographs. Due to wartime conditions, and the age of the photos available, or, in the case of photos from the 1994 voyage back to Normandy which were taken from newspapers of the day, a number are of lesser quality. They have nevertheless been used.

Dedication

To all the friends of the *Jeremiah O'Brien*
— past, present and future.

~

To Shelley

Other works by the same author.

Non-fiction:
The Last Mission Tanker
The Lane Victory, *the Last Victory Ship in War and in Peace*
The Last Liberty, the Biography of the SS Jeremiah O'Brien
Appointment in Normandy
The Track of the Golden Bear, *the Training Ships of California Maritime Academy*
The Presidential Yacht Potomac
Heritage of the Sea, the Training Ships of Maine Maritime Academy
Steel Shark in the Pacific, USS Pampanito
Recipes From a Coal-fired Stove
The Liberty Ships From A to Z

Fiction
Union Gold (as Mark West)

Editor
The Glencannon Encyclopedia
The Diogenes Club Speaks (co-editor)

Contributor
Naval Warfare, An International Encyclopedia
[VMI Encyclopedia of Naval History]

The pathway of man's journey through the ages is littered with the wreckage of nations which, in their hour of glory, forgot their dependence on the sea.

Brigadier General J.D. Little, USMC

ACKNOWLEDGMENTS

This book would not have been possible without the kind help and cooperation of many people. Among them are: Lisbet Bailey, Dan Bandy, Robert Blake, Bob Burnett, Vincent Carista, Rosario Carista, Nicholas Carista, Bob Crocker, John Crosby, Tom Ender, Francis Erdman, Albert Haas, Judy Hitzeman, Ken Holsapple, Marci Hooper, Charles Hord, Captain George Jahn, Henry Kusel, Ted Martin, Tom McGeehan, Robert Milby, Harry Morgan, Joanie Morgan, Ernest Murdock, Captain James Nolan, Admiral Thomas J. Patterson, Norman Robinson, Rochelle Rose, Carl Scharpf, Coleman Schneider, Phil Sinnott, E. Ray Sharpe, Jerome Shaw, Neil Thomeson, William Watson and Morgan Williams.

The quotes by Bill Boissonneault in chapter three are taken from the book, *Portland Ships Are Good Ships*, by Herbert G. Jones.

Robert T. Young, President of the American Bureau of Shipping is quoted from his article, "The Lessons of the Liberties," published by that organization in 1974.

The section on the Neptune ceremony appearing in chapter 13 is adapted from copies of such ceremonies which were conducted during World War II on the *President Polk* and the *Carlos Carillo*.

Many of the quotes by Admiral Tom Patterson in chapter fifteen are taken from an article titled "How We Saved the *Jeremiah O'Brien*" which appeared in *Sea History* in the Winter 1988-89 edition. I am grateful to the National Maritime Historical Society and Peter Stanford for granting permission to quote from the article.

A special thanks to Albert Haas for providing copies of his diary, Captain De Smedt's voyage letter and other valuable information.

Award-winning photographer George Bonawit graciously provided the photos for both the front and back covers of the dustjacket.

A special note of thanks to the *San Francisco Chronicle* for allowing me to reproduce portions of articles and to Phil Frank for his permission to include Bruce the Raven on our crew list. Bruce is actually one of only two permanent crew of the *O'Brien* (the other is Miss Jerry O'Brien who occupies the forward guntub). Bruce is berthed in the crow's nest on the foremast.

Finally, I would like to thank my editor who prodded, poked, cajoled, sympathized and encouraged me to keep on track and finish. Without her help it might never have been done.

CONTENTS

FOREWORD

The SS *Jeremiah O'Brien* occupies a unique historical berth. She is the last active ship in the world that took part in the greatest sea assault in history — the invasion of Northern France and the liberation of Europe that began on D-Day, June 6, 1944. Of the more than 5,000 ships that supported that epic battle, only she remains. She is the last unaltered Liberty in existence; others were modified during or after that war.

The *O'Brien* also was the first of the World War II merchant marine museum ships. She tested the waters for those to follow. The Liberty ship *John W. Brown*, berthed in Baltimore, Maryland and the Victory ships *American Victory, Lane Victory* and *Red Oak Victory* are maritime museums in their own right, but the *Jeremiah O'Brien* began it all. Her champions conceived the idea, secured support, guided bills through Congress, raised grants and finally established the vessel at a permanent berth, surveying the figuratively unexplored seas so that the ships that followed found themselves sailing through charted waters.

I first met the SS *Jeremiah O'Brien* in 1986. I boarded her not expecting much. Freighters are freighters. They earn their keep by carrying cargo of all types. In the course of their working lives little time is available for cosmetics — making the ship look clean and nice. Tight cargo schedules, heavy seas and extremes in weather make more than basic maintenance impractical. In addition, I knew she had languished at the Suisun Bay Reserve Fleet for thirty-three years and had been out of "mothball" status for only seven years. So I expected to see a working freighter with rust streaks, more than a few dents and scrapes, a ship well-used but sturdy.

On stepping aboard my first impression was surprise at her immaculate condition. You could almost literally eat off her decks. She looked as pristine as she must have on her launching day in 1943. Her deck was spotless, inside and out her brass gleamed, paint was fresh and her engine purred.

Eventually I got to know the ship and her crew and found her appearance epitomized the care, pride and professionalism of her volunteers. They were Liberty ship sailors. They had suffered the rigors of a global war on the oceans of the world. From the Admiralty Islands and the Philippines to Normandy and Murmansk, they knew what it was like to see their shipmates work and fight and die and wonder if their number would be the next to be called.

The SS *Jeremiah O'Brien* had also been there. She was part of the lore of World War II. She had been through the rigors of "Winter North Atlantic," the submarine-infested waters of the North Sea, the bombing attacks on the beaches of Normandy, the hardships of the South Pacific. Fifty years later she made an epic voyage returning to the beaches of Normandy for the 50th Anniversary commemorations of the D-Day landings.

The *Jeremiah O'Brien* is not only a museum ship. She is a labor of love and a memorial to all the ships and men who had given their lives in service to our country.

W.W.J.
Menlo Park, Calif.
2004

INTRODUCTION

The Greeks had a phrase for it — "the defects of our virtues." In today's parlance it is "the downside." Applied in historical context to the United States, it means we are blessed with a high degree of native intelligence, ingenuity and an abundance of raw materials. Unfortunately, these strengths have caused us to develop a national carelessness, a lack of discipline, a failure to plan ahead. Instead, we trust to luck and rely on our wealth and resources to extricate us from the consequences of our failures. America's maritime policy at the outbreak of World War I is a classic example of this pattern.

Before that war, federal maritime policy stated that foreign-built ships could not be registered in the United States. The intent was to protect the shipbuilding industry. Yet, other than that policy statement, the government did little to encourage ship-building. Seeking more immediate profits in other arenas, American businessmen looked to non-maritime investments.

When war broke out in 1914, only 9% of our foreign commerce was carried on American ships. Almost immediately the foreign flag ships, which carried the other 91% of American cargo, withdrew to their homelands, leaving American piers glutted with ever-growing piles of cargo.

Reacting to this, Congress passed a series of bills and emergency measures allowing American registration of foreign-flag ships and supporting the construction of new American ships. Under the Shipping Act of 1916 the United States spent $3.3 billion to build 2,300 vessels. The number of shipyards increased from 61 to 341 in just one year.

Unfortunately, it was a case of too much too late. Lacking a coherent plan, the nation reacted in haste, once more without considering the long-term effect of its precipitous actions. First, most of the ships weren't completed until the war was over. In fact, one third weren't even started until after the war ended. Further compounding these errors was the fact that most of our newly-built ships were coal-fired. The international maritime industry, however, was moving towards oil as the fuel for marine power plants. By 1929 the United States was again paying the price for its failure to plan. The backwaters of America's ports became clogged with obsolete, laid-up ships.

There was, however, a value to all this. As the next war approached, it appeared that we had finally learned the folly of simply reacting to events when they occurred, that we now recognized the importance of planning and foresight. In Europe, the rumbles of war could already be heard. Spain was serving as the testing ground as its Fascist dictator practiced the arts of war drenched in Spanish blood while the most monstrous Fascist of all watched and analyzed from his aerie in Berchtesgaden. In the Far East, the Japanese Imperial forces were refining in Manchuria the terrors that would be expanded to all of Southeast Asia.

For a while it looked like the lessons of history had been learned. The United States would be ready for the next war.

1

THE LESSONS OF WAR

And so, the Merchant Marine Act of 1936 was passed. Considered by many as the *Magna Carta* of the United States Merchant Marine, the Act took as its three critical principles:

1. A modern, efficient merchant marine was necessary for national defense and the development of overseas and domestic commerce.
2. The ships of such a merchant marine must be built so that they could be converted to naval auxiliaries in a war or national emergency.
3. All such ships must be built in the United States and owned and operated under the American flag.

To accomplish its intent, the Act created operating and construction differential subsidies. These allowed American ships to compete in a world market where ship construction costs were half, and ship operating expenses two-thirds, that of the United States.

The average remaining useful life of ships in the American Merchant Marine at the time was considered to be five years. Beginning in 1937, the Act called for a ten-year program in which fifty new ships a year would be built. The new fleet would be made up of fast tankers and three types of freighters (C1, C2 and C3) each powered by economical geared turbines, producing a relatively high sea speed. At the time there were only ten ship-yards capable of building ships more than 400 feet long. Containing forty-six slipways, half of these were already occupied with navy production.

In 1939, before war was declared in Europe, recognizing the importance of controlling our own commerce, the production schedule of the ten-year program was doubled to 100 ships a year. In August 1940 it was doubled again, with construction orders for 200 ships a year being distributed between 19 shipyards.

As country after country fell under Hitler's iron hand, England fought alone while the United States remained neutral. During the first nine months of war English losses totaled 150 ships, more than 1 million tons. In April 1941 alone, 800,000 deadweight tons of shipping was lost. German U-boats sank ships faster than England could build them.

In desperation, England turned for help to America, with her vast supply of natural resources and unequalled ability to accomplish large-scale projects. In September 1940 the British Merchant Shipbuilding Mission approached the United States about the possibility of building ships for Great Britain. Bringing with them their own plans for a ship design, they proposed a vessel similar to the *Dorington Court*, built in 1938. It had evolved from an old tramp ship design first conceived in England in 1879 and later modified. Initially dubbed the "Ocean" class, the ship was rated at 10,000 deadweight tons with a 2,500 horsepower engine that produced a speed of 10 knots. The design was slow, but the construction simple. Driven by an obsolete

The Liberty ship design was similar to the Dorington Court, *launched in 1938 by J.L. Thompson, Sunderland, England. She was torpedoed and sunk off Africa in November 1942.* Author's collection.

reciprocating engine with coal burning fire-tube boilers, the vessel had been built, year after year, on the River Tyne and had proven its reliability. England wanted sixty of them.

According to Admiral Emory Scott Land, Chairman of the United States Maritime Commission, the quickest way to produce the ships was for Britain to buy them outright, rather than go through the U.S. government. But no construction berths were available. New yards would have to be created in which to build the new ships. To accommodate the sixty-ship order for "Ocean" class vessels, a conglomerate of West Coast construction and engineering firms was called in. Known as the Six Services or Six Companies it included the general contracting firms that built the Hoover and Grand Coulee Dams and was headed by Henry Kaiser. Within months it would include Todd Shipyards Inc. in New York and the Bath Iron Works in Maine, among the oldest and most venerable shipbuilders in the United States.

Even without England's sixty ship order, however, the accelerating construction of new hulls outstripped the industry's ability to provide engines for them. There were not enough turbines to propel the new "C" types, let alone modify an additional sixty ships for Great Britain, and the demand for more tonnage was growing daily. It soon became apparent that the sophisticated, well-made ships envisioned by the Maritime Commission in 1936 would have to wait. Quantity, rather than quality, became the overriding goal.

To produce in quantity meant that existing ship designs had to be modified for immediate construction. The time necessary to design and develop a new ship was a luxury no one could afford. With the Battle of the Atlantic already raging, construction timetables were also critical. To reduce production time and costs, it was decided to weld the new ships rather than use the traditional, and time-consuming, riveted method.

The best design available was that brought over by the British for their "Ocean" class. It had adequate horsepower and carrying capacity for its intended purpose. In addition, the *Dorington Court* hull and engine were simplicity incarnate. First, the simple hull lines conformed easily to the new concept of welding, keeping construction costs relatively low and construction time minimal. Second, the reciprocating engine used in the British design was an uncomplicated piece of equipment that could be built in any machine shop. Unlike the high-speed turbines designed for the "C" ships, no special techniques were needed for manufacture and the capacity to produce them was available. The same was true of the engine's steam boilers, especially considering the relatively moderate pressures associated with reciprocating engines. Third, the ship was easy to operate. Operation of the steam reciprocating engine required a minimum of training.

In early 1941 Admiral Land showed President Roosevelt the plans for the British design with the intent of modifying them to produce a quickly-built, efficient American ship to meet the needs of the war effort. Roosevelt's comment was, "Admiral, I think this ship will do us very well. She'll carry a good load. She

The Ocean Vanguard *on builder's trials shortly after her launching on August 16, 1941.* Kaiser Shipyards.

isn't much to look at, though, is she? A real ugly duckling." As soon as the press heard the comment, the name stuck. The ships were affectionately known ever after as "ugly ducklings."[1]

The president announced construction of the new emergency class of ship in February 1941. Describing them as "dreadful looking objects," he set the first construction goal at 200 emergency cargo vessels. This would soon be increased to 2300 vessels totalling 23 million deadweight tons for 1942 and 1943.

Trying to change the public's image of the new emergency ship, which was soon to be the mainstay of American ship construction, Admiral Land referred to the 200-ship order as the Liberty Fleet and declared September 27, 1941 as "Liberty Fleet Day." On that day fourteen "emergency" ships were launched across the nation. The first of these, the *Patrick Henry*, provided the inspiration for the event. It was the ship's namesake who said "Give me liberty or give me death." A month later, on October 15, 1941, the first of Britain's "Ocean" ships came off the ways. Named the *Ocean Vanguard*, it was launched by Mrs. Emory Land.

The strategy of building ships faster than they could be sunk would prove to be an effective concept. An equally valid counter-objective is to sink them faster than they can be built, and that was precisely the strategy of the German Navy. In May 1942 German Admiral Dönitz said, "The total tonnage the enemy can build will be about 8.2 million tons in 1942, and about 10.4 million tons in 1943. This would mean that we would have to sink approximately

---

[1] To a seaman's eye the ships were actually smart looking with their raked bow, cruiser stern and well-designed sheer line.

Prefabrication became an artform during the war. Here, a midship section for a C4 is put in place. National Liberty Ship Memorial.

700,000 tons per month in order to offset new construction; only what is in excess of this amount would constitute a decrease in enemy tonnage. However, we are already sinking these 700,000 tons per month now." His mistake was in underestimating the shipbuilding capacity of American yards.

In gearing up for Liberty ship production, the art of shipbuilding was revolutionized. Old-line shipbuilders contributed their knowledge and experience. New organizations developed new techniques, their very lack of preconceived ideas about shipbuilding creating new methods and innovations in an old profession.

The art of welding had only recently been developed to the point where it could be used in shipbuilding and the first all-welded ship came off the ways in November 1940.[2] With welding

---

[2] Welding provided a savings in weight of 600 tons compared to the older method of riveting.

Prefabrication meant reduced construction time. Here, a transverse bulkhead is lowered into position. National Liberty Ship Memorial.

came prefabrication. Sun Shipbuilding of Chester, Pennsylvania developed the process of building a ship's bow section on the ground, then adding it to the ship under construction on the ways. Soon, bulkheads and sections of inner bottoms were being built in shops of various shipyards and set on the ways, rather than the old plate-by-plate, frame-by-frame methods. The Bethlehem-Fairfield yard at Baltimore was in the vanguard of this type of construction. In their fabricating shops they assembled materials for eight ships at a time: double bottoms with fuel and drainage pipes already installed, sections of deck structure complete with framing and bulkheads intact. From the shop the complete section was transported to the ways where it was set in place and welded to other sections. Meanwhile, construction began on the next section.

In Oregon, the entire Portland plant was revised to the new prefabricated, assembly-line method of ship construction. Here, the sections were prefabricated as completely as possible reaching the point where the entire superstructure, with living quarters and navigation equipment, was built in the shop, lifted by gigantic cranes, and lowered into place as the hull of the already-launched ship floated under the crane. In North Carolina, the Newport News Shipbuilding Company went so far in its newly-constructed Wilmington yard as to preassemble almost the entire sides of their ships. Once assembled, they were cut into manageable sections and the sections were then rejoined by welders on the launching ways. Delivery time, originally expected to be 110 days, averaged about 40 days for the new vessels.

Slowly, the new ship caught on. Originally designed to have a life of five years, it was often said during the war that if a Liberty delivered its cargo once, it had paid for itself. Few people would have guessed that the ship would outlast these pessimistic predictions and become the mainstay of the world's merchant fleets for the next twenty-five years. They hadn't counted on American workmanship and know-how — the ability to do the job, do it quickly, and do it well when the chips were down. This unique American quality, harnessed with a national policy and detailed planning, was to be an insurmountable force.

2

A SHIP FOR ALL SEASONS

Adapting the British "Ocean" design to American standards required some effort. To ensure that the conversion went smoothly and efficiently, the Maritime Commission called on the firm of Gibbs and Cox in New York, the naval architects who had done such a superb job on the original designs of the SS *America*. Their modifications gave a ship suited to the requirements of the times. The simplicity of their design made it easy to weld and facilitated the prefabrication process.

The split house used in the British design was consolidated into one midships house bringing the unlicensed crew into the same structure as the officers rather than having them occupy the fantail area below decks, as they did on the British version. This was considered safer for North Atlantic voyages. It also reduced the amount of piping, wiring and outfitting needed to build the ship.

Because of the extreme shortage of turbine and diesel power plants, the obsolete triple-expansion steam engine was retained. The original design was altered from coal to oil-burning and from fire tube to water tube boilers, but the engine itself continued to be the triple expansion steam reciprocating type developed in Britain by the North Eastern Marine Engineering Co. Ltd. It was adapted for American construction by Hooven, Owens & Rentschler, a subsidiary of the General Machinery Company of Cincinnati, Ohio. The fully assembled engine weighed 270,000 pounds, stood 19 feet high and was 21 feet long. It turned the four-bladed propeller at 76 RPM, giving the ship a design speed of 11 knots.

The fact that the Liberty burned oil, rather than coal, required other changes. Fixed ballast in the double bottoms was replaced with fuel tanks. Two deep tanks were added in No. 1 hold for water ballast. Without coal bunkers, there was room to lengthen No. 3 hold and single masts replaced kingposts.

Other modifications added to the Americanization of the British model. Steel decks replaced wood in the original design and steel bulwarks were substituted for chain rails. The original canvas wind dodgers on the bridge were replaced with steel. Separate access ladders were provided to the cargo holds so they could be reached without removing the hatch covers. An emergency steering station was included on the stern. The ship was given searchlights, refrigeration for the crew's food, and running water in the cabins. The engine, boilers, pumps and deck equipment were all built to one standard specification so that they could be made anywhere in the world and fit on any Liberty.

To facilitate the welding process and mass production, the hull was designed so that most of it could be built with simple hull plating. In other words, because the hull design lacked the twists and turns and double bow and stern curves of a more complex vessel, it was far quicker to build. The only two plates on the Liberty that required special processing were those adjacent to the forefoot.

Welding was a new technology. The process of welding a ship together, however, rather than riveting it, locked a great deal of stress into the hull. When the hull was subjected to the additional stress of freezing temperatures, improper loading and an unkindly sea, something occasionally gave way. Some Libertys developed cracks under heavy use. These usually occurred in the unstrengthened square hatch corners and that area of the sheer strake (the uppermost band of plating around the hull, just below the level of the main deck) which was cut to house the accommodation ladder. It was found that if a Liberty ship was going to crack, it would usually occur in near-freezing temperatures or during heavy seas, or both.

The solution was a device known as the "crack-arrestor." By riveting steel reinforcing straps (riveting allows for more "give" than welding) on the main deck the tendency to crack was stopped. In addition, the hatch corners were reinforced and gunwale bars were added. Stronger steel was used in areas of stress concentration.

It wasn't all bad news. There were unforeseen advantages to welding. A welded seam is often stronger than the plates it connects. When a welded ship was subjected to the sudden and cataclysmic effects of torpedoes or bombs, it was often more capable of holding together and making port in a damaged condition than its riveted sister. A ship's plating might be torn apart by the force of an explosion but the welded seams generally held. Side plates and bulkheads were often blown in without breaking the welds, and many a welded ship was saved because compartments remained watertight to keep the ship afloat. By contrast, a riveted ship would have sprung rivets and broken seams, with a correspondingly lessened chance of the vessel's reaching port.

Robert T. Young, President of the American Bureau of Shipping said,

> The record of these quickly-built welded ships has more than justified the adoption of welding in view of the number of vessels built, their ability to withstand enemy action without fatal damage,

and the comparative ease with which repairs can be made to them. In fact, considering the 5,000 or more welded ships built under the most adverse conditions, the loss through structural failure of a half dozen is less to be wondered at than the entirely satisfactory service given by hundreds of them when they were urgently needed.

In the end, the result was a ship that was quick and easy to build and uncomplicated to operate. According to Admiral Tom Patterson, "The Libertys were to steamships what the Model T was to cars. They were simple to build and simple to operate. You could teach a farm boy to operate one."

The greatest virtue of the basic Liberty design was its versatility. Because the design was simple and easily adaptable, Liberty hulls could be converted to other uses. In the sixty-two Liberty tankers built, the hull type was modified to carry petroleum products while retaining the outward appearances of a freighter. Deck piping was hidden and dummy cargo gear installed. But internally the ship's cargo holds had become large oil tanks. Liberty tankers had a cargo capacity of 2,722,692 gallons or 64,826 barrels.[1]

In colliers, the engine room was moved aft, leaving a small midships house for deck officers and navigation that didn't interfere with loading and discharge or reduce cargo capacity. The ships proved invaluable, loading larger quantities of coal in less time per ton, travelling at 12 knots, versus the pre-war 10, operating at reduced fuel consumption, and providing a rapid rate of discharge.

Thirty-six Libertys were delivered as boxed aircraft transports. The basic freighter design was modified to four hatches versus the original five. The hatch openings were made larger and the cargo gear was reinforced to handle up to thirty tons on kingposts, rather than the original centerline masts. Many of

---

[1] A barrel equals 42 gallons.

these ships were converted by the Navy to radar picket ships after the war.

Six Libertys were converted after construction to hospital ships (the *Jeremiah O'Brien* was almost one of these). This involved stripping the ship to a bare hull, adding a strengthening band around 80 percent of the hull and on the upper deck, the installation of steel girders and strengtheners at points of stress, installing new decks and bulkheads and adding rooms. The result was more than three hundred areas of rooms, corridors, wards, clinics and laboratories. Designed to handle 600 patients, the hospital ship carried a medical staff of 17 officers, 39 nurses, 159 attendants and a crew of 123.

More than 100 Libertys were built as, or later converted to, troopships. Initially, many of them carried prisoners-of-war but as the war drew to a close the need arose to carry more Allied troops. This involved another conversion, modifying the POW spaces to provide greater comfort for the troops.

Four Libertys were converted to the special purpose of carrying war brides and military dependents. Eight ships were converted as animal transports, carrying horses, mules and cattle.

Officially, the basic freight-carrying Liberty was an EC2-S-C1 class freighter. "E" represented Emergency, "C" cargo and 2 designated a waterline length between 400 and 450 feet. The "S" meant the vessel was both steam powered and single screw. "C1" referred to the design number. Because of their blunt, box-like appearance, the ships were at first called "Plain Janes" or "Sea Scows" or "Ugly Ducklings." It was only after Admiral Land's speech that the term "Liberty" stuck.

The basic Liberty freighter had an overall length of 441 feet 6 inches, a beam of 56 feet 10 and 3/4 inches and drew 27 feet 9 and 1/4 inches when fully loaded. Her deadweight tonnage (the ship's actual weight in tons) was 10,920, gross tonnage (roughly the internal volume in tons of 100 cubic feet each) about 7,500 and displacement tonnage (the weight in tons of the amount of water she displaced) 14,300. With a full load of fuel a Liberty carried 9,146 tons of cargo when down to her Plimsoll marks, but in wartime it was common to load them deeper than that. The basic crew complement on Liberty ships was as follows:

Master	1
Chief Mate	1
2nd Mate	1
3rd Mate	1
Deck Maintenance	1
Bosun (Boatswain)	1
A.B. (Able-Bodied Seaman)	1
O.S. (Ordinary Seaman)	1
Purser	1
Radio Officer	1[2]
Chief Engineer	1
1st Assistant Engineer	1
2nd Assistant Engineer	1
3rd Assistant Engineer	1
Deck Engineer	1
Oilers	3
FWT (Firemen/Water Tenders)	3
Wipers	2
Chief Steward	1
Chief Cook	1
Cooks & Bakers	2
Mess Utility Men	5
Armed Guard	26
Total	58

If the ship carried an Armed Guard gun crew, an extra messman was carried. If the ship was designed to carry tanks and planes, an additional Deck Maintenance man was carried. If the ship was a collier, the Deck Maintenance and Deck Engineer were not carried.

---

[2] In some wartime conditions the Armed Guard supplied additional radiomen so the ship's radio could be manned twenty-four hours a day.

Within three years from the day the first contract was signed, fifteen shipyards devoted to the production of Liberty ships had been created, employing over three hundred thousand men and women. They produced more than 2,700 Liberty ships. Each ship contained 52.08 miles of welding, 28,000 rivets, 3,200 tons of steel, 7.5 miles of pipe, 4.75 miles of electrical wiring, was covered with 25 tons of paint and used 900,000 cubic feet of oxygen and 250,000 cubic feet of acetylene gas in its construction.

The Libertys were a great fleet of cargo vessels whose success in supplying our own forces and our allies with the materials of war and with food for civilian populations was an indispensable factor in winning the war.

General Dwight D. Eisenhower had this to say: "Every man in the Allied command is quick to express his admiration for the loyalty, courage, and fortitude of the officers and men of the Merchant Marine. ... they have never failed us ... When final victory is ours there is no organization that will share its credit more deservedly than the Merchant Marine."

General Douglas MacArthur: "... they shared the heaviest enemy fire ... they have suffered in bloodshed and in death ... They have contributed tremendously to our success. I hold no branch in higher esteem than the Merchant Marine Services."

Of the 2,710 built during the war fewer than 200 were lost. Only two of these ships, the *Jeremiah O'Brien* and the *John W. Brown*, are still active today, the last of that massive fleet of Libertys. But initially they were just two of the thousands that were "built by the mile and chopped off by the yard."

The first day on the ways for a new Liberty ship shows much of the keel and bottom plating in place. National Liberty Ship Memorial.

The same ship, after about two weeks, looking forward. The second deck is in place in the foreground, the third deck beyond that. National Liberty Ship Memorial.

Looking toward the stern about three weeks after keel-laying. The hull begins to take shape. National Liberty Ship Memorial.

In less than a month the main deck, superstructure, masts and gun tubs are in place. National Liberty Ship Memorial.

3

THE SHIPYARDS

The sixty-ship order placed by Great Britain on December 10, 1940 became the impetus for the creation of two new shipbuilding concerns — both affiliated with Todd Shipyards Corporation, one of the oldest and most respected ship builders and repairers in America. On the West Coast, Todd-California Shipbuilding Corporation was formed with Henry Kaiser as its president and its initial yard in Richmond, California. (In October 1941 the name of the yard was changed to Permanente Metals Corporation.) On the East Coast, the Bath Iron Works Corporation joined Todd and the West Coast yards to form the Todd-Bath Iron Shipbuilding Corporation. This yard was to be located on Casco Bay, at South Portland, Maine. Each yard was to build thirty vessels for the British.

While the California yard was to have traditional slanting launching ways, the topography and extreme tidal range of Maine called for something different. It was decided to build a basin or graving dock. Beneath a bit of underdeveloped shoreline in South Portland was a solid rock ledge. By shoveling down through twenty feet of mud and sand to the rock, ships could be built; not on conventional ways, but in an open-water slip. Simply hoisting the flood gates on the seaward end of such ways when the job was finished would allow the ship to be towed right out into the harbor.

Work started immediately. The area was cleared and construction began. After building a 1,500-foot cofferdam in a mere four weeks, a three-compartment basin 750 feet wide by 450 feet long was excavated. The design was such that seven 416-foot Liberty ships could be built at one time, any two or three of which could be floated without disturbing the work in the adjacent compartments. Ten months later the yard was complete.

Although, compared to the standard launching ways in California, the process of building a graving dock was necessarily longer, the first British Liberty keel for the *Ocean Liberty* was laid on May 24, 1941, a mere six weeks after the laying of the first keel in the California yard. By the end of June four keels were in place. The thirtieth ship was delivered 466 days later on November 18, 1942.

At first, few people in the area knew anything about shipbuilding. Bill Boissonneault, a leadman welder:

> We were all learning together. The shipfitters were as green as the rest of us. On Hulls 1 and 2 everything was put together piece by piece like a puzzle.
>
> After they started welding, I knew I wanted to do that, so I went to the welding school. The welding shed, with twenty-five machines, was between Flat 1 and Flat 2. We had no office. The leadman made out the slips and we went to work. The lines had to go right from there down into the basins. Sometimes it took three or four leads to reach all the way to the other end of the basin.

The need for American ships in the coming conflict grew. In January 1941 Admiral Vickery of the Maritime Commission called on the nation's shipbuilders for increased production. The response was the creation of three new yards: Oregon Ship Building Corporation at Portland, California Shipbuilding in Los Angeles and the Houston Shipbuilding Corporation in Texas. Although construction on these yards began at once, the Commission soon decided it needed yet more shipbuilding capability. The new yards were expanded and two additional companies were created: Richmond Shipbuilding Corporation to adjoin the Todd-California Shipbuilding Corporation, and South Portland Shipyard Corporation to be adjacent to the Todd-Bath Iron Shipbuilding Corporation.

As the new site had traditional launching ways, the result was two launching systems under one management in South Portland. The Todd-Bath facility with its graving dock was known as the "East Yard" and continued working on the British contract. The South Portland facility, with its traditional ways, was known as the "West Yard." It built Liberty ships for America under the supervision of the Maritime Commission. It was thought that having the two competing on construction schedules was a good stimulus to production.

South Portland's initial order was for forty-four Libertys. Its first hull was the *John Davenport* launched on May 16, 1941. When the British contract was completed, the East and West yards were combined by the Maritime Commission and on April 1, 1943 the entire organization became the New England Shipbuilding Corporation (N.E.S.C.), an affiliate of Todd Shipyards Corporation of New York City.

At one time South Portland employed 29,680 people in building ships. Eighty-five percent of their workers were unskilled and had to be trained. Training that many people in a short period of time was a challenge against scarcity of materials and lack of suitable yard machinery. Another factor was the

Women were a significant part of the workforce during World War II. Janet Doyle, shown in her welding gear in 1942, was a welder on Liberty ships in Richmond, California. She was a longtime volunteer on the Jeremiah O'Brien. National Liberty Ship Memorial.

weather. Winter temperatures of 20 to 40 degrees below zero were common. Yet, South Portland achieved a remarkable record. According to Agnes E. Meyer in *Journey Through Chaos*, "the absenteeism and turnover in the N.E.S.C. yards were below that of other yards in the sunny West Coast and the Gulf States."

Among the labor force of nearly 30,000 were 3,700 women, the second largest number of women employed in any shipyard in America at the time. Initially trained as tackers and burners, they eventually became machine workers, pipe coverers, spray painters, even crane operators. Bill Boissonneault supervised the first groups of women welders at the yard. "If she's sincerely in here to do the work, a woman is more conscientious than a man on the same job. I never felt that the women were coming here to take

Edna Slocum was California's "welding Queen." A press release explained how she managed welding and being a housewife. "Her whole family joins in the housework, but she does the cooking, Mr. Slocum does the shopping and their two boys wash the dishes. Each family member cleans a different room of the house, Wash comes from the laundry rough-dry, and Edna squeezes in the ironing. 'And I still have time for a hair wave,' she said." G.G.N.R.A.

jobs away from men. There was enough work for everybody and the women came in just the same as the men — to help with the war effort and do the job that had to be done."

The final output of the South Portland yard was 236 Liberty ships and 30 British "Oceans." This was boosted with a cash incentive program. The government offered a fast delivery bonus of $60,000 to $140,000 for each ship. The average cost for the American Libertys at South Portland was $1,892,000. The first ship took 279 days from keel to delivery. By December 1944 this figure averaged 52.5 days for each ship.

The keel of the SS *Jeremiah O'Brien* was laid on May 6, 1943. It was the thirtieth hull built in the new "West" yard and was constructed on launching way number 1.

The Kaiser shipyard in Richmond, California showing twelve Liberty ships under construction. National Liberty Ship Memorial.

4

BUILDING THE
SS *JEREMIAH O'BRIEN*

When ships are mass-produced to the same design, like cookies punched out with a cutter, they're indistinguishable until something is done to give them a separate identity. The first thing that marks a ship, that makes her different from her sisters, is the assignment of a hull number. On January 14, 1943 a nameless Liberty hull that existed only on paper at South Portland, Maine, was assigned Maritime Commission Emergency (MCE) hull number 806 and New England Shipbuilding hull number 230. (Like all shipbuilders, New England Shipbuilding assigned its own hull number to the vessel in addition to that of the Maritime Commission). Little else happened for the next several months although plans, parts and pieces began to be designated as being for hull 806.

On May 6, the keel was laid. With the laying of the first piece of the keel comes reality and a name — in this case, *Jeremiah*

The SS Jeremiah O'Brien *just before launching.* San Francisco Maritime National Historical Park.

O'Brien, after a hero of the Revolutionary War. With the assignment of a name, things began happening with increasing speed. The hull was quickly assembled on the launching ways — double bottoms, frames, hull plating and decks.

The first official record of the ship occurred on May 20, 1943 when the Master Carpenter's Certificate, also known as the builder's certificate, was delivered to the Treasury Department. In it the vessel *SS Jeremiah O'Brien*, hull No. 230, is valued at $1,750,000.

Having a vessel on the ways and soon to be launched meant a steamship company must be selected to operate it. On May 26, 1943 the War Shipping Administration (WSA) advised Grace

Line, Inc. that the new ship was allocated to them under their Service Agreement, (Contract 363) dated January 1, 1942.[1]

The Irish say that luck is something you're born with. If so, the *O'Brien*'s luck must have started with the laying of her keel, for she seemed protected by good fortune throughout her career. It started with her naming — a good, lucky, Irish name. Then she was assigned, not to some fly-by-night newcomer started up to take advantage of the war, but to Grace Line which had been in the business since 1869. The *O'Brien* was one of two dozen ships eventually operated by Grace for the WSA.

On June 3, 1943, the vessel was assigned official number 243622 and call letters KXCH, the number and letters registered with the Collector of Customs. At the same time, the home port of Portland, Maine was designated.[2] The WSA advised Grace Line to obtain the necessary insurance and to send them copies of the policy, to become effective when the first crew member was placed on board. Grace Line was also instructed to have the master and chief engineer report aboard "on or about June 12, 1943" (15 days prior to scheduled delivery on June 27). The clerk-typist or purser was to be aboard ten days in advance, or about June 17. So that he would have time to learn Grace Line's operations, he was also allowed time to train in the company office.

The following ratings were assigned five days prior to delivery of the vessel: Chief Mate, First Assistant Engineer, Second Mate, Second Assistant Engineer, Third Mate, Third Assistant Engineer, Radio Operator, Chief Steward. The WSA allowed each of the newly-assigned crew members a subsistence

---

[1] The Service Agreement was a "blanket" agreement for a company to operate a ship or ships to be named at future dates. This way a separate agreement does not have to be drawn up for each vessel.

[2] In peacetime the port of registration is the city in which the owner (usually a corporation) resides. Many American ships are registered in the little-known seaport but well-known corporate headquarters of Wilmington, Delaware. In wartime, however, the government, which technically owned the ship, elected to use the port in which the ship was built as the port of registration rather than Washington, D.C., its residence.

rate of $4 per day to cover their meals and lodging while they waited for the new ship to become habitable.

Because the ship was government-owned and because the government had just established a new federal Merchant Marine Academy at Kings Point, New York, arrangements were made for a maximum of two deck and four engine cadets, or no less than two deck and two engine cadets, if available, to be part of the first crew.

On Saturday, June 19, 1943 the *Jeremiah O'Brien* was launched by Mrs. Ida Lee Starling, wife of the head of the White House Secret Service. She held the bottle by the neck and awaited the first movement of the vessel before beginning the ritual. A ribbon-covered chain secured the bottle to the deckrail of the ship. At a signal, she crashed the ribbon-bound bottle against the steel bow and in a spray of white foam, the *Jeremiah O'Brien* was on her way. Whistles from the ways, from the harbor and the yard roared a salute as the ship cocked gently, then settled with poise and confidence in her new element. With wartime efficiency upper-most in everyone's mind, the first piece of keel for the next ship was probably set in place on launching way No. 1 of the new West yard that same day.

Demands of war and the production of so many ships made christening ceremonies brief and simple but to the men who built the ships and those who sailed them, there was always dignity in the rites of launching. For they, more than others, sensed the miracle of birth when dead tons of steel became a living, floating ship.

The yard's tugs carefully guided the new vessel to the fitting-out berth where she would spend the next few weeks. The crew began to arrive before the ship was ready. After a week at the fitting out-berth, the *O'Brien's* engines were operated for the first time on June 26 when the Builder's Dock Trial was held. This important first testing of the main engine and auxiliary machinery consisted of running the main engine ahead for 2½ hours at 68 r.p.m. and one-half hour astern at 60 r.p.m. At the same time all the support machinery — pumps, motors, circuits, plumbing and hydraulics — was tested. To be sure everything was up to specification, indicator cards were taken showing operating

Mrs, Ida Lee Starling, whose husband was head of the White House Secret Service, launches the SS Jeremiah O'Brien *on June 19, 1943.* San Francisco Maritime National Historical Park.

Sliding down the ways, the SS Jeremiah O'Brien *makes contact with the ocean for the first time.* National Liberty Ship Memorial.

Just launched and moving toward the fitting out berth, the SS Jeremiah O'Brien *shows the fine lines of a well-made Liberty ship.* San Francisco Maritime National Historical Park.

readings. These were compared with standard readings for Libertys to ensure proper operation. The engines were balanced and all was proven satisfactory to the Inspectors and Trial Board Engineer. The *O'Brien* was ready for the next set of tests, the official trials.

The official dock trial was conducted on June 28 between 0600 (6 a.m.) and 1300 (1 p.m.), EWT (Eastern War Time)[3] The engine was run six hours ahead at an average of 68.8 r.p.m. and one hour astern at 60.8 r.p.m., developing 1597 IHP (Indicated Horse Power) ahead and 945 IHP astern. Indicator cards and all data were taken every half hour. The evaporator and distiller capacity was measured at 360 gal. per hour. These devices were critical, for the former created fresh water for the engines while the later made potable water for the crew. Each main feed water pump and fuel pump was run one-half the time of the trial (there are two sets). The soot blowers were tested and the three electric generators were run in parallel.

---

[3] Just after the United States entered the war the country was put on War Time. It was the equivalent of double daylight savings time. All the clocks were moved ahead two hours. This allowed for more daylight working hours and increased productivity and efficiency. War Time was a year-round condition and stayed in effect until the war was over.

Official Sea Trials were held on June 29 and June 30, 1943. During these trials a bevy of officials had to pass judgement on the capabilities of the new vessel; a trial board represented the Maritime Commission; the builders, by New England Shipbuilding Corporation; Grace Line was represented by the master, Capt. O. Southerland, and the chief engineer, R. G. Montgomery; and an American Bureau of Shipping representative. The Coast Guard had two officials in attendance.

The vessel was ballasted with fresh water so that the propeller would be submerged deep enough to get a good "bite" yet maintain a realistic trim. Ballast water was carried in reserve feed water tanks, port and starboard, and in the after peak tank. The fuel oil settling tanks had approximately 500 barrels, and No. 3 Port and Starboard tanks were partly filled with fuel oil.

One of the first tests was of the emergency steering gear. Located aft, on the deck above the gunners' quarters, it contains a wheel that enables the ship to be steered from that location. There is also a compass to mark the ship's course and a telephone to communicate with the engine room. Should the navigation bridge be destroyed by enemy action, the emergency steering station could be manned to steer the vessel. This was an important safety measure in the submarine-infested North Atlantic. The emergency steering gear was satisfactorily tested at the dock on June 30, 1943 in the presence of the American Bureau of Shipping surveyor, USCG Inspectors, U.S. Maritime Commission Inspectors and the Resident Trial Board Member.

Once the vessel left the dock, other tests could be conducted. One of the first was the anchor windlass. Both anchors were lowered until thirty fathoms of chain were out. Then the windlass was engaged and the anchors raised. Both anchors came up from 30 fathoms to 0 fathoms in four minutes with a chain speed of 45 feet per minute, well within specifications.

Certain other facts about the new ship had to be determined beyond question before she could be delivered. Could she withstand the shocks and stresses, the heavy structural strains that come in an emergency when her engines must be suddenly reversed from full speed ahead to full speed astern? Was she easily maneuverable? To find out, the engine and main steering were tested. Running ahead at 72 r.p.m., with steam pressure at 80 pounds (the *O'Brien's* steering gear is steam-operated), the steering wheel was swung to hard left. It took seven seconds for the rudder to reach that position. From hard left to hard right took 15 seconds and from hard right to hard left 14 seconds. Returning the rudder from hard left to midships required six seconds.

Once it was established that the ship answered properly going ahead, it remained to be discovered if she was equally responsive going astern. With the engines running 60 r.p.m. astern at a steam pressure of 82 pounds it took six seconds to go from midships to hard left; hard left to hard right 14 seconds; and hard right to hard left 14 seconds. Finally, the wheel was brought to midships from hard left, with the rudder following in six seconds.

Many a collision has been avoided by a quick response of the ship's engines. Recognizing this, one of the basic tests required by regulatory agencies is the Emergency Ahead and Astern Test. The *O'Brien's* engines were reversed from 72 r.p.m. ahead to 60 r.p.m. astern in 21 seconds. The propeller shaft stopped in four seconds. Then, once the ship was well underway astern, the engines were put ahead. Reversing direction from 60 r.p.m astern to 72 r.p.m. ahead required 14 seconds with the shaft stopping in the first four seconds of the maneuver.

A steel ship has a lot of built-in magnetism. In fact, the direction it's pointing when it's built determines the residual magnetic field it will have. The wiring in a vessel also adds to this magnetism. Sending a ship, carrying its own magnetic field, to the coasts of Europe or the islands of the Pacific, both areas strewn with magnetic mines, was a recipe for disaster. To neutralize the ship's built-in magnetism it was sent over a degaussing course. Consisting of electrically-charged underwater cables, this had the effect of negating the ship's natural magnetism. Once that was completed, the magnetic compass could be adjusted and the radio direction finder calibrated. Incoming radio signals were also subject to deflection, and subsequent erroneous readings, by the vessel's built-in magnetic field. Knowing what the deflection was allowed the ship's officers to accurately predict the margin of error when they took readings.

The Official Sea Trials were complete at 0905 (9:05 a.m.) on June 30 when the *Jeremiah O'Brien* returned to the dock, a broom at her truck, indicating a clean sweep of all tests.

A few formalities remained. A complete inspection of the vessel was made and unfinished items were noted and referred to the builder for completion. The Navy Armed Guard crew had arrived before the ship was finished. Billeted ashore, they helped with the trial runs and even in putting the finishing touches on the ship.

With all tests complete and all paperwork filled out, the ship was delivered at 1400 (2 p.m.) E.W.T., June 30, 1943. It had been just 56 days since her keel was laid.

Several things then happened simultaneously: the ship was transferred to the new owners, the Maritime Commission; the Maritime Commission gave title of the ship to its operating division, the War Shipping Administration (WSA); the War Shipping Administration transferred possession of the vessel to Grace Line, Inc. under Service Agreement, Form GAA (General Agency Agreement).[4] All of this occurred at 1400, E.W.T. At the time of transfer consumable stores, fuel and water on board were valued at $6,607.67.

---

[4]   The General Agency Agreement is a device still used by the government for the operation of merchant ships during wartime. Basically, it authorizes a steamship company, because of its expertise in operating ships, to receive the ship from the government and operate it on their behalf. The steamship company provides all the same services its other ships receive — manning, maintenance, insurance and so on — and receives a daily cost-plus payment for doing so. Initially, the payment was based on the amount of deadweight tonnage assigned to an operator with rates of 50 cents a ton for the first 50,000 tons, 40 cents a ton for the next forty thousand tons, and so on. This was changed in December 1943 to a flat rate of $65 per day per ship plus $15 per day per ship to cover accounting costs. Fixed rates per ton of cargo handled were also paid. Ninety percent of all amounts over $15 per day per ship were subject to recapture by the government.

The *Jeremiah O'Brien* was ready. Her machinery hummed, her decks swarmed with people, she was alive. Built to last one voyage, five years at the most, she began what would be a long, long life. Named after a Revolutionary War hero, she embodied the spirit of her namesake — Jeremiah O'Brien of Machias, Maine.

5

JEREMIAH O'BRIEN

A Scots-Irish lumberjack from Machias, in the "Province of Main," Jeremiah O'Brien was the offspring of a family that settled in the area in 1765. For ten years the O'Briens peacefully made their living logging the pine forests of the northeast, providing lumber for the local colonists.

In 1775, long-festering problems with the British Crown reached the breaking point. In the spring of that year a shipment of Machias pine was loaded into two sloops belonging to Captain Ichabod Jones. Normally, the lumber would be sold in Boston for the account of the townspeople of Machias but being firmly pro-colonist and unsure of the situation in Boston, they instructed Jones to sell the lumber along the coast. Captain Jones, however, had another agenda. His family lived in Boston. Anxious to move them out of harm's way, he ignored the instructions and sailed directly into Boston Harbor. He sold the cargo and made a deal with the British. In exchange for the promise that he would return with another load of lumber to build barracks for British troops, he was allowed to move his family.

Loading his sloops with badly-needed supplies for Machias, Captain Jones sailed for Maine. Admiral Graves of the British Navy, wanting to be sure the colonist kept his word, instructed the armed schooner *Margaretta*, under command of Captain Moore, to escort Jones' ships.

On June 2, 1775 the people of Machias were angered to see the *Margaretta* enter their harbor escorting the two sloops, *Polly* and *Unity*. Captain Jones tried to talk the townspeople into supplying lumber in exchange for food. The good people of Machias had a mere three weeks' rations left, but they knew the lumber was for Boston, which had recently fallen to the British, and they wanted no part of the deal.

Refusing to be bullied, the townspeople erected a Liberty Pole as a symbol of their defiance. When Captain Moore saw it he was incensed. Moving his ship into position to fire on the village, he ordered the Liberty Pole taken down and demanded that trade begin immediately. A few of Machias' more influential (and cautious) townsfolk agreed to the trade and the sloops' cargo was discharged and loading began. Others were less fearful and more determined. On June 11, while the commander of the British schooner was ashore attending Protestant services in the local church, they decided the timing was right to put the British bully in his place. As he looked out the window of the church, the commander of the schooner saw several colonists swimming toward the *Margaretta* on logs. Quickly returning to his vessel, he weighed anchor and sailed farther downstream, threatening again to burn the town if anyone interfered with the loading of the sloops. Firm in their resolve, the men of Machias located the schooner at its new anchorage. They began a small arms fire from a bluff whose elevation was too high for the ship's cannon to reach. The ship was forced to up anchor again and look for safety still farther downstream. In the haste of departing, with musket fire raining down from above, the ship's main boom snapped, seriously crippling her.

The following day the *Unity* was commandeered at anchor and brought alongside the town dock. Rapidly loading the ship with arms and ammunition (there was no time to remove the cargo of lumber) the ship sailed with the idea of capturing the *Margaretta* anchored downstream. Jeremiah O'Brien, a man of thirty-one, was chosen captain. His crew of thirty-five included his five brothers. For victuals they carried one loaf of bread, a few pieces of pork and a barrel of water. Their weaponry consisted of 20 shotguns with three rounds of ball and powder each, a small cannon, a few axes and swords and some thirty pitchforks. What they lacked in provisions and arms they more than made up for in conviction. As the *Unity* rapidly gained on the *Margaretta*, which had weighed anchor and was now running slowly toward the safety of the open sea, Jeremiah O'Brien shouted, "Now, my brave fellows ... our first business will be to get alongside of the schooner yonder; and the first man to board her shall be entitled to the palm of honor."

Ordering the cargo of lumber to be placed as a breastworks around the vessel for protection, O'Brien quickly gained hailing distance.

"In America's name, I demand you surrender," he shouted.

The British answered with a volley from the stern gun that killed two men. A backwoods moosehunter by the name of Knight manned the *Unity's* gun and picked off the British helmsman. This cleared that vessel's quarterdeck, leaving the ship wallowing out of control and caused her to broach. As the two ships crashed into each other, Capt. O'Brien lashed them together.

John O'Brien, younger brother of Jeremiah, with 49-year-old Joseph Getchell, was the first to set foot on the *Margaretta*. They were met with heavy small arms fire from the British captain and crew. Leading a select group of twenty pitchforkmen, they boarded the British vessel and fought hand to hand for a full hour. At the end, Jeremiah O'Brien personally hauled down the British Ensign,

Exterior of the Burnham Tavern, where the wounded were taken for treatment after the first naval engagement of the Revolutionary War with the British armed schooner, Margaretta. *Author's collection.*

Interior of the Burnham Tavern. Built in 1770, the building is now a museum of Machias history, in which Jeremiah O'Brien played such an important part. Author's collection.

winning the first naval battle of the Revolutionary War. Following this battle, Jeremiah became known as Colonel O'Brien.

Subsequently, the *Unity* was outfitted with the armament from the *Margaretta* and became the armed cruiser *Machias Liberty*, the first American armed cruiser of the Revolution (and, in a sense, the first true Liberty ship).

In mid-July 1776, Colonel O'Brien, in command of the *Machias Liberty*, with the aid of Capt. Benjamin Foster on the *Falmouth Packet,* captured the British vessels *Diligent* and *Tapnaquish*, both of which had been sent for the express purpose of bringing "... the obstreperous Irish Yankee in for trial."

Following this success, Jeremiah O'Brien patrolled the North Atlantic in the *Machias Liberty*. Later, he commanded the privateers *Little Vincent, Cyrus* and *Tiger.* After a year-and-a-half he was given command of *Hannibal,* mounting twenty guns and manned by one hundred and thirty men and brought many prizes into Machias.

Two years later the *Hannibal* fell in with an English fleet of merchantmen off New York, sailing in convoy. She was immediately chased by two British frigates and after a forty-eight hour running battle, taken. Jeremiah O'Brien was captured. Following detainment in the infamous guard ship *Jersey*, O'Brien was transferred to Mill Prison in England. His brother John, in a memoir written several years later, recounted what happened next.

> He purposely neglected his dress and whole personal appearance for a month. The afternoon before making his escape he shaved and dressed in decent clothes, so as to alter very much his personal appearance, and walked out with the other prisoners in the jail yard. Having secreted himself under a platform in the yard, and thus escaping the notice of the keepers at the evening round-up, he was left out of the cells after they were locked for the night. He escaped from the yard by passing through the principal keeper's house in the dusk of evening. Although he made a little stay in the barroom of the house, he was not detected, being taken for a British soldier. In company with a Captain Lyon and another American who also had escaped

from the prison and were concealed somewhere in the vicinity, he crossed the English Channel to France in a boat and thence came to America, just about the time the hostilities ceased.

During the War of 1812, when the British again threatened to take Machias, Colonel Jeremiah O'Brien, still dauntless despite his advanced years, defiantly brandished the same sword he so capably used in the Revolutionary War.

Seemingly imbued with the same spirit and determination, the *SS Jeremiah O'Brien* lives, honoring her illustrious 18th century namesake into the 21st century — a name — and a ship — for all time.

Jeremiah O'Brien's tombstone at Machias, Maine. The inscription reads, "Sacred to the memory of Capt. Jeremiah O'Brien who died Sept. 5, 1818 in the 79th year of his age." Author's collection.

6

BREAKING IN

With the war on, Grace Line lost no time in getting the ship outfitted and ready. The day after the *O'Brien's* delivery, the first crew signed on for voyage No.1. Comprised of some forty-four merchant seaman and a gun crew of twenty-eight Navy sailors, their commander was Captain Oscar Southerland. The shipping articles were a far cry from those issued in peacetime which typically said:

> ...now bound from the port of New York to a port or ports of loading in the continental United States if so ordered or directed by the U.S. Government or any department, commission or agency thereof, thence to (or as may be ordered by the U.S. Government or any department, commission or agency thereof) such other ports and places in any part of the world as the master may direct and back to the final port of discharge in the United States, for a term of time not exceeding twelve (12) calendar months.

But this was wartime and the articles were terse: they were signing on for twelve months and the final port of discharge would be in the "USA." Leaving Portland, the articles were a technicality for the coastwise voyage to Boston. Once there and ready to sail to a foreign port, a new set of articles with the same brief wording would be signed.

On July 2, 1943, while the merchant crew readied the ship for sea, the gun crew loaded ammunition. Ordnance for the two 3-inch cannons and eight 20 mm machine guns included: three hundred 3-inch 50[1] anti-aircraft projectiles; one hundred fifty 3-inch 50 common projectiles; two 3-inch 50 short projectiles for firing out lodged projectiles; two auxiliary fuze setting wrenches, 30 seconds each; 13,500 20 mm cartridges, high explosive, anti-aircraft, tracer; 27,000 20 mm cartridges high explosive, anti-aircraft, incendiary and two hundred forty 20 mm cartridges, target projectiles. In addition, there were eighteen snowflake rockets with cartridges and one hundred twenty .38 caliber ball cartridges. The ship departed Portland, Maine at 2230 the evening of July 2nd.

At this stage of the war, the threat of enemy submarines was everywhere, even along the coast of Maine. Despite the fact she was only going coastwise from Portland to Boston the ship sailed in a blacked-out condition and the Armed Guard stood their watches at the guns.

At 0900 on July 3, 1943 the *Jeremiah O'Brien* arrived at Boston, Massachusetts and anchored. She remained at anchor through the following day, then, at 1730 on July 5, she went to the Bethlehem Steel Docks. There she loaded a partial cargo of steel for England.

It isn't difficult to imagine the feelings of most of the crew at this time. Made up of Midwest farm boys who had never seen the ocean before, young men from New England and the deep South, veteran seamen and "first-trippers," some were excited, looking forward to the adventure to come. Others were afraid. Still others, those who had served before, looked on it as routine. A few certainly

---

[1] Three inches in diameter by 50 millimeters in length.

thought it might be their last voyage and were determined to live life to the fullest before they sailed. So it was that on July 6 one of the Armed Guard Seaman First Class reported aboard after being AWOL. The log does not document what, if any, discipline was administered to the miscreant who felt his time ashore was more important than reporting on board on time.

Also on board were young officers-in-training. Just across Long Island from Brooklyn, at Great Neck, stands the United States Merchant Marine Academy, then the newest federal service academy. The shipbuilding industry had risen magnificently to the challenge of building ships faster than they could be sunk and merchant vessels were rolling down the ways on both coasts. As many as three ships a day were being launched with an eventual output that would total more than 2,700 Libertys and more than 500 Victorys. All those ships needed officers and the function of the new academy was the training of those officers. The Merchant Marine Academy at Kings Point, New York, was established in the same manner as the earlier federal academies at West Point, New York (Army), Annapolis, Maryland (Navy) and New London, Connecticut (Coast Guard), drawing its student body from the nation through nominations by U.S. senators and representatives. It required a rigorous course of study including ship handling, navigation, marine engineering, cargo stowage, chemistry and physics and culminated in a license as a merchant marine officer. But during World War II its student body did not have the luxury of four years to complete the course. Mirroring the urgency to get the job done in the shipyards, the four-year course was compressed into two years combining academics with military discipline and producing more than a thousand merchant marine officers every six months (in some periods, two thousand). Part of the training included sailing as a cadet on board active merchant ships.[2]

---

[2] Because of the requirement to sail in the merchant marine as part of their education, Kings Point cadets are the only students from federal academies to potentially face battle as part of their training. During World War II, 212 cadets were lost at sea.

While longshoremen loaded the cargo, the Armed Guard crew was occupied with stowing a secret experimental anti-submarine device known as the Mark-29 gear. Basically a combination sonar/anti-torpedo device it was designed to detect propeller noise and explode approaching torpedoes. It consisted of two paravanes[3] equipped with explosive charges and sensors which were towed behind them and to the side of the ship. When armed, the sensor detonated the explosive charge when it detected an approaching torpedo. In addition, a hydrophone was towed off the stern. Electric wiring ran from it to a listening panel on the bridge which allowed an operator to detect the sounds of enemy submarines or torpedoes without the interference of the ship's engines. Because it was a secret device, the listening panel was guarded by a sailor carrying a sidearm while the ship was in port.

On July 9 the cargo of steel was on board and the ship shifted to the grain elevator at Charlestown, in Boston Harbor.

Britain was in a state of siege. Rationing came into effect in 1940 on most foodstuffs and the amount each person was allowed steadily diminished. Eggs were unobtainable and worst of all, for the English, tea was limited to two ounces per person per week. By 1942 the United States had committed itself to supplying Great Britain with one-fourth of its food supply. This translated to 500,000,000 dozen eggs, 18,000,000 pounds of chicken, 759,000,000 pounds of pork and lard and canned fruits and vegetables. Beef was high on the desired list but as America had no surplus, 9,000,000 hogs were substituted resulting in new foods such as "Spam fritters." Powdered egg omelets became the

---

[3] Shaped much like airplane wing tanks, paravanes are usually towed in pairs by a wire rope fastened to the bottom of the stem of the ship. At the stem the wire rope is mounted to a fastening called a paravene skeg. Paravanes have tail fins which give them direction, causing them to swing out toward the sides of the ship rather than being towed directly behind. A more common use of paravanes was to sever the anchor lines holding mines to the bottom of the sea.

subject of a major British publicity campaign. By March of 1943, because of the U-boat menace, Britain was consuming 750,000 more tons of food, oil and military supplies than it was importing.

As the grain came aboard during the following days the merchant crew spent their time stowing gear and learning the intricacies of their new ship. The Armed Guard spent most of their time stowing ammunition, painting the new Mark-29 gear and cleaning guns.

On July 12, with all cargo on board and the hatches battened, the ship shifted to the Mystic coal docks. This was simply a staging area, a place for the *O'Brien* to wait while enough ships were gathered for a convoy.

The Armed Guard had their hands full learning how to operate the cannons and guns that many of them had never seen before. On July 15th they bore-sighted the 3-inch guns. This is a process whereby the accuracy of the guns is set. By sighting through the bore at a fixed target, the guns' sights are adjusted for accuracy. Although they didn't do any shooting, they did become accustomed to the hard metal sounds of the guns' breeches, springs and mechanisms, and the smell and feel of the oil and grease.

On July 17, the Armed Guard went through anti-aircraft training on the Polaroid trainer. This is a shoreside simulation of shipboard anti-aircraft firing. The crew was placed in a large room with a 20 millimeter gun emplacement in its center. As each member of the gun crew sat at the gun, silhouettes of enemy planes flew past which they shot at. The effect was realistic and three-dimensional with mock tracers darting from the barrels and "kills" recorded automatically. It was an effective way to hone the crew's skill both in coordination and plane recognition.

One of the last merchant crewmembers to join the ship was Frederick C. Warren. He signed on as Fireman Water/Tender. His career in the merchant marine began just over a year earlier with a letter from the Coast Guard Recruiting Office in Portland, Oregon. It was the maritime equivalent of a draft notice.

Dear Sir:

You are hereby instructed to report to this office at 8:00 a.m., Saturday morning, May 2nd, to be sworn in as an Apprentice Seaman in the U.S. Maritime Service.

Completion of your enrollment papers will be made and you will be sent to the training school at Port Hueneme, California next day, Sunday, May 3rd.

Upon receipt of this letter, please inform us by phone or in person of your intentions to be here on that date.

> Respectfully,
> (signed)
> L. H. Painter
> Officer in Charge
> U.S. Maritime Service

Other ships gathered as time drew close for departure. On July 20, 1943 the captain, radio operator and Armed Guard officer attended a convoy conference.

On July 21, the Mark-29 gear was laid out on deck in preparation for streaming. As the crew took in the lines, the *Jeremiah O'Brien* slowly eased away from the wharf and glided out of Boston Harbor. Departure was taken at 1618. In this first convoy were twenty-three ships and three escorts. The speed was set at 8 knots.

Captain Ralph "Buck" Wilson, master of the *Jeremiah O'Brien* after she became a museum ship, recalled his wartime convoys. "We sailed 400 yards apart. No lights. It was pitch-black at nights. We were supposed to run at a certain speed, but sometimes in the engine room they'd let the rpms build up."

Traveling in convoy was a nerve-wracking experience. A sharp watch had to be kept on all four sides to ensure that no ship drifted out of its "slot" in the convoy. Four hundred yards' separation between 440+ foot ships is a figurative "arm's length" with little margin for error. If the master or mate on watch saw that his ship was creeping up on the one ahead, he had to adjust.

For the Mark-29 gear to work as an anti-torpedo device it had to be able to explode an approaching torpedo. To do this required that the lines trailing from the paravanes have detonators and booster charges called armed covers. Through an oversight these weren't sent on board. The result was that although the Mark-29 devices were on deck and ready to run, they weren't put over the side.

Although the anti-torpedo section of the Mark-29 gear couldn't be streamed, the hydrophone could. After dinner that first day, the crew, struggling with unfamiliar equipment, got it rigged to tow 500 feet astern of the ship. The listening panel and hydrophone were tested and found in good working order. After a thorough two-hour test the gear was brought back on board by the exhausted crew.

During the night fog set in. The normal anxiety of night convoy travel was exacerbated by the fog. The morning of July 22nd the fog was so thick that none of the other ships in the convoy could be seen although they were traveling within a few hundred feet of one another. Each ship in the convoy had been assigned a position number at the convoy conference and throughout the day the sound of foghorns permeated the air as ship after ship periodically sounded its number on the whistle.

The morning of July 23 was dark and thick again, the fog persisting. At 1330 the *O'Brien* received radio orders from the convoy commodore to heave to. Normally fog wouldn't be a deterrent to a single ship. But somewhere ahead lay Nova Scotia. The commodore didn't want to risk running his twenty-six ships aground because of thick visibility. In the afternoon the fog broke. The *O'Brien* found herself separated slightly from the rest of the fleet and increased speed to half ahead to regain her convoy position. At 1820 the ships arrived at the pilot station at Halifax, Nova Scotia only to find that no pilots were available. The *O'Brien* hove to for the night. After waiting all night and most of the next day, July 24, a pilot finally came aboard and directed the *Jeremiah O'Brien* to an anchorage.

That evening a conference was held ashore for all the ships in the convoy including those that were joining at Halifax. Captain Southerland returned to the ship with orders to leave two hours ahead of the main convoy in order to allow time to stream the

Mark-29 gear. Apparently the missing equipment for the device was on its way. The *O'Brien* was the only ship in the convoy with such an apparatus and everyone was anxious to see it work. After streaming the gear, the ship could take her position in the assembled convoy.

On July 25, before sailing from Nova Scotia, three explosive streamers and six armed covers (detonators and booster charges) were brought aboard for the Mark-29 gear. The *O'Brien* sailed, official departure from Halifax being taken at 1116. They sailed into a fog again with 32 ships and two escorts. Speed was set at 10 knots.

At 1300 that day, in a thick fog and with a rough sea throwing spray on the main deck, the Armed Guard crew began launching the Mark-29 gear. It was miserable work, straining on slippery decks, their hands numb with cold, as they wrestled the bulky gear. Because of the constant pitching and the wet deck, the port and starboard sides of the gear were streamed separately. Then they noticed that the port gear wasn't working. It couldn't be retrieved without slowing the ship down and dropping out of the convoy. Rather than risk losing sight of the other ships, Captain Southerland decided to leave the gear out all night. Chilled to the bone, the crew retreated to their cramped quarters.

Jerome Shaw:

> We had that Mark 29 gear on there. When we went into a convoy they always put us in the 'coffin corner,' in the back right or left corner, so we could stream that gear. We'd have to slow down to put it out and then the convoy was over the horizon. Then we'd try to catch up and about the time we caught the convoy we'd have to slow down again to take it in. We spent a lot of time out there by ourselves, watching that convoy disappear.
>
> That was a real doozey to put out. The paravanes run almost parallel to the boom they came off of. And each one had a sensor and three detonators running back, all the same length, almost as long as the ship. They were extremely heavy and it was back-breaking work. The idea was when a torpedo went over the sensor the detonator charge would blow it.

The next day the fog cleared and the Halifax group joined a fleet of ships which came up from New York. The full convoy was an impressive sight. A total of seventy-three ships and ten escort vessels now proceeded across the North Atlantic toward England at a speed of 10 knots.

At 1030 the *O'Brien's* speed was reduced to 4 knots. The Mark-29 gear on the port side was partially retrieved and the armed cover on the inboard explosive streamer was changed. By the time the gear was relaunched it was noon and the *O'Brien* was six miles astern of the rest of the convoy. The streamer on the port side still wasn't operating.

The rest of the afternoon and evening were spent catching up. The following morning Captain Southerland requested permission from the convoy commodore to decrease speed again to 4 knots in order to repair the Mark-29 gear. The commodore granted permission by flashing light but also signaled that he had no idea what a Mark-29 gear was! The device was so secret that few people were aware of its existence.

The *Jeremiah O'Brien* again slowed down and at 1000 started the retrieving process. When the gear was pulled in it was found that the faired[4] towing line and several electrical conductors had breaks in them. A spare faired towing line was substituted and the gear relaunched. By 1130 the gear was once again out and the ship had dropped eight miles astern of the convoy. This time they were successful. The Mark-29 gear operated perfectly.

Unfortunately, the convoy commodore had become increasingly impatient with the lagging ship. At 1400 a blinker message was received from the convoy escort saying the *O'Brien* would be placed in a slower convoy next time. It was impossible to explain why the ship was out of position since the escort commander had never heard of Mark-29 gear and conditions

---

[4] Faired in this sense means streamlined. The towing line offered little resistance to the water it was being towed through.

didn't allow for a lengthy explanation by blinker light. Breaking radio silence was out of the question.

It took until 2300 to regain the proper position in the convoy. In the back of everyone's mind was the knowledge that a favorite U-boat tactic was to shadow convoys and pick off stragglers.

With so much time spent on the Mark-29 gear the Armed Guard crew had little time to organize and practice responding to an attack, but on July 30, 1943 at 1300 the first gun drill was held. The ship's general alarm bells were used to signal a surface attack. The crew's response was enthusiastic and eager. The gunnery officer was so impressed that he made the following entry in his daily log: "Ship's crew participating and showing considerable interest."

The escort ships were still puzzling over the strange equipment the *Jeremiah O'Brien* carried. The following evening a blinker message was received from one of the escort vessels. "Senior escort commander requests 'What is Mark 29'?" A quick reply was flashed back, "An anti-torpedo device."

On August 1st a signal was received from the commodore of the convoy that guns might be test-fired. With so many ships traveling close together it was prudent not to fire the guns unless everyone knew it was going to happen otherwise someone might think an attack was taking place and respond accordingly.

The 20 mm. guns were test-fired with a total of 330 rounds of ammunition being shot. Since these were automatic guns, this was not much firing, but it was enough to ensure that everything was in good operating condition.

As the convoy neared the coast of England the threat of attack became more real and excitement grew. On August 2, at 0930 eight of the ten escort vessels were seen sweeping astern of the convoy. Two white flares went up. Although no depth charges were heard, the gun crew went to battle stations. At 1200 two more white flares were shot from an escort vessel astern of the convoy. Just after four in the afternoon roaring sounds were heard on the Mark-29 hydrophone. The panel was armed in case it was

Loch Ewe on the west coast of Scotland as seen from the boat deck of the SS Jeremiah O'Brien *in 1943.* Coleman Schneider.

a submarine attack but after nothing happened it was decided that the sounds were depth charges. These incidents, nevertheless, were an ongoing reminder that the convoy was in a war zone and helped keep everyone alert. Statistics on sinkings weren't released until after the war, but during this same month of July 1943, sixty-one ships totaling more than 350,000 tons were sunk by enemy action.

Just after noon on August 5, the *Jeremiah O'Brien* arrived at her first foreign port, Aultbea, Loch Ewe, Scotland, situated on the northwest coast of Scotland, across from the Outer Hebrides.

The ship was fitted with a barrage balloon and that same evening she departed with sixteen other merchant ships and two escort vessels at a speed of nine knots. Proceeding northeast and then in an easterly direction, the convoy rounded the northern tip of Scotland.

At 0745, August 6, the convoy arrived at Methill, near Edinburgh, in the Firth of Forth, Scotland. This wide bay was mined by the German submarine *U-31* in late 1939, and one of its mines sank the brand-new cruiser *Belfast*. Fortunately the area was well swept and several other ships were peacefully at anchor.

A convoy conference ashore took up most of the day. These conferences were a source of information and the captain brought back the news that the convoy ahead had been attacked by German E-boats[5] with only two ships surviving.

That evening the convoy, now consisting of thirty-seven ships and one escort vessel, sailed at a speed of 7.5 knots for London and arrived just before noon on August 9, with the ships disbursing to various docks and anchorages.

The cargo was discharged and on August 16th the anchor was weighed and the ship departed London. The *O'Brien* was one of thirty ships in convoy with two escorts, proceeding at a speed of 7.5 knots. The course was north, to pass over the top of Scotland and then east toward the United States. All the ships were in ballast.

With the cargo discharged and the vessel homewardbound it might be thought the worst was over with. In fact, danger loomed just over the horizon and set in quickly. Late that evening, while passing offshore of Great Yarmouth, the firing of big guns and loud explosions on shore were heard, raising speculation around the ship. The crew would later learn the port of Hull was under air attack. The next morning a loud explosion shook the ship bringing everyone to battle stations. There were no submarines or planes around but minesweepers were working the area the convoy traveled. They had detonated a mine directly in the *O'Brien's* path.

The following evening the convoy arrived at Methil. Here, the ships were separated according to destination and new convoys assembled. The *Jeremiah O'Brien*, along with twenty-three other ships and four escorts was assigned to a northbound convoy that traveled at an agonizingly slow speed of 4.5 knots. The crew settled in for the evening reading, writing letters or in journals, playing poker.

---

[5] The E-boat or *schnellboot* was a motor torpedo boat used by the Germans as an escort and combatant against British naval units, merchant ships and aircraft and, eventually, against the Normandy Invasion shipping.

The reality of war was never far away. Although a different ship in a different convoy, this Liberty with No. 2 hold on fire is a vivid example of what the O'Brien's crew often feared would happen to them. National Archives.

The morning of the 19th came peacefully with the ships plodding their way northward. At 1030 friendly planes flew over, giving everyone a feeling of confidence. Then, just as supper was over and the convoy was off the Buchan Ness Light near Aberdeen, a periscope was sighted. Three depth charges were dropped by the escort vessels, and the *O'Brien* made a 45 degree emergency turn to starboard as general quarters was sounded on the ship's alarm. Ten minutes of anxious watchfulness followed but apparently the submarine was driven off and the convoy returned to base course.

At 2050 the same night the escort vessel's signal lights began flashing across the water. Enemy aircraft were in the area. The convoy commodore ordered all ships to man their guns. General quarters was again sounded and the Armed Guard crew manned their guns. At 2150 the "all clear" was received from the escort ships on the radio-telephone. By this time even the novices were getting used to the mentally demanding routine — long hours of boredom killing time with card games, messroom conversation or paperback books, broken by hours on watch which could also be boring (unless they were on the Mark-29 detail), interrupted by frequent alarms, which everyone hoped wouldn't be "for real."

To this point, the *O'Brien* had performed admirably. Except for the problems with the Mark-29, her maiden voyage had proceeded remarkably smoothly. Then her luck changed. Captain Southerland received a call from the engine room. Both boilers were leaking badly, the ship couldn't maintain speed. This was transmitted to the convoy Commodore who signaled, "Return to port now." The *Jeremiah O'Brien* slowed down and came about. The captain's sealed sailing orders had specific instructions for such eventualities. Stragglers were to proceed to the Firth of Clyde. As an escort couldn't be spared for a single ship, the *O'Brien* sailed back alone. Fortunately it wasn't far. In the morning of August 23, 1943 the *O'Brien* arrived at Gourock, on the Firth of Clyde, Scotland.

While the boilers were being repaired, a conference was held concerning the Mark-29 gear, the problems the ship had with the gear and the time involved in rigging it, which slowed the ship down. The Royal Navy was especially concerned with knowing the difficulties encountered in streaming the gear while in convoy. Tentative plans were made for the ship to have a rear flank position in the next convoy so the gear could be put to use in such a manner as to protect the bulk of the ships in the grid.

Captain Southerland received the following instruction:

> To: Master, S.S. Jeremiah O'Brien
> From: N.C.S.O., The Clyde
> You are to await orders from the Commodore before streaming your Helm Apparatum (MK-29) gear. If not received by the time you reach 10 degrees west then ask permission to go ahead and stream gear.

August 22nd saw ships for the new convoy converging from three areas: Loch Ewe and the Mersey and Clyde Rivers. It took three hours to form a broad front and get all the ships in their

Losing convoy position made a ship a "sitting duck" for Nazi U-boats. The intensity of the fire on this Liberty would indicate something burning at high temperature, such as manganese. Smithsonian Institution.

proper convoy positions. This took place off Oversay light. The result was a gigantic square of sixty ships and five escort vessels sailing at 9.5 knots for the east coast of the United States.

After supper that evening the chief engineer reported that despite the repairs made in Gourock, four tubes in the starboard boiler still leaked. He thought it significant but not serious enough to prevent the *Jeremiah O'Brien* from maintaining convoy speed without difficulty — providing the weather held.

It didn't.

By August 29 the ship was pitching and rolling badly in a very heavy sea. Captain Southerland decided not to stream the Mark-29 gear since the ship's speed could not be decreased and still allow it to retain position in the convoy. At 1400 that afternoon a message was relayed from the convoy Commodore.

> From Comm.
> To: 1-6 (the *Jeremiah O'Brien's* position in the convoy)
> Have you special gear in operation. If not stream it at your convenience and warn other ships regarding apparatus.

Captain Southerland sent an immediate reply:

> From: 1-6
> To: Comm.
> Gear not in operation at present will stream gear as soon as sea moderates.

The next morning Chief Montgomery reported that as long as full speed was maintained and no fires extinguished under the boilers, the leaking of tubes could be held to a minimum. Apparently the fires were hot enough to vaporize the water as soon as it leaked out of the tubes. He planned to continue the voyage without attempting repairs.

The convoy commodore signaled that convoy speed would be reduced to 6 knots at 0800 so that ships with net defenses might stream nets.[6]

---

[6] Some ships were equipped with nets that could be rigged over the side. The idea was for the nets to catch and/or deflect any torpedo that was fired at a ship. For the nets to function the ship was forced to travel at a slow speed which made it more susceptible to submarine attack as submarines had a relatively slow underwater speed at this time. It was questionable whether the reduction in speed was a worthwhile trade-off.

The *Jeremiah O'Brien* didn't have nets, but at 0800 the Armed Guard crew began streaming the Mark-29 gear. In lowering the paravane on the starboard side, the faired towing line was torn so badly as to render it useless. Abandoning the starboard gear, the crew rigged out the port paravane. Two hours later the gear was out and running. But when the circuits were tested they didn't work. Fortunately, because of the slow convoy speed, the ship had not lost convoy position.

That quickly changed. Fifteen minutes later the convoy increased speed to 9.5 knots. The *O'Brien* tried to stay with the group but finally, at 1300, Captain Southerland decided to reduce speed to pull in the useless Mark-29 gear. Engine speed was decreased to four knots and the Mark-29 paravane on the port side was retrieved. The faired towing line was found to have several torn sections that had filled with salt water. All the Mark-29 gear was stowed on deck, engine speed was increased and five hours later the ship regained its position in the convoy.

The bad weather continued. On August 31 the conditions were logged as "Very heavy sea. Ship rolling badly."

By 1100 the weather abated slightly and the seas were calmer. But this was the North Atlantic and calm weather is short-lived. By 1400 it was again blowing a moderate gale with the wind at a Beaufort force of 7-8 (28-40 knots) and the ship was again rolling severely.

From the Armed Guard Log: "1900. Difficult for ship to make headway. Became separated from main body of convoy. Placed 2 men on wings of navigational bridge and 2 men on main deck below after 3" gun platform. Difficult for men to maintain footing on wet decks."

By the following morning the *O'Brien* found herself in company with four other ships that were unable to keep up. Fortunately, an escort vessel spotted them and signaled that the main convoy was just ahead over the horizon. By 1000 the main convoy was sighted, the sea moderated and the wind dropped to a force of 3 (7-10 knots) on the Beaufort Scale. Chief

Montgomery informed everyone it would be necessary to ration water, since the boilers were using more than twice the regular amount.

On September 4, just after midnight, two white flares were spotted on the starboard side of the convoy. An emergency turn was made. Apparently a ship had been torpedoed somewhere forward of their position for, an hour and a half later, the *O'Brien* went through a heavy oil slick. Due to radio silence, the crew was left to wonder what had happened.

Just after noon the same day a heavy fog set in. Once again the air was filled with the sound of ships' whistles as each vessel periodically sounded its convoy position.

After days of pitching, rolling and being battered about in heavy seas and violent winds, a weather advisory was received on September 5, and the commodore obediently relayed it to all the ships in the fleet: a hurricane warning had been received. It was about four days too late.

On September 6, at suppertime, the fog set in again. Although there was no wind, the ship was rolling badly in heavy swells. On September 7, fifteen ships detached themselves for Halifax, Nova Scotia but in the fog no one saw them leave.

Finally, on September 10, 1943, just after midnight, the convoy and the *Jeremiah O'Brien* arrived at New York City. At 1800 she docked at Pier 57 in the North River.

Voyage One was over.

7

VOYAGE TWO

At Pier 57, North River, New York City, the *Jeremiah O'Brien* immediately began preparing for a load of general cargo and ammunition. Having completed their first voyage to the war zone successfully, some of the crew were naturally inclined to celebrate their survival. Unfortunately, some celebrated too much and had to face the consequences.

On September 14 the *O'Brien* shifted to Pier F, Jersey City, New Jersey to load explosives[1], then shifted back to Pier 57, North River the following day to finish off her load with a deck cargo of vehicles and general cargo.

---

[1] It was common practice at that time to load explosives and ammunition in the upper tween deck on the square of each of the hatches. This allowed for quick access when discharging, thus almost immediately removing the hazard from the ship when it arrived at its discharge port.

The crew continued to decompress. To Ensign Charles Foote, Armed Guard Commanding Officer, fell the not inconsiderable task of maintaining discipline in the Armed Guard. On September 19, one seaman was absent at morning muster. He reported aboard the following day and was restricted to the ship and given extra duty. Another seaman returned aboard 5 hours late. He was placed on report for being absent over leave (AOL). Most of the Navy gunmen didn't seem to resent the discipline. It was simply the price one paid for not following the rules.

As on the previous voyage, the crew signed 12-month articles for a foreign voyage with final discharge port once more being simply "USA."

By September 21, the deck cargo had been loaded and lashed in place with chains.

In the early morning the *O'Brien* shifted to an anchorage off the Statue of Liberty to await the formation of a convoy. Official departure from New York was taken on September 22 at 0630. The *Jeremiah O'Brien* left in a convoy of forty-eight ships with speed set at 10 knots. Four escort vessels accompanied them as they headed into the open sea bound for England.

The concept of convoys dated from World War I when England was losing one out of every four ships to submarines. They organized the convoy system in 1917, and found it reduced their losses by 80 percent. When aircraft were added to the protection, the losses became negligible. The effect of sighting an airplane, civilian or military, by a surfaced U-boat, was an immediate dive to deep water with the accompanying loss of opportunity for the submarine and the disclosure of its location to the plane and, shortly thereafter, to the naval escorts.

During World War II the convoy system was refined. After lengthy analysis, the British concluded that the number of vessels lost in any convoy was proportional to the number of attacking submarines and the size of the escort, not to the number of ships in the convoy. That is, if a wolf pack attacked a group of twenty-

Statistically, convoys meant fewer ships were subject to attack. Unfortunately, the weather was rarely as pleasant as depicted in this photo. National Archives.

five ships it might sink twelve, yet if the convoy contained seventy-five ships it would still only sink twelve. The result was larger convoys with more escorts. The strategy proved effective. Of the 215 merchant ships sunk during the first nine months of the Battle of the Atlantic, only twenty-one were escorted in convoy.

Basically, a convoy sailed in a square of rows and columns. Typically, a group of sixty ships would have a front consisting of a row of twelve ships across with each ship having a row of four ships behind it — a grid measuring twelve ships across by five ships deep. A ship presents the largest target from the side, therefore having only five rows of ships minimized the number of targets.

The convoy commodore would be a merchant ship whose master was assigned responsibility for the other merchant ships in the convoy. Located in the center of the front row, he also had to see to it that the ships stayed in position. The merchant ships traveled 500 yards apart fore and aft and 1,000 yards apart side to side. Ammunition ships, troop transports and tankers would be placed in the center of the grid with the rule that ammunition ships were never placed side by side or next to a tanker to reduce the possibility of a chain reaction should one be hit.

Five thousand yards diagonally off each point of the rectangle of ships would be a destroyer or corvette.[2] With their great speed and armed with "ash cans" or depth charges, they patrolled in an elliptical pattern protecting the front and back of the convoy. In addition, two or more escorts patrolled the convoy's flanks, 10,000 yards out, in long rectangular patterns. The distance between the two flank escorts was about 18 miles with the convoy halfway between them. The escort commander was usually the naval vessel patrolling the left front corner of the convoy. When under attack he took charge of the entire convoy, including the merchant ships.

Keeping station in a large convoy, often sailing through stormy weather, heavy seas, in darkness or blinding fog was a formidable enterprise. In addition to the difficulties of keeping position, shipmasters had to be sure their ships didn't show smoke by day or lights at night. They were warned not to throw rubbish overboard or pump bilges during the day so that floating waste or oily slick wouldn't betray the convoy's route.

That first morning out, the *O'Brien* ran ahead of the convoy, the crew preparing to launch the by-now-accursed Mark-29 gear. Its reputation had run before it and even the new crew knew about all the problems it caused on voyage No. 1. But the submarine danger in the North Atlantic was increasing and every possible anti-torpedo device available, flawed or not, had to be employed.

---

[2] At the beginning of the war Great Britain was short on escorts, the basic defense of the convoy system. Prime Minister Winston Churchill ordered fifty-six escorts based on a whalecatcher, the *Southern Pride*, then in use by Smith's Docks Ltd. of Middlesborough. These became the "Flower Class Corvettes," and quickly filled a serious need. Although three knots slower than the U-boat's surface speed, the design existed and could be produced cheaply at £90,000 with only slight modification for armament. Eventually, 288 corvettes were built in England and Canada and accounted for the destruction of fifty U-boats. Churchill referred to them as "Cheap and Nasties."

The Riviere du Loup, *an Increased Endurance Flower class corvette, was built in 1942-43. Here, she looks rather weather worn.* Author's collection.

With grim determination the Armed Guard began streaming the paravanes, faired lines and hydrophone just after noon. They finished at 1400 only to learn the paravane on the starboard side had broached and needed to be pulled in. Finishing that task, the crew hoped they were through for the day and enjoyed a warm supper, anticipating a well-earned rest. But the rest was short-lived. During the night it was discovered that the gear retarded the speed of the ship to less than the speed of the convoy so they were called out and the remaining paravane was taken in. The log does not detail their state of mind nor the remarks that were made, although Morgan Williams recorded the following in his personal diary: "I sure don't think much of MK-29 and neither do the other boys or even the Ensign."

Because of the need for radio silence, communication between ships was difficult. Most messages were transmitted by flashing light or semaphore. This method of "pass it along" was slow, inefficient and prone to errors or misunderstanding. Situations frequently occurred in which the escorts simply couldn't stay up with what each ship was doing at any given time. This was sometimes frustrating and at other times comical. For example, the following morning one of the escorts called by blinker.

"Take in your special gear and take your position in convoy."

In 1943 a corvette signals the SS Jeremiah O'Brien *while negotiating a rough sea in the North Atlantic. Coleman Schneider.*

One can envision Captain Southerland on the bridge, "Grr-r-r-r-e-e-a-t Scott. What do they think we've been doing for the last twenty-four hours?"

But the official reply was business-like.

"Gear has been retrieved and we are proceeding at utmost speed."

The hydrophone was allowed to stream from the stern and a continuous watch was kept at the listening panel. This was the only component of the system that performed to expectations and it didn't slow the ship down, unlike the paravanes with their additional paraphernalia of faired towing lines and explosive charges. Nonetheless, it took until mid-afternoon to regain position in the convoy.

At this time almost the entire North Atlantic was a minefield. In addition to stationery mines planted by both the Allies and the Axis at every harbor entrance, German U-boats prowled the ocean in wolfpacks, loaded with enough torpedoes to sink entire fleets. Add the dangers in the depths to those on the surface — bitter cold, blinding fogs, fierce storms and wild seas — and the Atlantic run was a perilous one, indeed.

This British tanker, exploding after being hit by a German torpedo, vividly depicts the impact of the Nazi U-boat. U.S. Naval Historical Center.

Every seaman's greatest fear was of being torpedoed. The freezing water temperatures were as great a threat to life as any bomb or torpedo. As the war progressed, stories of days, weeks and even months in lifeboats on cold, fog-bound waters added to the lore of Atlantic mariners — stories like that of the Liberty ship *Stephen Hopkins* which, sailing alone westbound in the South Atlantic in 1942, sighted what appeared to be two cargo vessels. One of the ships stripped away its disguise, raised the Nazi flag and revealed its true identity as a merchant raider, the *Stier*. Armed with six 5.9 inch guns and two torpedo tubes the raider and her supply ship, *Tannenfels,* ordered the Liberty to surrender. Paul Buck, the *Hopkins'* skipper, raised the American flag and turned his ship with its single 4-inch gun toward the Germans and for twenty minutes the ships exchanged fire. Both ships (*Stier* and *Stephen Hopkins*) sank, the crew from the *Hopkins* spending four weeks in a lifeboat before reaching the coast of Brazil.

To enhance the chances of survival, the Coast Guard issued new regulations based on the lessons learned in earlier sinkings.

Part 153 of Coast Guard wartime regulations created new standards based on the "Unlimited National Emergency" proclaimed by President Roosevelt on May 27, 1941. In addition to the standard requirement that a ship carry lifeboats on each side for 100% of the crew, ships were also required to carry a minimum of four rafts, each capable of carrying between fifteen and twenty persons. These had to be carried so they would float free if the ship sank. In addition to the standard requirement of one life preserver for each member of the crew, ships were now required to carry additional life preservers on the boat deck equivalent to twenty-five percent of the crew. These were to be stowed so they would float free if the ship sank. Lifeboats were carried at the boat deck railing and griped in or held there for immediate lowering and air tanks were required so that the boat would float, even when filled with water. Made of metal, these were strapped or otherwise fastened to the undersides of the thwarts.

Because of the severe weather conditions more than two-thirds of those who survived a sinking in the Atlantic usually died of exposure. So the equipment list for lifeboats was adjusted to enhance survival at sea over long periods of time in cold and adverse weather. This included: blankets, chart, drinking cups, first aid kit, flashlight batteries, canvas hood and sidespray curtain, lamp wicks, massage oil, (to combat "immersion foot"), mast and sail, matches, provisions (biscuits, pemmican, chocolate tablets, milk tablets), signal flag, water containers, signal pistol (with 12 parachute red signal cartridges), fishing kit (containing gloves, knife, sinkers, sharpening stone, pork rinds bait, hooks, instructions, dip net, cord, line, winders and bib), daytime distress signals, portable identification boards[3], life preserver covering, life preserver light, lifesaving suits (exposure suit), whistles and jackknives, abandon-ship kit (20 syrettes of morphine, 48 tablets sulfadiazine, 10 packages containing 2½

---

[3] In peacetime ships are required to show the vessel's name and home port on each lifeboat and on the bow and stern of the ship itself. These were painted over in wartime.

grams of crystalline sulfanilamide, 4 ounces oil cleaning solution, 5 tubes 5 percent sulfadiazine, tannic acid 10 percent jelly, 2 chemical heating pads), lifesaving nets, signal mirrors.

Ken Holsapple, Seaman First Class: "It was cold on almost every trip we made. We had to wear that foul weather gear all the time. We didn't take our clothes off, slept in our lifejackets when we got in close [to England]."

John Crosby, third mate on voyage #6 of the *O'Brien* recalled his Atlantic crossings: "I never showered and always slept in my clothes out of fear of being hit and not adequately dressed for the cold weather in the life boat. The North Atlantic was always high winds, heavy seas, 150 ships in convoy and constantly under submarine and air attack."

In the early evening of September 24, 1943, sixteen ships from Halifax joined the convoy off Sable Island making a total of sixty-four ships traveling together. Little happened for the next few days. On September 28, the 20 mm. guns were test fired. Two days later, Chief Engineer Montgomery reported that the boiler tubes were leaking again and using excessive amounts of water. The weather grew worse and by evening the seas were heavy. The *O'Brien* was forced to drop two miles astern of the convoy in order to lash down some of the deck cargo of military vehicles that had worked loose. It was difficult scrambling around the pitching deck dodging loose cargo, trying to refasten lashings in what dim light they were allowed, punctuated here and there by the eerie glow of luminous tape. Eventually they got the job done and caught up with the rest of the ships.

That same evening an aircraft carrier and several additional escorts joined the convoy, bolstering the crew's confidence. There was something very reassuring about having the might of a carrier in their midst. In the morning of October 1, the carrier sent up two planes which searched the water ahead for submarines. During the day, for unknown reasons, it left the convoy, but rejoined it that evening. The next morning the carrier again dispatched several planes. The ships were closer to Europe and the danger was growing greater. Nine escort vessels now protected the convoy. Two days later the Loch Ewe portion of the group broke off, heading for Scotland. The remaining ships formed into three columns.

Late in the evening of October 4, forty-three depth charges were heard exploding off Tory Island, Ireland. After launching the Mark-29 hydrophone, the Armed Guard manned their guns, ready for action. Although another false alarm, it was a reminder that the crew was in waters that could at any moment spit up a torpedo.

In the early morning of October 5 the Mark-29 hydrophone was retrieved. As usual, it was difficult work. The crew had been at battle stations most of the night and the seas were heavy, so heavy, in fact, that many of the ships had difficulty maneuvering. Several ships signaled the convoy Commodore for instructions. None were forthcoming.

It was one of the ironies of wartime crossings that although ships were surrounded by scores of convoy sisters, most had little or no idea what might be occurring around them. Each ship was a virtual island, sufficient unto herself and knowing only what was happening on her own decks. Explosions, alerts and alarms, the appearance and disappearance of carriers, escorts, and planes and even members of the convoy were only to be conjectured at with no answer forthcoming. The more curious or persistent might find out some information later, but after awhile, each ship's crew simply settled into their own world and looked after themselves.

The *Jeremiah O'Brien* arrived at Liverpool, England on October 6, 1943 at 0730, anchored awaiting a berth and docked the same afternoon at Gladstone dock No. 1. With the ship safely in port, the crew's interests quickly turned to the enticements ashore and the following afternoon six of the Armed Guard seaman were discovered drinking whiskey and restricted to the vessel.

The last of the cargo was offloaded on October 18 and the *O'Brien* departed from Liverpool in ballast. So many ships were running in and out of English ports they no longer steamed at night in the nearby waters in blackout. This was partly because the Royal Air Force had won the battle of the British skies and was carrying the attack into European airspace, giving the homefront a measure of security. Then, in the relative safety of English waters, an unexpected disaster struck the convoy. The morning after departure, as the convoy tried to get into their assigned positions for the voyage home, two ships collided and one ship caught on fire. Why or how the collision occurred was never determined. Presumably, it was from the intricacies of too many ships maneuvering too closely together. The collision was another reminder that there were dangers besides U-boats and mines and that a high state of alertness had to be constantly maintained. There was just too much going on.

The convoy finally formed off Oversay Light, on the north-west coast of Scotland, a total of sixty-eight merchant ships with six "close" escorts all traveling at a speed of 9.5 knots.

Crews on board merchant ships lived in an atmosphere of suppressed danger. There was the constant fear that at any moment they might be bombed by enemy planes or struck by a torpedo and if this happened they had to be ready to abandon ship on a moment's notice. But the reality of day-to-day life was long stretches of routine watchstanding and boredom spiced with the unpredictable sounds of depth charges and the general alarm signaling "G.Q." The paradox was that life aboard ship continued in a relatively normal manner, yet one always had to be ready because the next alert might very well be for the torpedo with "*Jeremiah O'Brien*" written on its nose.

As the convoy pushed north the barometer fell and the seas rose — the curse of North Atlantic weather again bedeviling the ships. The crew groaned as the ships rolled heavily homeward. On the *Jeremiah O'Brien* the men staggered across the heaving decks and the engine room floor plates, the constant rolling making the simple task of getting from one place to another almost impossible. The *Jeremiah O'Brien* was known as a "feeder." She had a good galley and cooks who dished up two meats on the menu and three vegetables. Breakfast was bacon or sausage or hotcakes and eggs any way the crewmen wanted. Dinner could be steak. But, in very heavy weather soup and sandwiches were all that could be prepared for meals, pots and pans wouldn't stay on the stove long enough to cook anything.

At night the crew cursed the sea, wedging themselves into their bunks with lifejackets under the mattresses as they tried to get a few hours' fitful sleep. In extreme rolls, the sounds of crockery breaking, punctuated by the reverberant clang of falling pots and pans, echoed throughout the midship house.

An aircraft carrier joined the convoy, taking position in Column 6. The sense of security the massive warship's presence gave the *O'Brien's* crew was short-lived. Heavy seas made it impossible to hold position and the convoy was forced to scatter. During the night the weather abated enough to regroup. Early in the morning of October 21 a signal came by convoy light[4] for all ships to execute three 20 degree turns to starboard. Had a submarine been spotted? Again, communications were almost nonexistent and there was no way of knowing. The ships did as they were ordered and the turns were made quickly, one after the other. The following day a second aircraft carrier joined the convoy. At this time, standing on the flying bridge, Captain Southerland counted fifty ships around the horizon.

When they awoke on the morning of October 25, the crew discovered that one of the aircraft carriers had left the convoy during the night. Where had it gone and why? No one knew. The remaining carrier dispatched planes at intervals throughout the day. A flying boat was seen patrolling over the convoy during the morning. The following day, in the early afternoon, the seaman at

---

[4] All ships carried a "Christmas Tree" of convoy lights on a mast on the flying bridge. Three red and three green lights were displayed in a vertical line, side by side. Various turns and directions were indicated by the combinations of red and green shown at any given time.

Even approaching the east coast of the United States a convoy couldn't let its guard down. U-boats could strike anywhere, any time. National Archives.

the listening panel of the Mark-29 heard sounds resembling exploding depth charges. Some 60-70 sounds were heard during the afternoon. The escorts were in position. None of them was dropping depth charges. As there were no other indications of activity the ensign decided the noises were probably due to mechanical defects in the hydrophone. It was another cry of "wolf" by the mechanical monster.

A signal was sent from the convoy commodore to all vessels for "New Defense" ships to stream nets at 1500. The *O'Brien* signaled "Shall we stream our Mk-29 gear at 1500?"

The reply was "No," with no explanations. By now most of the crew had given up on the Mark-29 gear as being any kind of help.

That evening two white flares were seen, apparently from a ship on the forward port corner of the convoy, followed in quick succession by three sets of two white flares fired together and a Roman candle fired singly. The general alarm was sounded and the gun crew went to battle stations. No explosions and no depth charges were heard. An hour later the crew secured from battle stations. Once more, it was the old complaint, "Hurry up and wait."

On October 27 Captain Southerland decided to stop listening to the Mark-29 hydrophone. The constant mechanical noises coming through the listening panel were more of a distraction than a help.

Finally, the convoy approached the east coast of the United States. The ships formed into long columns to negotiate the narrow approach area to New York, which was constantly patrolled and swept for mines. For the first time the running lights were turned on, dimmed, during the night. The Atlantic seaboard of America was still a shooting gallery for Nazi submarines at this time, however, and even this close to home there could be danger. In the four months that the *Jeremiah O'Brien* had plied the seas since her launching in June, 134 Allied ships totalling 750,000 tons had been sunk.

The *Jeremiah O'Brien* took official arrival in New York at 1400 on November 2, 1943 and at 2100 she docked at Pier 58 North River. Voyage No. 2 ended at midnight.

8

WINTER NORTH ATLANTIC

Voyage No. 3 should have started at one minute after midnight on November 4, 1943. Instead, several days passed with the ship tied up to Pier 58 in the North River, New York City. This was significant for during wartime there was seldom a wait for cargo to be loaded. Delays were common in unloading, especially in Europe or the South Pacific where a ship might have to wait her turn at a berth but a delay in loading in a U.S. port was rare and a source of speculation.

The first sign of any kind of action was on November 10 and was most unwelcome — additional Mark 29 gear was brought on board including a complete new instrument rack assembly, a new angle indicator panel, four detector streamers, two faired towing lines and four paravanes. Apparently the ship was being prepared for another run.

That evening the ship shifted from Pier 10, Erie Basin to Pier 58, North River where it began loading a cargo of trucks, tanks and mail. The gunnery crew was sent ashore to hone their skills on their weapons and for the next week they practiced at 3-inch and 20 mm mounts. On November 18, 1943 foreign articles for 12 months were signed. The voyage, which began at one minute after midnight on November 19, was to be from "a point in the Atlantic Ocean to the Eastward of New York and thence to such ports and places in any part of the world as the Master may direct or as may be ordered or directed by the United States Government or any department, commission or agency thereof."

It was increasingly clear that an Allied invasion of Europe would occur in the near future. There were obvious signs — the cargoes being sent to England consisted more of military equipment and less of civilian commodities than earlier in the war. England was surviving, now she needed to be fortified. On board the *O'Brien* discipline and security measures tightened and the rules for standing watch were strictly enforced. The watchstander was required to literally stand and watch for strangers loitering, for unusual incidents, for anything out of the ordinary.

New York was far from the battlefields of Europe, but everyone was constantly aware of the war. Sabotage was a prime concern. Every merchant ship received a list of security instructions from the Captain of the Port on arrival. These covered every eventuality from swimmers in the water to sabateurs to direct attack and fire.

It was especially important that the enemy not learn what cargoes were loaded on which merchant ships nor their destinations. "Loose lips sink ships," was the credo of the waterfront. Most cargoes were crated and marked in code. A person could not tell from the outside what was in a given container. Sealed sailing orders were given to the master to be opened only after the ship was at sea. When the *O'Brien* finished loading her cargo on November 24, the Army restricted everyone to the ship.

The following day was filled with pre-sailing conferences. In his book, *Eastward the Convoys*, William G. Schofield described the convoy conferences:

> In New York or Boston or Norfolk or Halifax, there was an electricity to those conferences. They were held in well-lighted surroundings, amidst great wall maps and marine charts, where mock-up convoy formations were moved about and where late reports on the location of submarine wolfpacks were illustrated by lights and models. When you left to return to the ship and await departure time, you went out feeling the way a well-trained football team does when it runs from the locker room onto the playing field for the start of the second half. You felt alive and confident and ready for hard action.

The *Jeremiah O'Brien* set sail on voyage No. 3 on November 26, 1943, departing from New York at 0845 in a convoy of thirty-seven ships. Her assigned position was No. 91, meaning she was the lead ship in column number 9. There were four escort vessels and the convoy speed was set at 9.5 knots.

On November 29 the fleet was joined by twenty-three ships from Halifax, Nova Scotia, making a total of sixty merchant ships. As they proceeded eastward the weather, as usual, deteriorated and with winter coming on, the usual bad weather could be expected to be even worse. The North Atlantic did not disappoint. The next day the beam seas were extremely rough causing the ship to roll heavily. There was so much water on deck and footing was so difficult that the sea watch was secured from the forward gun and posted on the flying bridge.

By December 1 the *O'Brien* was separated from the main body of the convoy. Only five other ships were in sight. A hurricane warning (more timely than those on previous voyages) was issued. The sea watch on the after gun was secured and brought to the flying bridge and at 1000 everyone in the quarters aft (the Armed Guard gun crew) was moved amidships because of heavy seas. With saltwater coursing from one end of the ship to the other, Captain Southerland feared for their safety and he was right. Only a few hours later the wooden catwalk built over the after deck cargo of tanks and trucks washed away. By the following morning the seas had moderated enough that watches could be posted at the forward and after guns and the gun crew was allowed to return to their quarters. But now they faced a new problem. There wasn't a ship in sight. Such contingencies were covered in the sailing orders. If separated, a ship was to sail to a rendezvous position. However, due to an error in the rendezvous position the *O'Brien* found only empty ocean at the appointed time and place. A second contingency called for a ship to take a "straggler's route" to her destination. The *O'Brien* set course on this route and at 1630 sighted a plane and one ship, hull down (only masts and superstructure showing above the horizon). On December 3 two merchant ships and an escort vessel were sighted. Receiving word from the escort that the convoy was astern, the *Jeremiah O'Brien* slowed down to let the bulk of the fleet catch up and eventually she regained her position.

On December 10 the escort vessel left the convoy and shortly thereafter the ships arrived at Loch Ewe, Aultbea, Scotland. As on previous trips, a barrage balloon was put aboard. The *O'Brien* and Convoy No. 29, now consisting of eleven ships and two escorts, departed from Loch Ewe traveling northward around Northern Scotland towards Methil.

On December 12, the ships arrived at Methil in the Firth of Forth, Scotland, picked up seventeen merchant ships and two escort vessels and departed maintaining a speed of 7.5 knots. The next evening the *Jeremiah O'Brien* left the main convoy for the Humber River and at 2000 she arrived at Immingham dock (across the river and downstream from Hull).

Merchant seamen are allowed an advance against their wages when they arrive in a foreign port. Called a "draw" because the advance is drawn against their earnings, it gives them money for excursions ashore. The crew was given a draw the following day at the official rate of exchange of one British pound = $4.035

(American). The captain received £286 and 10 shillings from the ship's agent for this purpose, and the crew were soon off to enjoy themselves ashore.

Cargo work went slowly because there were more ships in the harbor than there were berths and cranes to handle them. Civilians were augmented with U.S. Army personnel and the following week was spent discharging cargo and loading dunnage lumber as ballast.

On Christmas Day the *O'Brien* left the Immingham docks. Anchoring just inside the submarine nets[1] in the River Humber, she awaited the formation of a convoy. On board was a cargo of sand ballast and 150 tons of dunnage lumber. Christmas dinner included turkey, mashed potatoes, peas, dressing, cake and fruit. On December 31, 1943 the *Jeremiah O'Brien* arrived at Loch Ewe and departed with fourteen other merchant ships and one escort vessel. On New Year's Day, 1944 they joined the main convoy from the Clyde and Mersey Rivers off Oversay Light. Approximately fifty ships spread in a broad grid eighteen miles across were returning to the United States, shepherded by seven escort vessels and one aircraft carrier, speed set at 9.5 knots. They immediately ran into heavy weather. Being in ballast, the ship rolled badly.

The weather moderated slightly for the next two days. During that time aircraft, bombers and carrier-based planes were seen over the convoy at intervals. It was both reassuring to see so much protection on that side of the Atlantic and anxiety-inducing because it indicated a stepped-up level of submarine activity. Frequent changes of course were ordered by the commodore, adding to the tension. Fifty-seven ships of various tonnages and differing configurations, sailing in relatively close formation,

---

[1] Submarine nets were made of steel cable. With a mesh of about one foot between strands or links, they were suspended across harbors from buoys. At times of scheduled ship arrivals and departures a boat called a net tender opened the net by towing one end clear of the entryway. Many nets were equipped with acoustical devices to detect the approach of submarines.

trying to change course simultaneously while rolling in heavy seas was a real navigational challenge.

On January 5, the commodore suddenly became aware of the Mark-29 gear. At 1100 a message was received "Are you equipped with Mark-29 gear?"

The *Jeremiah O'Brien* replied "Yes."

After digesting this news for a few hours the commodore signaled at 1430, "What time would you require to stream gear?"

The *O'Brien* replied "2 hours' time at least."

This resulted in another two hours' rumination. Then at 1630 the Commodore flashed, "Take station 125. I will reduce speed of convoy if necessary."

The *O'Brien* signaled back "Are we to stream our Mark-29 gear tomorrow morning. Can not get ready before dark today. Our orders were not to stream gear. Have these orders been changed?"

The message traffic was interrupted at 1700 when a flag hoist went up indicating that enemy submarines were in the vicinity. The crew went to battle stations. Escort destroyers made wide sweeps, sonar pinging in all directions, trying to locate the elusive U-boats. Crews scanned every sector of the horizon searching for the periscopes.

But the commodore was not to be diverted from his discovery. At 1710 he continued with the new, more interesting business at hand. "As regard the last part of your signal are you allowed to run this now and who changed the orders?"

The ship replied, "Orders from Port Director, New York, on Nov. 25. Also Nov. 26. 'Do not, repeat not, stream Mark 29 gear until further orders.' We are not to stream gear."

That gave the commodore an all-night pause for reflection. On January 6, at 0730 he signaled, "Have read message to which you referred. You are not to stream gear. Take position 125, now."

The *Jeremiah O'Brien* took position 125.

A day later the weather came up again. Seas were heavy and the convoy was forced to reduce speed.

The bad weather continued and the pounding on the ships took its toll. The morning of January 11 found three ships showing breakdown lights and dropping astern of convoy. The seas were too rough to maintain speed without damaging the ship's hull and it became increasingly difficult for the *O'Brien* to maintain steerageway. As dawn broke, she had once again lost the other ships. That afternoon four vessels were sighted, two ahead and two astern. Apparently the convoy was scattered all over. The *O'Brien* plowed on relentlessly, shuddering as her bow plummeted into wave after wave, spray and saltwater making her decks and superstructure glisten in the sun.

The following afternoon one of the escort vessels came into view, giving a course to steer to find the rest of the convoy and by sunset the ship was once more in her assigned position. But the weather was unremitting and the *O'Brien* soon began to lag astern again because of the heavy head seas and strong winds. After another day of pounding, the commodore flashed a welcome signal, "Your destination is St. John, New Brunswick." This was happy news. It meant the voyage was almost over.

On January 15, the *Jeremiah O'Brien*, with seven other ships and one escort vessel, left the main convoy as the escort vessel signaled, "Proceed unescorted to St. John, N.B." Departing from the Halifax-bound ships, the *O'Brien's* group found themselves in a blinding snowstorm. Then, in the early morning of January 16 an SOS was received. "Collision - ship in sinking condition."

From 0200 to 0900 a series of radio signals was received from the distressed ship. After an initial hesitation the *O'Brien* broke radio silence and transmitted messages so that the sinking ship could take bearings on them. At 0900 the scene of the collision came into view. Two ships and one escort vessel were sighted, the escort standing by a British vessel with a caved-in bow and a pronounced list. The *Jeremiah O'Brien* stood by the *George Westinghouse*, a U.S. Liberty Ship, which had a full load of cargo and was leaking badly. She had been hit in number 1 hold and was listing badly by the bow. That afternoon the *Westinghouse* was

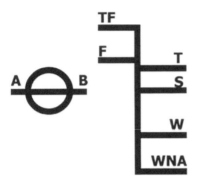

Plimsoll marks, as described above, were originally designed to prevent greedy shipowners from taking advantage of seamen by overloading their vessels. Author's collection.

taken in tow by a Canadian corvette and the *O'Brien* was released from standing by.

On January 17, 1944 at 0200, the *Jeremiah O'Brien* arrived at the Pilot Station for St. John Harbor, and that afternoon the ship was docked at Pier 5, West St. John.

The remainder of the month was spent loading a large cargo of grain, explosives and general cargo.

On February 1, the *Jeremiah O'Brien* left St. John, bound for the convoy rendezvous at Halifax with a full load of grain, general cargo and explosives. She was below her Plimsoll marks when she sailed.[2] The weather was freezing-cold with snow and biting wind. It was so bitterly numbing that the forward lookouts

---

[2] Plimsoll marks are the lines on the side of a ship that indicate the maximum depth to which she can be legally loaded in peacetime. The marks are calculated according to prevailing weather conditions and whether the ship is loaded in salt or fresh water. They also vary from trade to trade and ship to ship, but generally the highest mark, indicating the greatest load, will be marked "TF" for tropical fresh water. Below it may be "F" for fresh water, "T" for tropical below that, followed by "S" for salt water and "W" for winter. The lowest mark, indicating the lightest load, is "WNA": "winter, North Atlantic." During World War II Plimsoll marks were frequently ignored.

were moved to the flying bridge and later in the day the aft lookouts were also put on the flying bridge because of the weather.

Weather was the driving force on the voyage. Every plan and action — convoy instructions, the shipboard schedules, the watches and practices, the daily routines — all revolved around the weather. Fifty years later, the weather stories were still dominant in the mariners' recollections.

Ken Holsapple:

> It was so cold we stood fifteen minutes on fifteen minutes off. They had a line you had to hold on to to go from one place to another. Sometimes you couldn't stand watch on the bow. Sometimes you couldn't see one ship from the other. And sometimes they'd come close to you and you could almost read the names on the ship. Sometimes the weather was so bad you only made four miles during the day.

Dan Bandy:

> One of the things I remember so clearly going into Halifax was all the ice. Ice everywhere. That ice was six inches thick and thicker than that in some places. The standing rigging was full of ice. There was no question of anyone going out on deck. For a while it didn't look like the old ship was going to make it. The ship was so heavily coated with ice that people were concerned about it capsizing or not making port. There was just an unbelievable amount of ice on that trip. She must have been a well built old Liberty to survive that.

Arriving in Halifax on February 3 the *O'Brien* looked like a fairy-tale ice palace. The anchor was dropped and the crew put to work removing ice. It wasn't an easy task. Slipping and sliding across the deck, there was nothing to hold on to. The gunwales and rails were so thick with ice the men couldn't get their gloved hands around them to hold on. The Armed Guard spent the

Sea water froze on the main deck. Ice was so thick the crew couldn't get their hands around the railings. It took hours to chop the ice off. Above, two of the gunners work at it with long-handled scrapers. A major effort was needed to just stand upright on the slippery decks. Coleman Schneider.

afternoon breaking ice off the guns and cleaning the forward guns which had received the brunt of the weather.

The following day the Mark-29 gear was removed from the deck of the ship. The veterans in the crew watched with mixed feelings. The gear had been a royal pain to stream and retrieve, required constant maintenance, had caused the *Jeremiah O'Brien* to get a reputation as a slowpoke and never seemed to work properly. On the other hand, the fact that it was on board had saved the *O'Brien* from being converted into a hospital ship.[2]

---

[2] Between voyages No. 2 and No. 3 the *Jeremiah O'Brien* was taken off hire for a few days because the War Shipping Administration had designated her for conversion to a hospital ship. The fact that she was equipped with the highly secret Mark 29 gear prevented this from happening and ensured her continued career as a freighter.

The next day, just as when she was first launched, the ship weighed anchor and sailed across the degaussing range, realigning her polarity against magnetic mines for the voyage to come so that the ship's magnetic field would not interfere with the mines magnetism and cause them to explode. Sailing on February 7, the harbor's submarine nets were towed out of the way and she cleared the entrance at 1000. She was in a convoy of sixty-five ships, six corvettes, twelve destroyers and three aircraft carriers.

On February 8 each member of the Armed Guard crew was given a present, thanks to the Canadian Red Cross — six pounds of chocolate and five packages of chewing gum. The Armed Guard had perhaps the hardest, most uncomfortable duty aboard the *Jeremiah O'Brien* and no one begrudged them the gift.

As always in an outward-bound convoy, a great deal of time was spent in practice and preparation. On February 9, on instructions from the convoy commodore, the master of the *O'Brien* rang the general alarm to indicate the convoy was going to have target practice. Red flags or helium balloons would go up over the convoy. By the end of the afternoon all but six columns of ships had fired. The following day the gun crew fired six rounds of common ammunition from the after 3-inch 50. Their target was the windward edge of a smoke float dropped by one of the escorts. Lieutenant Memhard proudly recorded in his log: "Opening range 3000, closing 3800. 5 of 6 shots right on target, 6th being slightly off in deflection. Good shooting; favorable comments from master and other ship's officers. Gun OK."

The convoy sailed on, gunnery practice and watches alternating with hours off spent reading, writing letters, telling war stories and, of course, playing poker.

As always, when the convoy drew closer to England, the watchfulness increased and tension levels grew high.

On February 17, a warning was received that aircraft were approaching, possibly enemy. The escorts closed around the convoy for protection. Five planes from convoy carriers went up scarching and Condition II was set until general quarters was called. All the 20mm's were kept cocked and loaded. During the night more planes flew around the convoy and the jittery crew braced for an attack. None came and it was decided they must be from the convoy carriers which routinely sent up planes on patrol. The following day English bombers flew overhead, covering the group at intervals. This time there was no doubt. The crew could clearly see the markings and they welcomed the sight.

On February 19, at 1050, three loud explosions were heard, close enough to shake the ship. The weather was foggy and there was no way to know what they signified. Although by now experience should have taught them that communication and information was not to be expected, the speculation and rampant rumors never ceased. Each explosion, every maneuver of the escorts, every course change started a fresh wave of conjecture as to what was happening. No one questioned the importance of maintaining radio silence but being "kept in the dark" was a constant source of grousing among the crews.

John Crosby, third mate on the *Jeremiah O'Brien* on voyage No. 6 had this to say about North Atlantic convoys:

> All the radio traffic was incoming. We could never send a message, ever. Messages from the commodore would be by code flag and semaphore flags. If a ship was out of control in a convoy, they would put a couple of red lights. That was havoc when you'd see that and try to avoid a collision. Between the U-boats and the bad weather and the fog and the ships out of control, it was horrible. You never knew what happened, you never knew anything. The only thing you could do was assume and maybe talk to somebody on the other ships when you got into port.

The perspective from the engine room was even worse than up on deck. At least the deck crew could sometimes see what was happening. Bill Watson: "You're closed up and you're below water and every time an explosion or depth charge goes off outside, the hull of the ship acts like the skin of a drum. It just vibrates and magnifies the sound and scares the hell out of you, especially the first few times it happens. Eventually you just get so you wait for it to get over with."

Two hours later the fog lifted a little and, to their horror, the crew saw two floating mines only 1500 yards away. Attempting to explode the mines, one of the escorts dropped eight depth charges at the same time signalling the nearby ships to disregard its actions. The ships in the immediate vicinity, for once knowing the cause, could "disregard" the explosions. But for the rest of the convoy, the depth charges were yet another source of concern, tension and unanswered questions.

In the evening the *O'Brien* and her sisters arrived at Oban, on Scotland's west coast in the Firth of Lorne, anchored overnight, then proceeded around the northern tip of Scotland to Methil, on Britain's east coast, where they arrived in the morning of February 23. The crew eagerly prepared for shore leave, took their "draws" and went out on the town.

Rowdiness, fights and drunken episodes were not the only concerns when crews went ashore. Venereal disease was a serious problem. The Armed Guard crew was mustered at 1000 on February 27, and warned that each man going on liberty was to have sani-tubes and safeties (condoms) and, further, that the gangway watch was to check each man going ashore to be sure he had them. Lieutenant Memhard also noted that each man was to be checked for exposure when he returned on board. Just how this was to be accomplished isn't stated in the Armed Guard Log. The merchant crew was left to their own devices.

On March 2 the lieutenant held mast, the traditional Naval Board convened to hear reports of violations of regulations and to "award" punishment. A seaman first class was seen the previous evening coming aboard with several bottles of beer, having first left the ship without permission. The sailor was given a warning, fifty hours' extra duty and restricted to the ship. This was the only incident logged — not too bad a record for a Naval Armed Guard ashore in wartime.

In general the merchant and Naval crews of the *Jeremiah O'Brien* were not given to bad behavior ashore. The logs record some incidents of drinking, unruly behavior, some fights, but only to a relatively minor degree. The *O'Brien's* crews were professionals, deeply concerned with the serious business of the war — supplying the Allies, ever alert, carrying a strong feeling of patriotism and responsibility. As many of them said in later years, "We just wanted to get the job done."

Completing discharge, the *O'Brien* sailed in ballast on March 5, via Loch Ewe for the United States. She arrived in New York on March 22.

Left, left to right, gunners Serra (behind telegraph), Smedley and Shaw. Right, left to right, Serra and Shaw. Taken in New York, the relief at being safely home is apparent in the expressions on their faces. Jerome Shaw.

9

PRELUDE TO D-DAY

Voyage 3 ended at midnight on March 24, 1944; Voyage 4 began one minute later. The *Jeremiah O'Brien* was at the Bethlehem Steel Shipyard, Pier 57 in Brooklyn. Capt. De Smedt had replaced Capt. Southerland as master of the ship. According to his voyage letter, "The bottom was painted, strainers removed and cleaned, and the hull and screw inspected and found to be in good condition."

Shifting from the shipyard to Grace Line's pier in New York on March 29, the ship loaded stores and fuel and trimmed her ballast. The *Jeremiah O'Brien* was given deck and engine stores for six months and four months worth of commissary stores. At the same time fifteen hundred tons of ballast previously loaded in Great Britain was trimmed and leveled off in the lower holds: 350 tons in No. 2, 550 tons in No. 3 and 600 tons in No. 4. A three-inch plank floor was laid atop the ballast on which to stow cargo.

On April 1 deep tanks No. 1 and No. 2 were loaded with a cargo of 3952 barrels of diesel oil weighing 515 long tons. The consignee was the Petroleum Division of the British Ministry of Fuel and Power. April 4 found the ship loading army cargo at Pier 16 on Staten Island. As the ship neared completion of her loading, a convoy conference was called. The *Jeremiah O'Brien* was assigned to Task Unit W-1, HXF 287 consisting of eighty-one ships.[1] Her position was No. 132 (column 13, row 2).

Now, the orders became more stringent. Lieutenant Memhard returned from the conference with new instructions for his crew: any airplanes between 36 degrees west longitude and 7 degrees west longitude should be regarded as suspicious. East of 7 degrees west longitude *all* aircraft should be regarded as enemy. They were to open fire on any unidentified plane approaching within 1500 yards of the ship regardless of where it was encountered.

For the first few days, the voyage was relatively quiet. The merchant crew settled into a seagoing routine of four hours on watch and eight hours off — 12 to 4, 4 to 8 and 8 to 12. Breakfast was served from 0730 to 0830 in the morning to catch those going on and coming off watch. Lunch was served from 1130 to 1230 for the same reason. Dinner would run from 1700 to 1800 with a sailor, officer and black gang[2] member called out to relieve the watchstanders so they could eat supper. The Armed Guard easily fell into their routine of Condition I and Condition III, day and

---

[1] Convoys were assigned prefixes and numbers according to their routing. HXF indicated a convoy originating in Halifax (HF) bound for England (X). The number indicated it was the 287th convoy to eminate from Halifax since the war started. Other prefixes were OA (outbound from the Thames or east coast of England), OB or ON (outbound from Liverpool or the west coast of England), HX or KJ (inbound from Halifax), OG (outbound from Gibraltar), HG (homebound for Gibraltar) and SL (Sierra Leone).

[2] The unlicensed engine department crew is normally referred to as the "black gang." This comes from the days when ships' engines were coal-fired and the crew traditionally came off watch covered with soot and coal dust.

night, respectively. The Mark-29 hydrophone listening device, the only part of the maligned gear remaining on board, was streamed and put into operation.

Although the long-anticipated assault on the European continent was cloaked in deepest secrecy, it was becoming increasingly obvious that it was imminent. The convoys from America and Canada had been delivering supplies to England in a never-ending stream and British ports and warehouses were overflowing with millions of tons of food, medicines, ammunition, and vehicles of all types including tanks, half-tracks, armored cars, trucks, jeeps and even thousands of railroad locomotives and tanker and freight cars. The level of alertness was raised, discipline and order were stepped up and enforced, practices and precautions against gas and other hazards were increased and became part of the routine. Helmets and gas masks were distributed to the Navy crew and the anticipation of the impending campaign grew daily.

On April 16 the *O'Brien's* merchant crew held a meeting. There was a great deal of discussion and conjecture as to what lay ahead and what could be done to ensure the safety of the ship. Sixteen men volunteered for gun stations to back up the Navy Armed Guard and watchfulness increased.

A muster of the Armed Guard crew was also held to discuss how to prepare for the expected escalation of the war. The two leading petty officers were given morphine syrettes to sew into their lifejackets for use in emergency, another indication of mounting danger and necessary precautions.

A few days later both the ship's crew and the Armed Guard crew were given instruction on the effects of liquid and spray mustard gas. This was the first of many sessions regarding precautions against a gas attack, how to wear the protective clothing they had been issued and other training.

On April 27, the ship arrived at Newport, South Wales. From the Armed Guard log: "30 April 1944. Began to get feeling that we were going to be used in a coming invasion or some kind of special mission — procedure for special training course being outlined."

Twelve smoke generators[3] were placed on board the *O'Brien*. The Armed Guard crew began an intensified training schedule with classes on air recognition, plane spotting and practice abandoning ship. Air recognition consisted of identifying silhouettes of airplanes shown with flash cards or with slides through a projector. However, projectors weren't readily available. The crew of the *O'Brien* was resourceful. They built one using a pineapple can, a grapefruit juice can, two 500-watt bulbs, one magnifying glass and miscellaneous bits and pieces of wood and metal. The results, according to Lt. Memhard were, "excellent for both photos and silhouettes, of which collection over 200 shots. Noticeable increase in interest on part of men thru projection of planes."

The last of the cargo came off on May 8 and, according to Captain De Smedt's voyage letter, "the vessel was turned over to the U.S. Army to be outfitted and equipped for special operations." Three days later the ship shifted to mooring buoys just outside the harbor.

Gas training became the order of the day. May 12, 1944 found the crew engaged in gas and gas mask drill and instruction. Each man's mask was checked for adjustment and all hands were required to have their masks on within seven seconds from hearing the order "gas." Everyone except those on watch went ashore for special training in gas warfare, first aid, air recognition and abandoning ship.

The tempo of preparation increased. Five hundred twenty-five life jackets were placed on board for Army use. On May 14, the Armed Guard crew was mustered and advised that when troops came on board they would have added responsibilities. They were now to carry gas masks and lifejackets at all times.

---

[3] Smokescreens made it difficult for shore batteries to pinpoint the ship as a target.

The Germans were expected to use gas during the invasion. Here Radio Operator Robert Milby dons his full gas regalia for the camera. This was taken in 1944. Robert Milby.

May 14th to May 16th was designated as a practice period to get in the habit. In the afternoon a life boat was lowered for the Navy crew to practice rowing and boat handling. Nine men spent two hours rowing back and forth across the harbor. Later a class was held on identifying signal flags and semaphore.

The war was never far off. From Purser Albert Haas' personal diary, "Air raid in vicinity of Cardiff, Barry, and Bristol. Flashes of light were seen and the muffled thud of bombs heard throughout the night."

The intensity and urgency of training continued to increase. Now, daily classes were held in air recognition, flag and semaphore. Practice was conducted on the shoreside firing range and the ship's guns were operated daily. The crews didn't know it, but they were being prepared for their date with history.

On May 19 a waiver was obtained from the U.S. Coast Guard at Cardiff. According to Captain De Smedt's voyage letter this was to enable the ship to carry "troops and cargo, out of compliance with law, for the duration of military operation in which we were about to engage and to be effective until the return of the vessel to the United States."

At noon that day the degaussing was turned on and the *Jeremiah O'Brien* left Newport at 1840 that evening.

Oiler Francis Erdman: "The *Jeremiah O'Brien* was ordered to proceed to Gourock, Scotland. Gourock is on the South Shore of the Firth of Clyde.[4] Here the crew was sent to 'gas school' where we were taught about the different kinds of poison gas, the characteristics of each kind, how to contend with the stuff if it leaked, and so on. There was a strong feeling that the Germans would use gas."

The certainty was growing that the great invasion was now close at hand. The "harbor was full of Liberty ships and warships." From the Armed Guard Log: "We had training in military preparedness. What was happening was that we were preparing for the invasion of Europe — but we didn't know it. However, we drew our own conclusions." The crews practiced uncomplainingly, with great mental concentration, knowing that their fate — and that of the ship — could depend on how well they learned the lessons.

But there were lighter moments, too. Gunner's Mate Morgan Williams:

> Waiting to go into Scotland, we were at anchor and we had a deck light hanging over the stern of the ship. And you looked down and you could see all these salmon just rolling under the light. They came right up to that light. So we rigged some lines and you put a hook down with a rag or meat or anything on it and they'd bite it. We loaded up the whole ship, galley and everything with eight to ten pound silver salmon.

---

[4] According to Webster's Geographical Dictionary, "During World War II debarkation point for U.S. forces (in 2 1/2 years after May 1942, about 1,317,000 Americans landed here).

The ship went to the dock at Gourock-the-Clyde on Sunday, May 21. The first order of business was a "short arm inspection" for the Armed Guard crew by Army medics. Fortunately the results of this check for venereal disease were negative.

Three days later twenty-five additional lifejackets were placed on board for the Army by the Army. The Armed Guard crew was given a class in 30 cal. rifle instruction, including field stripping. June 1, 1944, came with more instructions on fighting the enemy. Under multiple air attack each man and unit was to act independently of bridge control. Instructions were issued on how to act under various circumstances and with reasons why. Each gun was assigned a sector, for example, from dead ahead to 45 degrees on the bow, they were told to concentrate on covering their sectors while under attack and cautioned not to be distracted by what was going on in adjacent sectors.

Another class in air recognition was held. Dan Bandy laughingly recalled those sessions: "Aircraft identification classes on board ship, well it was dark and some of the guys would fall asleep. But Memhard, he solved that by once in awhile throwing in a slide of a naked woman. That kept the guys up."

The classes continued. A fire and boat muster was held for the merchant crew. The Navy gun crew mustered on the aft gun platform in complete gas protective clothing for inspection by Lt. Memhard. Every man wore rubber boots, oilskin gear, gloves, mask and Army protective headgear. One of the greatest fears of the Allied Command was a poison gas attack and crews were heavily drilled on the use of gas suits and masks.

Now, seemingly all of Great Britain was buried in war matériel. Everywhere were lined up jeeps, tanks, trucks, half-tracks and ambulances, rations, canned goods, cannons, machine guns, rifles, pistols, ammunition, bombs, hand grenades, mines, mortars, uniforms, clothing, medicine, dental fillings, bandages, ointment, plasma, drugs, gasoline, kerosene, diesel fuel and hundreds of other necessary items were stacked in cans, boxes,

Radio Operator Robert Milby, on the left, and third assistant engineer William Watson. Taken on board before Operation Overlord. The Jeremiah O'Brien*'s engine room skylight can be seen behind them.* Robert Milby.

barrels, drums, kegs and cartons in the streets and alleys of the cities, along the highways and byways of the countryside, on the moors, in the valleys and hidden in the forests. The fortress called Great Britain was stockpiled with equipment and literally covered with supplies.

Third Engineer William Watson remembered, "There was so much material over there. 'My God,' we used to say, 'if they cut the barrage balloons loose, England would sink all the way to China.' Material stacked up everywhere."

All Petty Officers in the gun crew were advised of the necessity for special attention to proper lookout and the possibility of E-boat attack in the unspecified area the ship was leaving for. The latest advice from the British was that an E-boat attack was practically a certainty. Special instructions were given for E-boat fire control[5] and probability tactics.

By this time the status of the civilian merchant convoy had subtly changed.

Tom McGeehan:

> The army assigned us Army Transportation Service number MT 267. We were basically under the U. S. Army. We had lots of training there, lots of gas mask training. They put some extra guns on board ship. Army 40 millimeter mobile guns were put on deck. They tied them down and they were for extra protection on the invasion.
>
> We had hundreds of sand bags aboard for D-Day, for extra protection. There were all kinds of sandbags piled around the guns. Captain De Smedt's quarters were on the starboard side of the bridge deck, just under the flying bridge. He had these sandbags stacked above his quarters two or three high. There must have been a hundred of them, just over his room. The rest of the deck was bare.
>
> The *Jeremiah O'Brien* departed Gourock-the-Clyde, Scotland, on June 2nd. We sailed on down the Irish sea toward Land's End. And as we went we picked up an escort of naval vessels. So the mate on watch sent me back to the fantail to do the normal courtesy of dipping the flag. I saw the *Augusta* pass by and I dipped the ensign and watched as she lowered her ensign and raised it again. Then I raised ours. I found out in later years this was Admiral A. G. Kirk's flagship. So then a battleship came by and I dipped the ensign again and then another battleship, and then some cruisers and so on. I just kept dipping. I was at that for two hours before they all went past.

Saturday, June 3, 1944. The *Jeremiah O'Brien* and her convoy were covered by a heavy escort of ships and, in the air, by an umbrella of Spitfires, Hurricanes, B-24's and Mosquitos.

---

[5] Fire control in Navy parlance refers to the aiming and firing of guns, not, as a civilian might think, to controlling something on fire.

Part of the cargo and a few of the troops the Jeremiah O'Brien *would carry to Normandy wait on the dock at South-ampton as she prepares to load.* Robert Milby.

Robert Milby: "Four or five ships started down between the islands and ships kept coming and joining us and then we went around Land's End towards Southampton. And, my God, you never saw so many ships. Thousands, just thousands and thousands. It was incredible. The water level of the ocean must have gone up twenty feet with all those ships there."

Francis Erdman:

The *Jeremiah O'Brien* was at the head of the convoy — in the first wave of ships in the convoy. As we steered down the west coast of Great Britain, passing ports large and small, we picked up ships at each one until there were so many vessels that there was no end to the procession. As we passed around Land's End, entering the English Channel, different ones of us would go up on the flying bridge and use the mate's telescope. As far as you could see, for mile after mile in the distance, ships, ships, ships! The *O'Brien* was in the vanguard of perhaps the greatest flotilla ever assembled in history.

Tom McGeehan: "It was the biggest thing that any human being could ever see in the history of the world. There were so many ships that the curvature of the earth prevented you from seeing it all. It was just stupendous!"

Monday, June 5, 1944. At 0658 the *Jeremiah O'Brien* anchored in Poole Bay, outside the Solent of Southampton (at Bournemouth).

Francis Erdman: "Finally we started loading troops. No equipment. Just troops. I can only guess at the number of troops that came on board — they overflowed the ship. There were soldiers everywhere, crammed and crowded in. As I remember, they each carried their rations. No other provision was made for feeding them."

Heavy gunfire was observed in the distance from about 2300 on throughout the night. Allied bombardment of the French coast had started.

Albert Haas recorded in his diary, "Hundreds of aircraft passed overhead, enroute to the continent. Hundreds of small craft and some transports in the area. Warships seen in distance of English Channel and seemed to be heading toward continent. Glare from gunfire over the horizon of the Channel was visible."

Robert Milby:

> I distinctly remember the night before the invasion. We were sitting there in the harbor and thousands of planes went overhead. And two searchlights coming up in a V right over us. Squadrons of planes went overhead all night long. Hundreds and thousands of planes.
>
> Where we were at, you could see the explosions, ninety miles away. It was the bombs they were dropping. The whole area was lit up.

E. Ray Sharpe: "We saw the first salvo fired over there. We were in Southampton and we could see that all the way across the Channel."

It was early morning, Tuesday, June 6, 1944.

10

NORMANDY

Operation Overlord began at fifteen minutes after midnight with the dropping of two battalions of British and American pathfinders into the moonlit sky over Normandy. Their job was to light the drop zones on the French coast, roughly between Cherbourg and Le Havre, for the paratroopers and gliders filled with infantry who were soon to follow. Once landed, the airborne soldiers fought their way through the swamps and hedgerows toward their assigned sectors. Offshore, more than two hundred thousand soldiers rode more than five thousand ships across the Channel towards five beaches across 60 miles of French coast. The Americans landed at "Utah" and "Omaha," on the western shores of the coast, with the British and Canadians taking "Gold," "Juno" and "Sword," farther to the east.

The news that the invasion had begun sent an electric pulse of excitement throughout the ship. The *O'Brien's* crew and troops anxiously passed the day with one ear to the radio and the questions, "What's the latest?" and "When do we go?" on everyone's lips. A torrent of Spitfires, Hurricanes, Thunderbolts and Mustangs flew in thunderous waves overhead toward France. Across the globe, newspapers carried the momentous news in giant black type and millions held their breaths, glued to their radios, listening to the bulletins from England.

It was a day never to be forgotten — the skies dark with aircraft, ships stretching to the horizon and beyond — the invasion of Europe was unparalleled in scope, bold and magnificent, yet ominous with an "awful grandeur." A few beaches and inland areas were quickly and easily taken, but almost every other inch of ground had to be wrested from fierce defenders, captured with perseverance, sacrifice, blood and guts. By the end of what the author Cornelius Ryan called "the longest day in history" the Allied forces, under Commanding General Dwight D. Eisenhower, were on European soil and the liberation of the continent from Nazi domination had begun.

On the *Jeremiah O'Brien,* the deafening roar of the planes and the sight of the greatest armada in history raised a fevered desire in many who saw it, to rush out and be part of the historic day. Others were pale with fear. Some sat, silently writing letters or alone with their thoughts. Others exchanged names, addresses and messages for the folks back home, "just in case." Priests and chaplains walked among the troops reassuring, counseling, taking messages and doing what they could to encourage the men, many of whom were young, homesick soldiers, not long out of school. The gun crews checked and re-checked their equipment. The radio operator strained every sense to hear the traffic crashing over the airwaves, almost drowned out by the unceasing drone of thousands of airplane engines overhead. Captain De Smedt paced the bridge. The *Jeremiah O'Brien* waited for her orders.

Right, after shaving their heads, the Armed Guard called themselves "baldies."
Above, Morgan Freeman sporting the Mohawk favored by many of the
paratroopers at Normandy. Dan Bandy

The paratroopers who jumped behind the beaches of Normandy on the night before D-Day had cut their hair into "Mohawks," bald heads with a narrow brush of hair running from front to back. When the Armed Guard crew heard about this, they responded with a strong sense of camaraderie and *esprit de corps*.

Coxswain Dan Bandy: "We all had Lone Eagle haircuts [Mohawks] or baldies. And it caught on. First one gun crew and then another and pretty soon all the merchant gun crews did it. We just wanted to do it."

Once the beachhead was established, it was vital to keep a constant stream of troops and supplies supporting the advancing front line. There could be no interruption in the flow of men and matériel flooding the Normandy coast. This meant that some ships were scheduled to unload on the first day, others were scheduled for the second day, third, fourth, and so on. The success of the whole great enterprise rested on this unbroken stream of men and supplies.

D-Day+1, June 7, 1944. A Royal Navy officer came aboard with an exclusive radio receiver for the assault area. Labeled "Reception set R-109," it was tuned to special frequencies to

Landing craft at the docks in Southampton in early June. Imperial War Museum.

receive warnings of impending attacks, instructions for crossing the Channel and mooring at Normandy. There was always a large crowd gathered around it, listening to the developing news.

To relieve the tension and pass the time waiting for the coming battle the troops diverted themselves. Oiler Francis Erdman: "The night (before we left) the troops in the hold had themselves a jam session. Several had brought instruments — there were ten or twelve musicians. They played all night, partly out of fear, I guess. When they disembarked, the instruments were left on board — 'We won't be playing those any more!' they said."

In a different hatch, Dan Bandy watched G.I.s boxing.

> Those soldiers of ours were outstanding. We all heard what great fighting men the Japanese and Germans were, but the men that we had on the *O'Brien* the evening before we sailed were the best in the world. They were having elimination boxing matches in the square of the hatch! They'd have kept it up all night, but we finally turned the lights off on them. Those were soldiers. I will tell you, they would make you proud.

At 2210 on D-Day+2, the *Jeremiah O'Brien* left the dock at Southampton and anchored in the Solent, the area between the Isle of Wight and the south coast of England. On board, the several hundred Army troops checked their equipment one more time. This was the springboard for *their* assault.

The following day, D+3, the *Jeremiah O'Brien* sailed at 2220. Weighing anchor with hundreds of other vessels, she pointed her bow toward the assault area off the coast of Normandy — a place code-named "Omaha Beach." She had on board ten officers, 563 troops, 135 armored vehicles and 161 tons of explosives. At midnight the Armed Guard set Condition II. No one slept.

From Albert Haas' personal diary, "Friday, June 9, 1944. Sailed from Southampton enroute to France. Left about dusk."

In the early morning darkness of June 10, two mines were seen on the port side, less than 100 yards from the ship. Then a mine was seen on the starboard side less than 50 yards off. A ship a few miles away on the starboard beam suddenly exploded and burned brilliantly for several hours.

At 0330 the general alarm was sounded. Tracer fire was spotted about 4000 yards away on the port side. The Germans had mustered an E-Boat attack and the ships on the perimeter of the convoy were shooting at them. Twice more during the darkness of that early morning, tracers were seen firing at surface targets. Flares dropped frequently throughout the night, giving the scene an eerie, surreal quality.

Francis Erdman:

> Before we got to Omaha beach we encountered barrage balloons — hundreds of balloons up there to discourage air attack on the shipping. But the enemy was there and their planes had flares — it was as bright as noonday at three o'clock in the morning. We steamed on, toward the shore. It was a low coast line with hills and scattered in the hills, although we couldn't see them very distinctly, were numbers of pill boxes. But they didn't open fire right away.

At 0830 June 10, 1944 the *Jeremiah O'Brien* arrived at "Omaha." The sea had been rough and many of the soldiers were seasick. The first sight of their objective was not comforting.

Albert Haas' diary, "Saturday, June 10, 1944. Arrived at the 'Omaha' beachhead. Thousands of ships were in the harbor, of all types. Warships (mostly destroyers and D.E.'s) provided a semi-circle of protection."

Among the major difficulties that had to be overcome was getting the troops and cargo safely ashore. There were no piers or ports as such in that part of France. This meant troops and supplies had to be off-loaded from ships into amphibious craft which would then run the cargo ashore. The amphibious DUKWs ("ducks")[1] and landing craft were necessarily small and vulnerable to the rugged sea and swell coming in from the English Channel. To quickly create a safe harbor where none was before, the idea of sinking ships to form an instant breakwater was conceived. Known as the Gooseberry or "block" ships, they were sunk in rows to form breakwaters which provided protection for the unloading of troops and supplies. In the Omaha Beach area seventeen American-flag ships were sunk: *George S. Wasson, Benjamin Contee, Matt Rasnon, David O. Saylor, Vitruvius, West Nohno, West Cheswald, West Honaker, Victory Sword, James Iredell, George W. Childs, Artemus Ward, J. W. Marshall, Wilcox, Galveston, Courageous* and *West Grama*. As some of these broke up during ensuing storms others were added: *Alcoa Leader, Exford, Illinoian, Kentuckian, Kofresi, Lena Luckenbach, Pennsylvanian, Robin Grey, Sahale* and *West Nilus*.

Commander J.E. Taylor of the Royal Navy was part of the group responsible for setting these instant breakwaters. In his book, *The Last Passage*, he described what it was like putting ships to a use for which they were never intended.

---

[1] D represents the year of the vehicle's design, U indicates it is amphibious, K signifies front-wheel drive and W means rear-wheel drive.

To create the gooseberry breakwaters ships were put to a use for which they were never intended — resting on the bottom of the ocean. Nevertheless, the concept was quick and effective. Robert Milby.

A ship is designed to serve its life afloat and those who man her are trained to keep her in that state. A beach means only shipwreck and stranding to sailor minds. There were many who expressed surprise at (ships) sitting upright on a beach. They did not know that a merchant ship is a vessel of flat bottom, perfectly capable of sitting upright on a flat sandy shore. Sometimes, when the bottom on which they settled wasn't level, frames were strained, but few suffered major hurt. We passed one coaster that waited, and her captain leaned over the wing of his bridge and waved to us. He presented a vast and cheerful countenance that reflected a schoolboy relish in the unortho-doxy that had been brought into his life. This was no way for a master to treat his ship, not to have crowds of soldiers swarming over her; but he had no need to worry, everything had official sanction.

The process of lining up the Gooseberry ships and sinking them went with clock-work precision. Among the vessels was a French man-of-war, the battleship *Courbet*.

High up, from the top-most point, a gigantic flag of the Free French flaunted its colours. At the stern a huge tricolour flew.

The *Courbet* came on, persuaded steadily forward by four tugs. Around her dozens of ships busied themselves with the purpose that had brought them there. Yet the progress of that old battleship seemed to dwarf all other activities into insignificance. One felt that there ought to be a crashing of military music to accompany that flaunting Cross of Lorraine. And that last passage seemed too easy of accomplishment. Without a hitch of apparent difficulty the *Courbet* came right in, was turned with slow dignity, and pushed into position. Her bow came to rest on that of another ship already sunk. There was a great rending and tearing of steel as one bow scraped past another, and there was a strange unconcern in watching that buckling and tearing of a ship's bow, because it no longer mattered. No court of enquiry on the collision would follow. Then the *Courbet* was in position and once there she just stayed still as if conscious that this was the end and compliant in the matter. The explosion was sudden — just a dull thud and brief tremor, and then a quick settling of the three feet that separated her keel from the sea bed.

Of course, the explosive charges designed to sink the gooseberry ships didn't always go off as intended. Commander Taylor was on the *Durban* when she was planted.

And when the *Durban's* life ended in a sudden disruption it was a vast explosion that for a moment threatened collapse of the topmast. Instead of forcing its way outward through holes blown in the ship's side, the blast went inwards then sought escape by every possible egress. Up through vents and gratings rushed the force of explosion taking all movable debris with it. In its path it found a bundle of old clothing supplied for cleaning rags, and draped the rigging with an unseemly display of ancient and ragged underclothing. The ship's company had been moved to the empty gun platforms, and some did not escape. Those near the boiler-room vents emerged from the thinning cloud of dust like coal-trimmers from the bunkers. In five minutes the *Durban* was on the bottom and we waited to be taken away. There was an aimlessness about those who awaited on her upper deck. There was no further purpose in their presence on board, for the reason behind it had ceased. Like uncertain children they waited for the next move.

A newly-sunk ship had an other-worldly quality. Commander Taylor recalled boarding another vessel in which

... the water lapped at an upper deck and one could step aboard straight over the rails. Only twenty minutes ago she had been planted, and there were still signs of her dying. I walked along the deck and looked in at the galley. Food still simmered there for the mid-day meal that was never eaten. That galley had a strange empty look, for who sees a galley without its cook when the food is ready for dishing up? A long cube of corned beef waited for slicing, and the pots simmered on the stove. I almost expected the cook to burst in at any moment with a wrathful injunction to get out of his galley, and when lifting the lid to examine the contents of a pot there was a guilty feeling of trespass. But the authority had gone, and there was clear evidence of this in the 'midships house. The saloon was wrecked and on the deck half a dozen counterpanes torn from a cupboard, were strewn. In the pantry, the captain's cabin and officers' quarters it was the same. I felt a sudden anger at those who had despoiled her. It was like robbing a body that was not yet cold.

I looked in at the engine-room, and stepped on to the upper grating. Water was just lapping around the tops of the great cylinders in the gloom below. The engine room was full of sound, not great sound, but the tiny sounds of unseen movement in the water below: faint gurgles and bubblings and occasional plops, last dying murmurs where for years there had been the steady thud, thud, thud of massive machinery, and

The Mulberry harbor at Arromanches. Note the ships discharging at anchor, foreground, the sunken ships forming the breakwater and the long causeways to the piers inside the harbor. Author's collection.

constant suppressed murmur of high pressure. There was the funeral atmosphere of church beneath the blacked-out arch of the skylight. It was a place of departing souls that murmured in their passing. The sunlight outside was blinding in comparison.

With the breakwaters in place, large, prefabricated sections of piers were towed into position and partially submerged to facilitate the unloading process. Tom McGeehan: "I remember seeing the Mulberry harbors being towed across. They looked like the Empire State building lying on its side. They had railroad tracks already built into them so when they got there they just sunk them and they were ready to use."

The *O'Brien* anchored and discharging of cargo began. The crew secured from general quarters. The Armed Guard set Condition II.

Francis Erdman: "LSTs came out to meet us and take the troops off. The weather was very rough, swells that I recall as from fifteen to twenty feet. This made it very hard unloading the troops. All along one side we hung cargo nets and the soldiers scrambled down."

Not long after the initial landing, equipment offloaded from the ships in the background is lined up ready for the march inland and the liberation of Northern France. National Archives.

Throughout the day (D+4) air protection over the beachhead was excellent. Spitfires, Mustangs, Thunderbolts, Lightnings, Hurricanes and Typhoons were on constant patrol. At 2000 that evening the R-109 receiver came alive with the information that heavy German air attacks were expected as soon as weather permitted. At 2316 Anti-Aircraft firing broke out. Hostile planes were near the outer edges of the landing force. Although they weren't near enough to the ship to open fire, the general alarm was sounded and the crew went to general quarters.

Francis Erdman: "Before long all hell broke loose. I could never be sure where the shells from those pill boxes went. Over us? God knows, they really cut loose. The *O'Brien* was positioned close to the battleship *Texas* on one side and the cruiser *Augusta* on the other. The *Texas* was shelling the beach without let-up. The sounds of the war were coming from all directions —

The view from a slight elevation just beyond the beach proper, looking seaward. A few of the 5,000 ships which took part in the initial landing can be seen in the background. National Archives.

the pillboxes, machine guns on the planes — the *Texas* was enough all by herself to deafen you."

On June 11 at 0345 the general alarm again sounded. The *Jeremiah O'Brien* and the ships around her were under attack. According to Lt. Memhard's log:

> On 11 June 1944, at 'Omaha' beachhead, the USN Gun Crew was called to battle stations at 0345. Enemy planes were circling overhead, and some ships in the vicinity opened fire with 20mm's and larger AA guns. Following assault area instructions, since it was too dark to see clearly, this ship withheld fire. The enemy planes appeared to be flying over the anchorage at about 10,000 feet. At 0400 three planes came down lower and one was heard to go into a dive, in the direction of this ship. Two men on the aft 3"-50 saw it briefly as it passed from bow to stern, and the undersigned also observed it -- the

plane being identified as a JU-88. Four bombs were dropped, one splashing about 200 yards away on the port bow and the other three just the other side of another Liberty. About 0425 one FW 190 was seen flying from shore toward and over us, first at about 14,000 feet and subsequently lower -- for'd and aft 3"-50's opened fire and expended two rounds each. About 0500 at least three groups of FW 190's, three planes to a group, were seen coming in from the shore (the dark side) toward the ships at anchor. Heavy AA fire was thrown up. All guns on this ship opened fire, 12 rounds of 3"-50 and 500 rounds of 20 mm ammunition being expended.

Captain De Smedt, in a letter to Grace Line described it:

Shortly before dawn on June 11, while at the 'Omaha' beachhead, the vessel was attacked by enemy dive bombers. Bombs fell wide of their mark and the vessel, though shaken, was undamaged. The gun crew, commanded by Lt. Memhard, USNR, put up a heavy AA barrage and drove the enemy away preventing a second attack by the promptness and accuracy of their fire. An inspection of the vessel during the day revealed that the only damage was to No. 4 lifeboat which had been hit by shrapnel.

Francis Erdman:

I ran back and forth across the ship to see it all. But I gave that up. There was just too much. German planes were strafing whatever they could get their sights on. Our side was offering such a target that they could hardly miss, it seemed to me. But I really think that the barrage balloons on their long wires seriously hampered their planes from closing in. Something kept them away from the *O'Brien.*

At 0530, with the coming of dawn, the enemy planes disappeared.

Francis Erdman: "Now another astonishing scene was unfolding before us — within half an hour of our men hitting the beach we could see graders and bulldozers (ours) building roads." The military engineers (the Construction Battalion also known as Seabees) performed miracles, building roads and bridges with lightning speed over impossible terrain, often under murderous fire.

The crew secured from general quarters. Condition II was resumed. More troops and equipment went ashore.

Robert Milby: "We had a lot of soldiers and equipment. Some of the poor G.I.s were petrified. They had to beat them to go down the side of the ship. You know, the ropes [cargo nets hung over the ship's side]. Not many, but some of them. And I felt so sorry for them. They were beating their hands, step by step as they were going down. Otherwise they just froze."

Dan Bandy:

All the Navy men painted our hometown on the backs of our jackets so the soldiers could see it. That way if they were from your home town, they'd come over and talk to you. One guy I remember saw 'Columbus, Ohio' painted on my back and he came over and talked to me. I knew where he lived, too. So he asked me to go see his folks when I got back home. Then he went over the side. I never did see him again. I know that he got killed that day.

Francis Erdman: "Three or four LSTs came alongside to take on our troops. A couple of LSTs would be alongside and a couple of others standing by to take their place. It was all done very rapidly. No delay — none."

On June 13, with the coming of darkness, the menace from the air resumed. But, unlike the previous evening, the enemy, with one or two exceptions, stayed at a safe distance, circling just out of range. From Lieutenant Memhard's log:

During general quarters 13 June between 0345 and 0515, there were two alerts. On the first occasion three enemy planes

Above, two of the Armed Guard prepare one of the 3-inch 50s for action. Right, Seaman First Class Swanson completes loading just before firing. Dan Bandy.

were seen in the immediate area at about 8000 feet; later a single plane at the same height. The single plane flew directly overhead and was tracked, but fire was withheld since it appeared to be very unlikely that this ship or the others in the vicinity could be seen due to haze.

Normally, the Navy Armed Guard log entries were short, limited to simple fact. But on this occasion, the Lieutenant, recognizing the historical significance of the landing, added his observations.

In general, it was surprising that more determined and heavier enemy plane attacks were not encountered, particularly so soon after "D" Day and since enemy-held territory at this point was only a few miles inland. During the day excellent Allied plane coverage was maintained, mainly by Spitfires of several types, Mustangs, Thunderbolts, Lightnings and Typhoons in this area. At night, from dawn to dusk, enemy planes were always about and dropping flares, but practically no damage to Allied shipping was observed by the undersigned. "E" boats also made frequent attempts to penetrate the destroyer protective ring. On one occasion it appeared that a combination plane and "E" boat attack was being made on the protective ring outside the anchorages.

Albert Haas watched "terrific gunfire ashore, giving the impression of a terrific electrical storm."

At 1035 on the morning of June 13, the *Jeremiah O'Brien* weighed anchor and left the "Omaha" beachhead.

Francis Erdman: "We had our orders — we hauled up the anchor and headed back to England, to Southampton, to get another load. This time it was equipment and ammunition in the holds, and we loaded quite a bit of food, field rations."

The ship would know the beaches of Normandy well in the weeks ahead. The next morning the *O'Brien* was alongside the dock loading for Normandy. Her cargo was twelve officers, 453 troops and 217 vehicles.

Loading finished in the early morning of June 17. Part of the cargo was 50 cal. quadruple machine guns. Four of these were left on deck as additional armament for the ship and fire control procedure was explained to the gun crew on these weapons. Leaving the dock at 0645 the *O'Brien* anchored in the Solent, waiting for the convoy to form, and sailed at 0850. As on the previous voyage, twenty U.S. Army soldiers were given instructions for helping on the ship's guns.

Tom McGeehan: "Just outside Southampton harbor is the Isle of Wight. Going to Normandy we'd go out the starboard [west] side of the island and coming back we'd go in on the other [east] side, the port side. There was so much traffic it had to be one-way. By far the biggest amount of ship traffic for Normandy came out of Southampton. It was just continual."

At 1400 the general alarm was rung. An escort ship about a mile off on the starboard beam dropped several depth charges. Then four other escorts closed in, two of them flying black pennants indicating contact with a submarine. At 2025 the evening of June 17, the *Jeremiah O'Brien* arrived for the second time at "Omaha" beachhead. It had become the most active port in Northern France. From D-Day to June 18th 197,444 troops, 27,340 vehicles and 68,799 long tons of supplies were landed.

There was no respite from the heavy weather and to the weary crew the Channel was just another extension of the North Atlantic.

William Watson: "They [Liberty ships] rolled a lot. When we went across that Channel we took some pretty heavy seas. We went across on one trip and had wave crests about seventy feet high. When she came down the ship shook like a string on a violin."

That same evening the crew had their first experience with the V-1 rocket. Just before midnight, an object was seen coming in from seaward over the ship. It zipped overhead on a straight course, flying very fast, looking like a ball of fire in the night sky.

Dan Bandy: "We were on general quarters right off Normandy. It was pretty low, flying at about 2,000 or 3,000 feet. It looked just like a little airplane. Later on, the Germans used the V-2s. They were demoralizing 'cause you never saw them coming. By then the Germans knew they had no chance, but they used them anyway."

Albert Haas' diary: "Saturday, June 17, 1944. 'Flying bomb' was seen going across anchorage area. Flares were dropped by enemy planes, illuminating entire harbor. All ships except ours opened fire on approaching bomb and aircraft."

By midnight the crew had secured from general quarters. During the remainder of the night enemy planes were seen overhead but they merely dropped flares and fired from a distance. The crews were on duty virtually around the clock. They stood their assigned watches and spent the rest of the time in a perpetual state of watchfulness.

Left, constant attention to the armament ensured that it worked when needed. Seaman First Class E. Ray Sharpe cleaning one of the 20 mms. Dan Bandy.

Right, after cleaning the guns had to be oiled and greased. Seaman First Class Helbing lubricates a partly assembled 20 mm. Dan Bandy.

Left, assembled, the 20 mm. is loaded, aimed and ready to defend the ship. Dan Bandy.

Having discharged her cargo and loaded her passengers, the ship left "Omaha" in the early afternoon of June 19, 1944. She arrived at her Solent anchorage just after midnight and went alongside the dock in Southampton in the early afternoon of June 20th.

Francis Erdman:

> Every night after dinner in Southampton we would sit on the after hatch covers and watch the B-26's setting out across the English Channel to do their nightly bombing. On occasions, we counted fourteen hundred of them — this by counting the number of planes in

a squadron and then the number of squadrons. There was some argument over these counts, but fourteen hundred was about right.

Later on in the night you would have the enemy's retaliation — self-propelled bombs, buzz bombs. As long as you heard the motors you were all right — they were still coming. When the motor stopped you knew they were descending. But they were targeted for manufacturing plants, railroad marshalling yards and other targets inland. For some reason none of them landed in the Southampton Docks.

Captain De Smedt vividly recalled the buzz-bombs flying over.

On the night of June 20, while at anchorage at Southampton, a heavy raid by flying bombs was experienced. A total of 18 flying bombs passed directly over the vessel at high speed, in a northerly direction. Only one of these bombs fell in the Southampton area and caused damage, all others landed far inland. This was the last raid on this port as these bombs were launched from the Cherbourg Peninsula, which our troops captured soon afterward.

On June 22, just after breakfast, the *O'Brien* again sailed from Southampton, this time as commodore of the convoy. But rather than going south to Normandy, the destination was Belfast. On Independence day, July 4, 1944, after waiting at anchor for 11 days, the *O'Brien* went alongside the dock. On this same day, 29 days after D-Day, on the beaches of Normandy, the one millionth Allied soldier stepped ashore.

Cadet Tom McGeehan: "We got up to Belfast and anchored and went in on July 4th. There we picked up Patton's army. It was the first I ever heard about Patton."

The Allied offensive was now well underway, moving rapidly inland toward Germany. General George Patton's Third Army would play a major role and throw the term *"blitzkrieg"* right back into the faces of the Nazi Command.

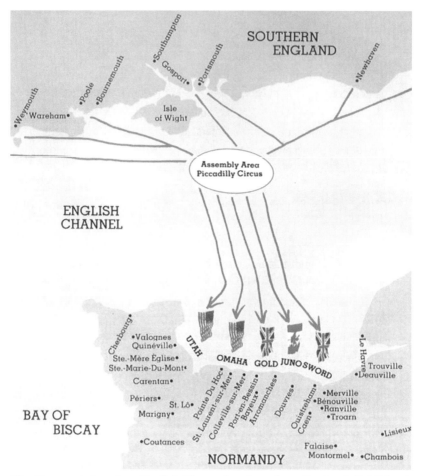

The Normandy beaches, English Channel and southern England. Publisher's collection.

After all the waiting, the loading was done quickly. Captain De Smedt received a briefing and the *O'Brien* sailed the following morning. On board were twenty-three officers, 386 troops, 227 armored vehicles and 160 tons of explosives. The soldiers were part of General Patton's Third Army, Fifth Division.

Cadet Tom McGeehan:

On each trip to the Omaha or Utah beaches the O'Brien *took several hundred troops and several hundred vehicles. Here, an Army truck is loaded in Southampton.* Dan Bandy.

We picked up a mascot in Southampton, a little terrier. De Smedt and the pilot are on the bridge and all the lines are gone and the pilot is backing off from the pier and someone sees the dog on the pier. One of the crew hollered up, 'The dog. Go back for the dog.' Pretty soon the whole crew and the Armed Guard is hollering, 'Get the dog.' We had all those soldiers on board and then *they* took up the cheer. You could hear it all over the harbor, 'Get the dog.' So Captain De Smedt talked to the pilot and they brought the ship back alongside. Someone put a jacobs ladder over and one of the navy guys went over and grabbed the dog and brought him on board.

After waiting a day at anchor outside Belfast a convoy was made up.

At the beachheads the O'Brien*'s heavy lift gear was used to off-load heavy equipment into landing craft alongside.* Dan Bandy.

The DUKW was an agile amphibious craft that could drive up the beach or into the water. This one heads toward the beach with a full load. National Archives.

All was quiet as the convoy worked its way toward Normandy. As the ship drew near the French coast, Captain De Smedt called the crew together to tell them what to expect. Numerous subs had been sighted and were active in the area from Lands End to beyond Portsmouth. In addition, the enemy had also recently laid several new mine fields in the area. At ten-thirty that night, the convoy commodore advised by signal light that the ships could expect an enemy air attack by dawn.

In the early morning of July 9 one of the escorts dropped several depth charges nearby. It was too dark to see what she was after but the alarm was rung for general quarters. So far the *O'Brien* had been lucky. Through all the Atlantic and Channel crossings, despite the mines, submarines, air attacks and V-1 rockets, she had not been in harm's way. But no one took this good luck for granted or relaxed their vigilance. At every sighting or unexplained event the crew went to general quarters, ready for anything that might happen. Far better to stand down from a score — or a hundred — false alarms than to risk not being ready in an emergency. A member of one crew remarked, "I'd rather have a false alarm any day than the real thing."

That evening, the convoy arrived at the "Utah" beachhead. They were part of the typical group of nine transports, twenty LCIs, twenty-five Liberty ships, forty LSTs, seventy-five LCTs and thirty-eight British coastal freighters to arrive at the Normandy assault areas during any one

The Rhino barge was large, bulky and unwieldy, but carried big loads. This one is only partially loaded. Note the large number of ships in the background. Robert Milby.

day. The total number of ships arriving from D-Day to the end of June was 180 troop transports, 570 Liberty ships, 372 LCIs, 905 LSTs, 1442 LCTs and 788 British coasters. The daily tonnage handled at Normandy was equal to one-third of the normal import capacity of the United Kingdom.

The day was spent discharging men and equipment. Here they were closer to the action than at Omaha but it was relatively quiet; the front had moved inland. One man was posted at each 3-inch 50 with battle phones while the remaining men on the Armed Guard watch were assigned to the 20 millimeter guns on the bridge. Shrapnel from shore batteries went whizzing past the ship, some of it falling on the deck.

"Utah" was known for the ferocity of its German air raids. The historian Samuel Elliot Morison described it in *The Invasion of France and Germany, 1944-1945*:

The really brisk time off Utah was the small hours of the morning, which the Luftwaffe chose for raiding. Plenty of warning was given to the invasion fleet by radar. The Luftwaffe ritual was to have a reconnaissance plane drop a line of float lights as a guide to the bombers. As soon as the first flare was seen, patrolling PTs began to shoot them out one by one and every vessel that could make smoke did so. In a few

Semaphore was a common means of communication. Seaman First Class Hardin "wig-wagging" to another ship. Dan Bandy.

minutes the bombers were overhead. The Army ashore and the ships afloat opened with antiaircraft fire, tracers crisscrossed the sky, burning planes plummeted into the ocean, exploding 1000-kilogram bombs sent up immense geysers. After half to three quarters of an hour the pandemonium ceased and the amphibious forces tried to grab a little sleep before unloading was resumed at daylight.

The *O'Brien's* crew performed valiantly. Nominally civilian,

A woman was a rarity at Normandy. This unidentified WAC lieutenant made one of the O'Brien's crossings. To her right is Gunner's Mate Second Class Dan Bandy; to her left, Seaman First Class Hardin. Dan Bandy.

the merchant marine served with such distinction and devotion to duty that they became indispensable to the military services. They faced the same dangers from the air and sea, they persevered under every condition to do their duty and they gave their lives in service to the nation. Few considered themselves heroes. Their heroes were those who went into battle. The merchant crews worked, sometimes around the clock, on what they began to call the "bus runs" to Normandy — routine, undramatic, unglamorous. No journalist covered their trips, no historian chronicled their quiet determination, but their role in the war and final victory was crucial.

At noon July 12, having finished her discharge, the *Jeremiah O'Brien* hoisted anchor and left the "Utah" beachhead. With the beaches secured, the supply effort increased in geometric proportions. Albert Haas noted in his diary, "During our passage, we passed six convoys enroute to France."

In general, the English and Americans got along well. Cooperation between the services was outstanding and the civilian population was friendly. But after several stress-filled years, everyone was getting weary of the crowding, the discomfort and the inevitable jealousies that arose. American servicemen and sailors are often noisy and boisterous and the more reserved British found this irritating. Even more irritating to the English men was the attraction the Americans had for many English women. So, while the English people continued to be friendly and welcoming, often there was no love lost between British and American soldiers, sailors and seamen.

The invasion had been underway for more than two months and the Allies now knew much more about the hazards of crossing the Channel and how to handle them. On August 12 the crew was gathered and given the results of the latest findings. Practically all casualties to Liberty ships on cross-Channel operations were from acoustic mines or torpedoes and the most serious and greatest number of injuries were to men on the stern. These occurred to lookouts whose hips were shattered when the explosion went off under them while they were standing in a rigid position. Captain De Smedt ordered that when underway on the cross-Channel shuttle, everybody was to keep out of the stern quarters and only the lookouts on the gun platform aft were to be allowed. These men were told to sit on the gun or lean in such a way as to be completely relaxed, not in a rigid upright position. Wearing life jackets at all times was imperative.

There were additional instructions for the Armed Guard. The two leading Petty Officers would be stationed on the bridge so that there would be no loss of sector coverage entailed by the stern lookout arrangement. Also, there had been several cases reported of the Germans at the beachheads using so-called "infernal machines" which were snipers disguised to resemble boxes, debris, etc. The Armed Guard was advised that two rifles would be kept on the flying bridge with an extra man, in case of a need to fire at suspicious objects.

As the *O'Brien* got underway for Normandy on Sunday, August 13, the usual church services were held — mass for Catholics with church service for Protestants following immediately afterward. The anxiety of the earlier Normandy runs having passed, the urgent requests for spiritual assistance and divine intervention had abated and the communicant population reverted to the pre-invasion few.

On August 25, the *Jeremiah O'Brien* went alongside the Southampton dock, loaded fifteen officers, 145 troops and 127 vehicles, which took one day and night, then anchored in the Solent on the morning of the 30th for her ninth trip to Normandy. The crew were beginning to feel like yo-yos.

The shuttle runs having become relatively routine, the crew's interests returned to life on board and "chow" resurfaced as a prime topic. During the excitement of the invasion it had momentarily slipped down the list of priorities but as the trips became ordinary, it resumed its rightful place.

Dan Bandy: "The food on the ship was very good until we got low on supplies in the U.K. because of the invasion and because we'd feed some of the army people when they were on board."

Captain De Smedt's voyage letter phrased it more diplomatically: "Commissary stores were supplemented from time to time as needed."

The crews generally had a high regard for the troops they came in contact with. Especially during the first weeks of the invasion, recognition of the great undertaking, the critical responsibility of the soldiers and the dangers, sacrifices and horrors they would face forged a bond of admiration, sympathy and understanding between them.

Sailing from the Solent on August 31, there was a minor mishap. At 1415 the general alarm was rung as a fire was reported in No. 4 hold. Vehicles in the hold had been stowed in a hurry and broke loose, smashing together due to the ship's rolling in choppy seas. Each time they hit, they threw sparks. As the vehicles were loaded with gasoline and some of it had spilled, the potential for fire was extreme. The captain had the ship heave to while the cargo was secured.

September 1 was spent unloading at "Utah" and all the cargo was off before midnight. The ship left the beachhead, anchored at the "Capetown" anchorage [also called Piccadilly Circus] for the night, crossed the Channel again on September 2, and arrived at the Solent just before 11 in the evening. Again, there were too many ships and not enough berths and it was September 6 before the O'Brien could go alongside the dock.

After one day of quick loading the ship left the dock and anchored in the Solent, awaiting the formation of a convoy. On board were 4 officers, 230 troops and 128 vehicles. As though playing a game of battledores and shuttlecocks, the ships once more left the Solent and arrived at "Utah" in the early evening. It was the O'Brien's tenth trip. After three days of unloading, the O'Brien left the beachhead on September 12, anchored at "Capetown," then crossed the Channel and arrived back at the

Some of the crew got ashore at Normandy while the ship was discharging on her last shuttle. Left, three of the O'Brien's *Armed Guard crew inspect a German gun emplacement on the beach. Right, one of the pillbox fortifications used by the Germans to defend the Normandy coast.* Dan Bandy.

Solent. This time the berth was vacant and the cargo ready and the next morning the ship was alongside the Southampton dock.

September 15 found the *Jeremiah O'Brien* once again anchoring in the Solent and on the 16th she sailed for "Utah" once more. It was to be the last time. She had on board twenty-three officers, 467 troops and 205 vehicles. The evening before sailing, a farewell dinner was held aboard the ship, attended by Army and Admiralty officers and the American Consul General. The vessel, her officers and crew were commended for their good work in bringing the mission to a successful conclusion.

After three and a half months, the beach was well secured. According to the Armed Guard Log, the Navy gun crew was allowed ashore at "Utah" beachhead, in the beach area only, for four hours at a time. But this entry was only for the official record. In reality, the crew had been going ashore since after the first few shuttles.

Morgan Williams:

> The last trip, Memhard let us take turns going ashore. A couple of us went through a minefield. We saw all these trip wires and everything, but you could see where the soldiers had walked there before us and we just walked where they did. So we got to the other side and some soldier yelled at us that two or three guys had been killed there just the day before." What the inexperienced men did not

know was that some mines are set to go off after a set number of passes — the fifth, tenth, etc. So, walking in another's steps was not necessarily proof that the path was not mined. Fortunately for the *O'Brien* gun crew, no mines exploded.

We saw some big bunkers and we did get some souvenirs. I got a potato masher [hand grenade] and different shells and so on. I still have them. So we went about ten miles into France, then caught a ride on a Sherman tank and he brought us back.

The cargo was discharged by September 23 and that morning the *O'Brien* sailed for Cherbourg, France where she arrived in mid-afternoon. During her eleven trips to the assault area the ship carried 3492 troops, 1746 vehicles, fourteen police dogs, 117 tons of special cargo and 341 tons of dynamite. On September 24, the *O'Brien* left Cherbourg and the next day arrived at Mumbles Point, off Swansea, Wales.

At about this time Grace Line received an unusual letter in its New York office from the U.S. Coast Guard.

"This office is in receipt of a confidential report from a reliable source, which states that a member of the crew of the *SS Jeremiah O'Brien*, under your operation, made the written statement that there is a still in the engine room of that vessel where the crew draw their own alcohol." The not-exactly-startling allegation was calmly acknowledged by Grace Line which promised to look into the matter.

The ship and crew had been out almost six months and worked hard in dangerous conditions in the greatest military maneuver in history. They looked forward to returning to their families and were overjoyed to sail just after midnight on September 29. The ship was homewardbound at last in a convoy toward New York.

Tom McGeehan: "The last thing we saw, we went through St. George Channel and the Irish Sea and all we could see of that was the loom of a light on the Irish Coast. Pellegrino and I were on the flying bridge, and he said, 'Well cadet, that's the last thing of Europe you'll see.'"

The crossing was uneventful except for some minor incidents. On October 6, at 1115, ship No. 46 of the convoy, the *SS William Ellery*, suddenly opened fire. No flag hoist was up, nor was one put up until 1120. They seemed to be having firing practice. Lieutenant Memhard noted in his log, "Opening fire in such fashion a particularly annoying violation of Mersig's (signaling instructions for merchant ships), since other ships in convoy initially can only go on assumption that firing is at a hostile target."

And, as always, the North Atlantic weather. Tom McGeehan: "There had been a hurricane that had passed through a few days earlier and done damage to the East Coast. I don't know if it was the aftereffects, but we were in mid-Atlantic and the ship was rolling terribly."

As the ship neared the East Coast the crew relaxed. Wartime precautions and military rules gave way to civilian concerns. What had happened while they were gone? Had their friends changed? Had *they* changed? Would their homecoming be welcomed?

Helmets and gas masks were collected from all personnel. A bulletin was posted advising the ship's company of federal ballot particulars and setting October 10th as voting day. Franklin D. Roosevelt was running for his fourth term with Harry Truman as his Vice-President.

Coming back to home port required that one final detail be attended to. Gunner's Mate Morgan Williams: "Miss O'Brien was a painting we had on the forward gun tub. Kind of a pin-up, like on the planes. Well, she was naked, bare-breasted and everything and there was a chance we'd get into trouble, so we had to paint her over with gray coming back into New York."

Finally, on October 12, at 1800 the *O'Brien* arrived at the Ambrose light ship, marking the approach to New York Harbor. The voyage was over. They had made it through. Seemingly protected by a lucky charm, the ship had triumphed over the worst the North Atlantic could give, braved the Nazi bombs, torpedoes and shelling barrages, delivered her cargo, and brought her crew safely home.

Dan Bandy: "I would have said it was a happy crew, the merchant crew got along good. Captain de Smedt was a good man, he was very accommodating, very good with the Navy crew. All the way through we had a good crew on that ship. She was a good old happy ship." It was high praise.

Miss Jerry O'Brien, the ship's pinup, had to be painted over before arrival in the United States. It was feared authorities might find her too risque. Dan Bandy.

On the day of payoff the crew filed through the saloon, collecting their wages. In the passageway outside, plans were made, goodbyes were said. One by one or in some cases in groups of two or three, seamen walked down the gangway, their belongings in a duffel bag slung over their shoulders or carried in suitcases. Some were happy to be getting off, others were sad at losing friendships. As they reached the end of the dock they turned for one last look at the ship, their home for the previous six months, a never-to-be-forgotten voyage.

But, as usual, when in port...

E. Ray Sharpe:

Al Helbling, from Ohio. He was young and heavy set. He and another guy went ashore in New York. They went up to this bar and there was all these Coastguardsmen in the place. You could tell them 'cause they had a shield on their uniform. So Helbling and this other guy says, "Move over shallow water, let the deep blue sea in." Well they moved over all right. All over them. They came back to the ship with the biggest shiners you ever saw. The shiners lasted about two weeks and every time we'd see one of them in the passageway we'd tell them, "Move over shallow water."

Francis Erdman: "The last time I saw her, looking back, the *O'Brien* was lying quietly, rusty sided and war-worn — but a good ship that had seen us through."

11

In The Shadow
Of The Andes

We rejoin the ship several days later at the Bethlehem Dry Docks in Hoboken, New Jersey, where she has just been given a "shave and a haircut." This is maritime slang for a quick, routine drydocking. The ship was showing the effects of the heavy duty. No major repairs were necessary. All she needed was the barnacles scraped off her hull and several coats of fresh paint.

On October 20 the *Jeremiah O'Brien* moved to Pier #3 on the North River in New York to load a mixed general cargo of trucks, foodstuffs and machinery for the Canal Zone. After the long, eventful voyage No. 4, many of the crew needed a vacation and the ship received almost an entirely new complement.

Voyage 5 began at midnight on November 1, 1944. Casting off her lines, the *O'Brien* passed through the submarine nets to New York harbor at 2034. For the first time in her career, she was traveling independently. According to the Secret Log[1] her course was s/c [steering course] 144 T. [true]. This is south-southeast from New York and toward Florida. As if in reward for her valiant service on the storm-lashed North Atlantic, the *O'Brien* was heading for warmer climes.

According to the Secret Log, at noon the first day out, the ship had steamed for 15 hours and 26 minutes since departure for a distance of 178 miles, making good a speed of 11.4 knots. Although it was November, the weather was warm and pleasant — a welcome change from New York's leaden skies and cold winds.

By November 6, the ship was in the Caribbean. The icy grey waters of the Atlantic had given way to a deep rich blue with pastel green shades in the shallower areas close to shore. Cuba was sighted off the starboard bow, a verdant green island mass, covered with lush foliage. The off-duty crew basked in the warm sun, glad to be away from the cold of the eastern seaboard. The war seemed far away. But it could not be completely forgotten. At 1105 the ship was challenged by a Navy patrol blimp. The answer was given by flag hoist. The blimp acknowledged the signal and quietly drifted away, continuing her patrol.

November 7, 1944. "Secret Log: St. Time 24h 00m, dist. 300 miles, speed 12.5 knots,[2] departure to noon st. time 5d 15h 26m, dist. 1599 miles, speed 11.8 knots."

Because the *O'Brien* was traveling alone in the still-potentially-dangerous waters of the Caribbean, she was required to zig-zag, a series of frequent course changes designed to thwart any submarine that might be lining the vessel up in her crosshairs.

---

[1] Secret Logs were carried on all merchant vessels during the war. Information relating to course steered, speed made good and prominent landmarks were entered in this log and not in the deck log as peacetime tradition dictates. The *Jeremiah O'Brien's* secret log for earlier voyages was not available as of this writing.

[2] This was the fastest day's run recorded in the Secret Log for the *O'Brien's* early years. She was probably being helped along by one of the coastal countercurrents from the Gulf Stream.

On the Atlantic seaboard and in the Caribbean challenge by blimp, as well as military vessels, was common. In this photo a Navy blimp checks the identity of two merchantmen. National Archives.

Once released, torpedoes travel in a straight line until they hit their target or run out of fuel and sink. Zig-zagging was thought to improve a ship's chances by confusing the submarine commander enough to make him reluctant to fire or turning the ship out of the path of an already-fired torpedo. The Germans had developed an acoustical torpedo that homed on the sound of a ship's propeller but zig-zagging was continued because not all U-boats had the newer device.

As they neared the Panama Canal Zone, security became tighter. On November 9, just outside Limon Bay the pilot came aboard. As he guided the ship through the breakwater, the crew had their first glimpse of Gatun Locks, the entrance to the Canal itself. This soon disappeared behind a lush, green hill as the ship eased to her left toward the commercial section of Cristobal. By 1530 the *O'Brien* was alongside the dock and tied up, preparing to discharge her cargo. The air was thick with the smells of the jungle, light perfumes from tropical flowers, the richness of growing plants and the underlying heavier miasma of decay.

German submarines were still operating on the Atlantic Coast and the United States was urgently aware of the potentially crippling effects of a successful attack on the Canal, the "crossroads of the world." The Allies (in reality, primarily the United States) were fighting a two-ocean war and the Canal was the supremely-critical, and extremely vulnerable, link, conduit and supply line between the Atlantic and the Pacific. Damage to the Canal would force ships to take an almost 8,000-mile journey around Cape Horn, subjected to conditions that were even worse than the notorious North Atlantic. Security — total, absolute and impenetrable — was required to safeguard this passage.

Cargo unloading proceeded slowly due to frequent and heavy downpours. Rainfall for the Atlantic side of the Canal is 130 inches each year.

An alert was called for the nights of the 15th, 16th and 17th of November and all hands were ordered to remain aboard ship during the hours of the alert. Shore leave was granted but on a limited basis. A memo from the Port Captain of the Canal Zone to all shipping agents stated:

> In the interest of security every vessel at any dock or mooring within Canal Zone waters shall be ready to move at all times on a moment's notice. At least one third of the ship's officers and crew must be kept on board at all times so that the ship may be ready to move on a moment's notice. The captains and crews of vessels should be on board at least 12 hours prior to going to sea or transiting the Panama Canal.

The humid air combined with the tropical temperatures gave Cristobal a pleasant, "shirtsleeve" atmosphere. The docks were in the heart of town and the *O'Brien's* crew, when allowed ashore, enjoyed brief excursions to the nearby restaurants and bars. These were either built without fronts or had large paneless windows to let the customers enjoy the balmy air and watch the passersby on the sidewalks. The overall feeling was one of pleasant lethargy, an oasis from the battles in the far reaches of the Atlantic and Pacific.

The Canal transit was scheduled for November 17, arranged in advance by Grace Line. The ship left the dock in ballast at 0628, dropped anchor in the stream at 0715, took on a Canal pilot and approached the first lock. In addition to native linehandlers, a detail of U.S. Marines was placed aboard. This relieved the Armed Guard crew of their duties and allowed them to watch the process of going through the locks. Many of the off-watch merchant crew also came out on deck to observe the fascinating procedure.

The first set of locks separate the Atlantic Ocean from Gatun Lake and, appropriately enough, are named Gatun Locks. As the *O'Brien* approached the open gates and eased into the lock, the linehandlers threw heaving lines to compatriots on the concrete walls on either side. The heaving lines were fastened to eyes in wire rope cables which ran off constant tension winches fastened to the "mules" running on tracks along both sides of the locks. The "mules" (named for the animals used to pull barges on the Erie Canal) were actually electric locomotives, each one weighing more than fifty tons and having more than thirty-five tons of pull or braking power. Once the heaving lines were fast, the linemen pulled the cable ends to the *Jeremiah O'Brien's* bow and stern. The ship was now held in place in the center of the lock basin with a mule on each side of the bow and stern keeping her in place with their constant tension winches. The floating gates, each weighing 720 tons, yet so finely engineered that they were moved with a 40 horsepower motor, were then closed.

Fresh water from Gatun Lake was pumped into the basin until the *O'Brien* floated at the same level as the water in the lock in front of her. The gates separating the two locks were opened and the mules carefully guided the ship into the next basin where the process was repeated. Exiting the final basin of Gatun Lock (there are three), the mules were cast off and the *O'Brien* found herself floating on Gatun Lake, eighty-five feet above the Atlantic. To their right they could see the top of the spillway to Gatun Dam. One and a half miles long and one-half mile wide at its base, it was the largest earthen dam in the world when built as part of the Canal project that opened a new era in global shipping on August 15, 1914.

The water in Gatun Lake is fresh and very pure. Merchant ships often take advantage of passing through the lake to fill their tanks and, if time allows, to wash down the ship with fire hoses.

Approaching the Canal proper, the *O'Brien* passed the largest island in the lake, Barro Colorado. Here, capuchin and howler monkeys chased each other through the treetops, ignored by the alligators and iguanas sunning themselves below. Then, as lush green hills and mountains rose abruptly on either side, the ship entered Gaillard Cut, the most difficult section of the Canal to engineer. Evidence of the 674 million yards of earth removed to dig the eight mile-long "ditch" was obvious in the broad sweeping cuts and terraces rising on either side, partially covered with meadows and groves of trees. From the banks of the encroaching jungle could be heard the lazy singing of the striped cuckoo, "Tres, tres, tres, pesos, pesos, pesos." Tiny birds, blue-black grassquits, popped out of the tall grass like buzzing black popcorn as the ship passed. Crewmembers pointed out the sights to one another: screeching flocks of parrots bounding from tree to tree, toucans calling across the treetop canopy, an iridescent blue butterfly flitting though the dark jungles, an occasional boa constrictor hanging in sinuous loops from a tree branch.

After crossing the continental divide, the ship approached Pedro Miguel Locks. Linehandlers rowed out to the ship and clambered aboard to receive the lines from the mules. The single basin at Pedro Miguel lowered the ship thirty-one feet to the level of Miraflores Lake. A short traverse then took the *O'Brien* to the double basin of Miraflores Lock. Here the ship was lowered in two stages the remaining sixty-four feet to the level of the Pacific.

The crew marveled at the massive eighty-two-foot gates that separate the final basin from the ocean.

"That's because the tidal range here is twenty-feet," the pilot explained. "On the Atlantic side, it's only three feet, so we don't need them so big there."

After clearing the last lock, the pilot, linehandlers and Marine detail were dropped off. The ship passed through the submarine nets and into the Pacific bound for Antofagasta, Chile. Secret Log: "Canal transit from 0922 to 1728. 1728 (2228 G.C.T.) departure Balboa."

Then it was back to routine days at sea, zig-zagging south toward Chile.

Robert Crocker:

> Our typical day was fairly quiet. The petty officer stood watch and you'd have shipboard watches. You'd make sure the men were awake and up on the guns and relieve each one for a coffee break. When they came back I'd go to the bridge, and then the stern, and relieve them. And another thing, you'd have to be sure the next watch was awake. At night I'd have to make sure they had half an hour to stand outside to get their eyes adjusted so when they went on watch they could see properly.
>
> We had eight men, one on each of the twenties. On the three inch there was one gun captain, one sighting, one pulling the trigger and at least two loaders — five or more. The aft gun would have five or six or even seven. The gunnery officer would be on the bridge. Then you had the signalman and the radiomen. The signalman would be up there on the bridge to handle the light and the flags. The radioman would alternate with the merchant marine in the radio room.

The voyage south was through calm, deep blue water. The skies were pale blue with wispy white clouds. At times pelicans flew in a straight line from one end of the horizon to the other. As the *Jeremiah O'Brien* approached, the line of birds bent farther and farther in the direction the ship was travelling until finally one bird took the initiative and broke the stream, passing astern of the ship with the remainder following it. The ship crossed the equator for the first time in her career, but the traditional ceremony was ignored. Captain Gunderson was against such "foolishness." As the ship passed the coast of Peru, the Andes were seen, tall, snow-covered, in the distance.

Eight days after leaving Panama, at 0425 on the morning of November 25, land was sighted off the port bow. At 0825 two patrol planes circled the ship asking for identification. The *O'Brien* answered and the planes flew off toward land. As the port of Antofagasta, Chile came into view the crew saw a barren plain beyond it that swooped quickly upward into high, scrub-covered coastal mountains and, in the distance, once again, the snow-capped Andes. By 1320 the ship was tied up fore and aft to the pier at Antofagasta.

It took three days to load the cargo of copper and lead ingots and plates. Loading went slowly due to security measures.

Sailing closer to shore now, the ship passed rugged, rocky terrain where the coastal mountains seemed to plunge into the sea. As the *O'Brien* approached Callao, the topography leveled off, revealing a well-protected natural harbor.

On December 1, the *Jeremiah O'Brien* entered Callao, Peru and was tied up fore and aft to pier No. 1 before noon. The ship would be in port only a day and the crew, each in his own way, tried to make the most of the time.

Departure was taken at 1948 the following evening, with the ship bound for Cristobal, on the Atlantic side of the Canal Zone. Perhaps due to the quick loading, the cargo had not been well-secured.

Ted Martin: "We had a problem with the ore. The cargo was big sheets of metal ore. It broke loose in the hold and had to be re-secured. That happened almost as soon as we left port. The strapping broke loose. In fact they had to strip the canvas off the hatches and secure the cargo with four by fours and come-alongs."

The rest of the run up the west coast of South America was peaceful. The deck department took advantage of the good weather to lubricate the cargo gear and touch up some of the paintwork. The traditional poker game resumed. Life aboard settled into a pleasant routine.

The *Jeremiah O'Brien* made her second transit of the Panama Canal on December 8, 1944 and up through the Gulf of Mexico in a hurricane.

On the morning of December 14, the low, broad entrance to the Mississippi River came into view — a welcome sight to all on board. By 1010 the pilot was aboard and the *O'Brien* was underway up river. The river delta came together in low banks dotted here and there with a ramshackle building or fishing shack. As the ship steamed farther upriver the banks became lined with vegetation and low trees hung with Spanish moss. Ships and barges passed, traveling downriver to the Gulf of Mexico and beyond. Just before midnight she moored fore and aft at the docks in West Wago, Louisiana. Then she shifted to the Market Street docks in New Orleans.

For most of the crew "New Orleans" was the old French Quarter — Dixieland jazz pouring out of every doorway and on every street corner, cajun and creole food — crayfish, jambalaya, alligator tail, filé gumbo, pralines — artists working at their easels, the finished paintings propped against the iron fence surrounding Jackson Square, old houses with ironwork grills, servicemen roaming the streets, noisy nights, bars everywhere, and girls, girls, girls.

It was almost the end of the year before the last of the copper and lead were unloaded. The crew took advantage of the long layover to celebrate the holidays and relax. With great reluctance they joined the ship on December 29 as she left the Market Street dock at New Orleans and headed downriver.

Voyage 5 had been an interesting, exotic, unique adventure. Voyage 6 would be a different story.

12

"ONE SHIP IN THE PACIFIC"

The *O'Brien* had just cleared the dock and was partway down river when a thick fog suddenly settled in from across the bayous forcing the ship to anchor. The crew waited, listening to the river surge past, through the night and into the next day. Just before noon on December 30th the fog lifted, the ship weighed anchor sailing downstream and cleared the Mississippi Delta a few hours later. There was no cargo on board and the only ballast was water.

After steaming a few hours in a westerly direction through the Gulf, the *Jeremiah O'Brien* anchored in Galveston Bay, Texas, on New Year's Eve. The crew was ready to celebrate, but it was not to be.

John Crosby, recently graduated from Kings Point, had joined the ship as third mate: "We loaded 10,000 tons of bombs, with the warheads in No. 3 hatch and a very high load of belly tanks on deck. During the time of loading none of the crew was allowed ashore."

Loading ammunition was a slow, careful process. First, the *O'Brien's* cargo holds were cleaned of all debris. Then, in each hatch, a solid plank deck was laid over the ship's steel deck and wooden bulkheads were erected attaching them to the inner sides of the hull, creating a wood box inside the hold. There would be no steel surfaces exposed for the metal-cased bombs to rub against, eliminating the possibility of sparking.

Then the bombs, without detonators and strapped to wooden skid pallets, were loaded. The pallets were flat on the bottom surface with heavy timbers at each end. The top surfaces of the timbers were cut in an arc so that the cylindrical bombs fit in the cutout and wouldn't roll. The bombs were strapped to each pallet to hold them in place. When they reached a certain height a new deck would be laid to distribute the weight evenly and additional tiers were added. As each cargo space was loaded, void areas were blocked to prevent the cargo from shifting horizontally and timbers, called "toms," were wedged between the cargo and the overhead to prevent it from shifting vertically.

The detonators or fuzes were loaded in a separate compartment from the bombs. Because of the extreme danger involved, smoking was allowed only in the *Jeremiah O'Brien's* midship house and at designated areas ashore. Most of the stevedores chewed tobacco, rather than smoke.

The crew watched the process with increasing disfavor. They calculated the tons of explosives contained in the bombs and translated that into equivalent tons of TNT. Restricted to the ship day after day, there was nothing to distract them while the loading continued. The stories and apprehensions grew, fed on themselves, and grew some more. Tales of "ammo ships" being hit by torpedoes and vaporizing into oblivion circulated.

Injuries and accidents began happening. Suddenly, the *O'Brien*, which had sailed through so much with a minimum of crew health problems, was becoming a floating infirmary.

According to John L. Crosby some of the injuries and illnesses were faked or deliberate. "During our stay in Houston ... several of the crew members inflicted injury to themselves by breaking an arm, etc., or causing a disability in order to get off the ship out of fear of the bombs as cargo. There was some secrecy about those bombs. We were not allowed shore leave all the time we were loading them."

On January 17, 1945, two weeks after the *O'Brien* arrived at the Ordnance Dock, her hatches were full. She sailed for Galveston, to finish off with a load of deck cargo.

The ship arrived at Panama early the morning of January 25th and transited the Canal that afternoon with the Marine guard assuming watch duties.

The ship's crew fell into a normal routine of standing watch, maintaining the engine and cargo gear and killing off-duty time by reading, playing cards, washing clothes, telling stories and writing letters home. The Armed Guard built a target for gunnery practice. Using two metal barrels as floats, they built a wooden frame around it with a painted bull's eye on top to shoot at.

The crossing was long, slow and relatively uneventful. The tide of the war was now in the Allies' favor. In the Pacific, the United States was driving the war onto the shores of Japan and for most of the way across, the ocean was relatively secure, both on the surface and underneath.

With little else to look forward to, meals are a big event on board ship. If the food is good, the crew is happy and you don't hear much about it. If not, they complain. Typically, the first few weeks of a voyage are pleasant — until the fresh produce and milk run out.

Some of the crew continued worrying about the cargo. Others were more fatalistic. Robert Crocker, Gunner's Mate Third Class: "We carried bombs that trip. As far as the gun crew was concerned it didn't matter. We didn't bother with lifejackets or anything, if we got hit it would all be over with anyway. We just made sure we spent all our money in whatever port we were in."

On February 16, at 0200 the *Jeremiah O'Brien* crossed the International Dateline for the first time in her career — February 16 became February 17. On troop ships and passenger liners, this passage into the "Realm of the Golden Dragon" was often celebrated with a ceremony and the issuing of certificates commemorating the occasion. But Captain Gunderson was not the type to indulge in such "nonsense."

On February 21st the ship crossed the equator for the third time in her career. On many ships this is cause for hazing and a ceremony making "polliwogs" who have not crossed before into "shellbacks." Again Captain Gunderson vetoed the "silly" ceremony.

On February 23, 1945 the *Jeremiah O'Brien* arrived at Seeadler Harbor, Manus, Admiralty Islands, New Guinea. Manus was merely a staging area, a port of call for further orders. The next day the ship departed in a small convoy for Hollandia, there to await assembly of yet a larger convoy for the Philippines.

By March 3 the convoy was assembled. The *Jeremiah O'Brien* left Hollandia with instructions to tow two Navy LCM's and carry their crews on board the ship, while in convoy with nine escorts and thirty-four other ships.

On March 7, as they passed off Palau Island, a second convoy was sighted off the port bow. By noon it had joined the *O'Brien's* group, adding twenty ships. This made a total of sixty-four vessels steaming together. Three days later land was raised off the starboard bow. That afternoon the "Tacloban convoy," consisting of twenty-eight ships, one of which was the *Jeremiah O'Brien*, broke away from rest of the fleet.

There was a great deal of confusion in the South Pacific at the time. The war itself was fought bravely and effectively, but the process of supplying the machinery of war, the matériel, was chaotic. Supplies seemed to be randomly routed in all directions at once with the result that some areas were awash in materials while others operated on bailing wire and chewing gum. The *Jeremiah O'Brien* sailed directly into the middle of a figurative sea of bedlam and disorder.

As the ship entered Tacloban harbor located on Samar Island, in the Philippines, Captain Gunderson couldn't get direction from the authorities ashore where to anchor. In disgust, he finally dropped the *O'Brien's* anchor where he thought it was safest. The following day he was instructed to up-anchor and move to a specified anchorage. On March 12, the shoreside authorities suddenly realized the *O'Brien* was carrying ammunition and she was ordered move to the explosives anchorage. One day later the ship was ordered back to the inner harbor to discharge part of her deck cargo. The deck cargo was partially unlashed when new orders came through. Captain Gunderson was told the previous order was a mistake. After spending the night re-lashing the cargo, the ship shifted back out to the explosives anchorage. And there it sat. The crew chafed, making derisive remarks about military efficiency and their chances of winning the war. A descriptive acronym had been coined, and was much used during the war, to describe normal military operations, especially as they existed in the South Pacific. The word was "SNAFU." It stood for "Situation Normal, All Fucked Up." The word was much used in crew conversation.

Someone then decided to send the *Jeremiah O'Brien* elsewhere. On March 15 the anchor was weighed and the ship began to move into convoy position but the convoy sailing was canceled and, once again, the ship returned to the anchorage.

Things finally came together on March 16 when the *O'Brien* moved out to join a northbound convoy. Thirty-three ships combined with a group of twenty-four ships coming up from New Guinea to form a convoy of fifty-seven ships headed for the Northern Philippines. The *O'Brien* had been in the war area three weeks and still carried her cargo of ammunition, airplane belly tanks and two LCMs.

Corregidor had been retaken by American forces under General Douglas MacArthur a few weeks earlier with Manila Bay itself opening to Allied shipping only a few days before the convoy sailed. Subic Bay was recently cleared but the Japanese forces had retreated to mountain strongholds throughout Luzon and continued a determined resistance. The recent kamikaze attacks at Lingayen were a new topic of conversation and concern, as were the continual threat of attacks by air or sea.

On Saint Patrick's day, 1945, as the convoy proceeded farther into the Philippines, there was a sudden alert. An emergency turn to starboard was ordered and a flag hoist (International Code Flag No. 2, indicating a submarine) went up on ship No. 21. General quarters (GQ) was called. This was followed by orders for an emergency turn to port and, two minutes later, another emergency turn to starboard and yet another emergency turn to port. Nothing else happened and eventuallly the ship secured from GQ. Later that day another submarine warning was hoisted. The tense alert turned into farce when it was heard over the TBY (radio telephone) that what the escorts thought was a submarine was in fact "Two whales and a floating swab handle".

On March 18, Mindoro was sighted just after noon. Taken by American forces in December 1944, the island had become a jungle stronghold of supplies feeding the efforts in Luzon. Suddenly, in addition to mines, submarines, depth charges, and enemy bombers — and swab handles — the new threat of kamikaze planes became a reality. The crew, which had grown more or less accustomed to the cargo — which they couldn't seem to get rid of — now had their earlier apprehensions resurface.

John Crosby: "We were told that the ammunition ship going into Mindoro prior to us was hit by a Japanese kamikaze and was completely destroyed."

In a desperate, last-ditch effort to prevent the Allies' determined advance toward their homeland, the Japanese had developed the kamikaze attack. The word means "divine wind" and stems from the 13th century when a typhoon destroyed an

This is what happened to the ship that preceded the SS Jeremiah O'Brien *carrying ammunition into Mindoro. It was hit by a kamikaze and disintegrated.* National Archives.

invading force of Mongols. The Japanese believed that the divine wind made their nation impervious to attack. To ensure their survival as the tide of war turned against them, the Japanese decided to create their own divine wind. Selecting their best pilots, the Imperial Japanese forces armed their planes with explosives and flew them directly into Allied ships. The young Japanese pilots vied for the honor of dying for emperor and country, believing such a heroic death guaranteed honor, glory and eternal life in the hereafter. The effect was dramatic but, overall, strategically impotent. Nevertheless, if one's ship was the target of a kamikaze, the danger was very real. The Liberty ship *John Burke*, fully loaded with ammunition, was hit by a suicide plane a few months earlier and vaporized, leaving not a trace of her presence when the smoke cleared. The Liberty ship *Lewis Dyche,* also loaded with ammo, suffered the same fate. According to the War Shipping Administration, merchant marine losses in the Mindoro landings were greater than those of the Armed Forces taking part in the D-Day invasion of Normandy and many of those losses were due to kamikaze attacks.

In the early afternoon the *Jeremiah O'Brien* broke away from the convoy and proceeded into the harbor area of San Jose, Mindoro.

The period between March 21st and March 26th was difficult. There was a strong offshore wind and a serious concern that the pilings or dolphins the *O'Brien's* mooring lines were tied to weren't strong enough or anchored firmly enough to hold the ship. A sharp watch had to be kept to ensure that the ship wasn't blown off the dock and back into the bay. Nevertheless, by March 27 the two LCMs, all the deck cargo and some of the cargo out of No. 4 hatch had been removed. All that remained was the ammunition. The ship moved from the dock to an anchorage to await the next north-bound convoy which she joined on March 30. A day later the *Jeremiah O'Brien* and thirteen ships broke off and entered Subic Bay, Luzon, with four escorts. She passed through the submarine nets protecting the harbor and two hours later was anchored and secured.

Subic Bay is a large, well-protected harbor with a narrow entrance surrounded by high, gently sloping coastal hills. The military base occupies the east end of the bay and just outside the gates lies the civilian town of Olongopo. The surrounding area was still infested with Japanese soldiers. Fighting was frequently seen and heard in the surrounding hills.

April 2 was spent discharging ammunition onto barges and mail sacks into LCMs. The discharge of the ammunition went quickly compared to the slow process of loading. The shoring and tomming were knocked out of the way and the pallets of bombs simply lifted out and set in the waiting LCMs. The ship then moved from the anchorage to the docks where cargo operations continued.

The last of the bombs was taken off and the ship moved from the cargo dock to the watering dock. All that remained on board was dunnage. The *O'Brien* rested alongside, all hatches secure, awaiting further orders. On April 17, she departed from Subic Bay to join a convoy bound for Hollandia, New Guinea, arriving there on April 27.

The *O'Brien* left Hollandia for Oro Bay, New Guinea, anchored overnight, then was called into the dock to commence loading the following day. Her scheduled cargo was oil, lubricants, gasoline in drums and a deck cargo of light and medium tanks and half-tracks.

On May 8, 1945, Germany surrendered.[1] It was noted in passing by the crew — half the war was over, but half was yet to go — as they continued with the routine but important task of getting the ship loaded.

With her hatches full of lubricants and gasoline, the *O'Brien* moved to a different pier to load tanks and half-tracks. That afternoon, while lifting an Army Sherman tank, the jumbo boom collapsed. The tank crashed through the dock into deep water and the falling boom struck the No. 1 (starboard forward) gun tub and the right hand half of the gun shield. The gun tub was crushed inward on the outboard side and the gun shield bent slightly inward although the gun itself was undamaged.

May 20 found the ship preparing for another convoy. Weighing anchor, the *O'Brien* departed with seventeen ships and three destroyer escorts. The ship's guns were elevated and trained through the full arc of fire and firing circuits were tested.

The convoy dispersed in San Pedro Bay, off Leyte, Philippines. All ships were ordered to proceed to their assigned destinations independently at their declared speed. It's an indication of how close to the end of the war it was and how safe conditions were considered that the ships were allowed to proceed alone and were allowed to use dim running lights at night.

---

[1] During the Battle of the Atlantic 2,603 merchant ships were sunk totalling more than 13.5 million tons. Of Allied merchant seamen, 30,248 lost their lives.

On May 29, the *O'Brien* arrived at Subic Bay to await the formation of a convoy proceeding North.

The next day, they arrived at San Fernando, Lingayen Gulf and anchored in the inner harbor. A floating crane came alongside to start removal of the deck cargo.

John Crosby:

> I was Acting Master and we went ashore and entered the arrival of the ship with the Captain of the Port. When they discovered our cargo they said, 'Why are you bringing more tanks here? We have enough for three wars.'" On the way back to the ship, I was shown a sea of tanks that were inactive and their tracks were half buried in the sand.

On June 1 the ship moved in to the dock, unloaded quickly and by June 6 was empty. It was one year since the historic events of D-Day.

On June 9, a blinker message from shore was sent asking if the ship was ready to join the convoy. Four ships were scheduled with one escort. They were all outside the harbor waiting for the *O'Brien* to join up. The *O'Brien* was to be commodore but other than that fact, knew nothing of the location of the ships or the early move. Apparently the other ships had gone out on their own initiative. Snafu.

Sailing in a northeasterly direction away from the war zone, the *Jeremiah O'Brien's* crew enjoyed a return to normal days at sea with the typical events that mark an easy passage across the Pacific.

Ted Martin: "In our off time we'd play pinochle or read or play poker. Sometimes we'd just go sit with a buddy on watch and talk. There wasn't that much to do. Some of the guys played checkers, but poker was the biggest game on the ship."

John Crosby: "The ship was a happy ship. The third engineer Roy Simpson and the third radio operator, Merrill Hubbard and I would meet after our watch and talk, play cards and have fun. We were constantly playing jokes on each other."

Robert Crocker:

> We expected danger constantly. We had no radar, no doctors, nothing. But it didn't seem to bother us. We were used to having very little, except ourselves. We relied on one another. The crews were good. The gun crews were very good. The merchant crews were very good. Sailing in the Far East didn't worry us that much. After all, one ship in the Pacific is pretty hard to find.

On June 26, 1945 a significant and very welcome message was received: "Resume traffic on 500 kcs." This is the standard calling frequency for merchant ships. For the first time since the war began it was back in use, clear proof that the war was over. V-E day had been May 8 and now this message truly marked the beginning of a return to normal. No longer would there be the fear of enemy submarines and air attacks. No longer would crews have to sleep in their clothes and lifejackets, ready to abandon ship on an instant's notice. After years of isolation, mis-information and no information, radio silence was no longer necessary and the crew would know what was going on around them and in the rest of the world. The Allies had won and the U.S. Merchant Marine had played an important part.

John Crosby: "Liberty ships, I have the greatest admiration for them. I know what they were and why they were built. I believe they were the backbone of the merchant fleet. They could get a big belly full of cargo. The engines were simple and engineers could be trained easily. The Liberty ship proved itself, the value they were in World War II in carrying supplies to the Allies. And I resent the term 'ugly duckling.'"

On July 5 the *O'Brien* approached the West Coast of the United States and ran into fog off San Francisco. Late in the afternoon a Navy patrol blimp appeared through the fog and disappeared again off the starboard bow. Forty minutes later the Farallon Island group appeared to port. A patrol vessel requested

"International Call." The ship took arrival at 1650 and anchored at 1830.

The war was nearly over, but the *Jeremiah O'Brien* was still serving the nation. Her next voyage would take her even farther.

13

DOWN UNDER
AND BEYOND

July 1945. The war in the Pacific was entering its final phase. Carrier-based planes from the U.S. Pacific Fleet and U.S. Army Air Force planes from the Marianas, Iwo Jima and Okinawa pounded the Japanese homeland without let-up while Pacific Fleet surface ships with the help of a British carrier task force bombarded its eastern coast. Planes from the Philippines hit Japanese shipping in the South China Sea, Formosa and the south coast of China as General Douglas MacArthur and Admiral Chester Nimitz expanded ports and bases in the Pacific to accommodate more than a million troops from Europe, the United States, Australia, New Zealand and other areas for the invasion of Japan, scheduled for November 1.

For the *Jeremiah O'Brien* and her crew, however, 5,000 miles away from the front, July was a welcome respite. R and R were the magic letters — repair for the ship, rest and relaxation for the crew. The last trip had been hard on both ship and crew. Yet, after six wartime voyages, battling the pounding seas of the North Atlantic, ferrying thousands of troops, ammunition, tanks, jeeps, LCMs and other heavy cargo, the *Jeremiah O'Brien* was still sound. It was a tribute to the skill and professionalism of the ship builders, who built the Libertys in mere days, envisioning a single voyage.

The crew's natural tendency to let go and celebrate on making home port was to be expected and some made up with a vengeance for the months of enforced abstinence and celibacy.

Almost "good as new," the *O'Brien* shifted back toward Pier 35 on the morning of July 24th to load cargo. The run down the California coast was pleasant, offering glimpses of the rugged shoreline and, farther south, low sandy beaches fringed with palm trees. The weather grew more pleasant as blue skies and sunshine replaced the grey overcast of San Francisco Bay. Arriving in San Pedro harbor on the morning of July 26, the ship anchored briefly then went alongside Pier 176 in the early evening.

A week later the first load of cargo was taken aboard and Articles for the coming voyage were signed stating that the vessel would sail on a voyage "From the port of Los Angeles, Calif., to a point in the Pacific Ocean to the westward of Los Angeles, Calif., and thence to such ports and places in any part of the world as the Master may direct, or as may be ordered or directed by the U.S. Government, or any Department, Commission or Agency thereof." And "Back to a final port of discharge in the United States, for a term of time not exceeding twelve (12) months."

Loading was quick. On August 3 at 1900 we find the ship casting off lines and getting underway. Her cargo was listed as "general" and partially consisted of beer and a deckload of jeeps; scheduled port of discharge was Calcutta, India.

Because the war in the Pacific still on, bonuses were paid to merchant seamen. That evening the Official log noted: "Leaving San Pedro, Cal. 33 1/3% bonus effective as of 2200 hrs this date." This was followed a few days later with two entries, "August 6, 1945. At sea. 33 1/3% Bonus terminates as of 2400 hours this date," and "August 7, 1945. At sea. 136 degrees long. passed this date at 1800 hrs. 66 2/3% bonus effective at 0001 hrs this date."

On August 6, 1945 the atomic bomb was dropped on Hiroshima and three days later the second atomic bomb was dropped on Nagasaki. The Japanese Empire was defeated and the Allies, now joined by Russia, moved to finish the campaign quickly and end the war.

But this was all far away. On board the *O'Brien*, the voyage continued in much the same way as the previous one. Ships were occasionally spotted, islands appeared on the horizon ahead and disappeared astern. Minor ailments and accidents occurred — One of the wipers was burned on the right forearm. The wound became infected, with complications, including septicemia, setting in. He was treated with a full course of sulfa drugs, recovered and returned to duty in two weeks. The log noted a few incidents: on August 8 another ship was sighted; that evening a Navy tug was seen four miles off the port bow; on August 11 the ship began zig-zagging; a tug towing two barges was sighted five miles off traveling away from the ship on August 12; in the afternoon of August 13, a tanker and tugboat were sighted bearing 270 degrees at a distance of five miles off going away from the *O'Brien...*

The merchant crew spent the time doing the age-old, never-ending shipboard chores — chipping, painting, varnishing woodwork and lubricating the cargo gear while the gun crew chipped, painted, varnished woodwork and lubricated the guns. The Armed Guard stood "G.Q." at sunrise and sunset and practiced shooting the guns. On August 15, they sent aloft six helium-filled balloons for target practice. Ten rounds were fired from the two 3-inch guns and 360 rounds from the 20mm. Four of the balloons were brought down.

V-J day, August 15, came and went with little notice on the ship. While back in the United States people were literally dancing in the streets, on board the *Jeremiah O'Brien* the reaction was much more blasé. Charles Hord, Fireman Watertender recalled: "The war ended somewhere between San Pedro and the Far East. We didn't really pay much attention to it at the time."

A few days later when the ship crossed the equator, Captain Gerdes held a "Crossing The Line" ceremony for those who were not yet "shellbacks." With the war over some of the foolish but fun ceremonies and traditions could be resumed.

The Neptune ceremony is a rite of passage that goes back several centuries to when seamen first passed into the unknown dangers that lay above and below the ocean. A sailor who hasn't crossed the equator is considered a "polliwog" and treated with disdain by the "shellbacks" who have. The process of becoming a shellback is strictly scripted and solemnly enacted. One of the crew, dressed as Davey Jones, appears on the foc'sle head and hails the bridge.

Davey Jones: "Ship ahoy."

Mate on watch: "Ahoy Davey Jones."

Davey Jones proceeds to the microphone in the wheelhouse while the mate announces, "Davey Jones has just come aboard the ship and is now talking to the chief mate. Let's listen in on the conversation."

Davey Jones: "Greetings sir. What ship is this?"

Mate: "This is the *SS Jeremiah O'Brien*."

Davey Jones: "Where are you bound?"

Mate: "Southwest Pacific on a War Mission."

Davey Jones: "Know ye on whose realm you are trespassing?"

Mate: "The realm of Neptune."

Davey Jones: "My congratulations to you sir. I hear you have an old friend of mine aboard, Captain George Gerdes. I first met him when he crossed the Equator and became a shellback many years ago. I have a summons for him from King Neptune."

Mate: "I will be glad to receive it for the captain."

Davey Jones:

Know All Men By These Presents: Tomorrow at five bells, his most titanic majesty, Neptunus Rex, King of all the waters that cover the earth and his most gracious and lovely spouse, Queen Amphitrite, than whom there is none fairer, will deign to visit this good ship *SS Jeremiah O'Brien* to examine and put to the test his neophytes, those kind and good souls whom he had never seen and who he hopes will answer for themselves.

Think well of your past sins, oh you neophytes, for King Neptune for all his graciousness is very stern with those who have transgressed against the written and unwritten laws of his realm, the seven seas. Think back to your days aboard this vessel and be prepared to answer for your sins tomorrow at five bells.

Given under my hand and seal, this 22nd day of July the year of our King Neptune, two million, one thousand, nine hundred and forty-five. Signed, King Neptune.

The following day at five bells Davey Jones appears and reports to the mate on watch that the captain is to be informed that Neptunus Rex and his party have been sighted ahead. The flag of Neptune is unfurled when Neptune appears on deck. A bugle call is sounded to call all hands to attention. The royal party then proceeds slowly aft to meet Davey Jones.[1]

Neptune to Davey Jones: "Well, well. What a fine ship and what a cargo of landlubbers!"

Mate, saluting: "The captain awaits the royal party."

Captain: "A sailor's welcome to you, Neptune Rex. It is a great pleasure to have you with us."

Neptune: "The pleasure is mine. I am glad to be with you again, captain. I have prepared for a very busy day in order to make your landlubbers fit subjects of my great Sea Domain."

Captain: "I am glad to hear that, Your Majesty, as I have quite a few young men of the crew aboard who have not been in the service long enough to have had the opportunity to visit your domain and become shellbacks. I beg of you to be as lenient as possible."

---

[1] Traditionally, crew members dress as Neptune, Amphitrite and members of the royal party, wearing mops for hair and sheets or tablecloths for robes and gowns.

Neptune: "I will be as severe as I can."

Captain: "I turn my ship over to you for as long as you wish."

Neptune: "Very well, Captain, I thank you. You may direct the ship on the course assigned. All polliwogs are ordered to the after deck. Policemen, take charge of the polliwogs."

The mate escorts Neptune to a throne on No. 4 hatch and the polliwogs are brought forth. Initiation consists of having their heads and/or eyebrows shaved, being forced to drink concoctions heavy with cod liver oil or cooking oil and tabasco and running a gauntlet of firehoses or rolling in bilge water and grease while their crewmates watch with great mirth and hilarity. When the rites are complete, the polliwogs are given cards certifying them to be shellbacks.

The *Jeremiah O'Brien* continued on in a southwesterly direction. As she neared Australia and the Great Barrier Reef, a stop was made on August 28 in the outer bay at Port Moresby, New Guinea, for a pilot. Extending 1,250 miles parallel to the Australian state of Queensland, the reef is thick with hull-piercing coral lying just below the surface and is considered one of the more treacherous areas of the world to navigate. The pilot guided the *O'Brien* through this obstacle and the Torres Strait and disembarked at Thursday Island.

Two days later, a second pilot came aboard to guide the ship into Darwin, and the *O'Brien* dropped anchor in Darwin harbor at 0600 the following morning. Her speed on the run from San Pedro was 11.4 knots.

Ted Martin:

> In Darwin we had real nice liberty. The people were very friendly. You could buy about a sixteen ounce T-bone steak and a quart of Black Horse ale for $2.50. Of course it was warm ale. They kept it all at well water temperature. But it was a good liberty, they used to have dances quite often. And we used to like the Sunday afternoons when they'd go into the parks with concerts in the

gazebos. Nine times out of ten, if you met somebody in the afternoon, they'd invite you to dinner. The families were all really friendly.

On September 2, Japan signed an unconditional surrender aboard the USS *Missouri* in Tokyo Bay. World War II was over. Little notice of the ceremony was taken on the *O'Brien*. As far as the crew was concerned, the war had been over for months. They lived in their own insulated, isolated world — a cocoon crossing vast distances of ocean and time peripherally touched by the world outside. Their world, of necessity, was limited to the rails of the ship and circumscribed by the horizon of the blue sea, as Omar Khayyám called it, "that inverted bowl, the sky." Their interests were in the functioning of the ship, the lives of the people on board, and outside events, in that order. It was the only way to survive. To become embroiled in distant events over which you had no control created anxiety and stress. The philosophy was, "do your job and let the world take care of itself. It will all work out somehow."

Sailing on September 4, at 2200 the ship continued westward, to Calcutta, India.

It was September 9, 1945 before the end of the war was officially acknowledged by the military. Late that evening a message was received from COMPHILSEAFRON (Commander of the Philippine Sea Frontier) dated 090153Z and addressed to all areas in the South Pacific. It stated that ships would no longer zigzag, blackout regulations were canceled, navigation lights were to be burned with full brilliancy, and guns no longer had to be manned. Now, the crew listened with great interest. Unlike most of the political and military information they heard, this was news that had relevance to them, on board their ship. Life really was returning to normal and they looked forward to going ashore at the next port. The vessel would load U.S. Army cargo at Calcutta for discharge at Shanghai, under the supervision of the U.S. War Department. All hands received initial immunization for cholera.

The Indian Ocean has some of the world's worst storms and typhoons. With nothing but water between Australia and Africa, waves travel long distances, building upon themselves to great heights. The typhoon's winds, without land masses on which to expend their energy, build and sustain for long stretches of time and ocean. A major storm in the Indian Ocean is an awesome — and wonderful — phenomenon, but one to be avoided, if at all possible. So, when, on September 18, Captain Gerdes received warning of a storm ahead, he immediately reversed the ship's course from north to south for eight hours. Resuming the original course the following day, he wisely reduced the ship's speed to ensure they didn't sail into the predicted maelstrom.

Storms aside, sailing on the Indian Ocean was monotonous, hot, humid and boring. There was little entertainment other than a short-wave radio piped into the messrooms from the radio shack. The crews often gathered in the evenings on the main deck aft of the midship house to talk and tell sea stories. The officers did the same on the boat deck. The latest issues of *Saturday Evening Post, Colliers* and *Life* were read and passed around. Some might read aloud the latest adventures of Tugboat Annie or Colin Glencannon, to the delight of their gathered shipmates.

The *O'Brien* arrived in India on September 21. She anchored outside the Hooghly River because the tidal current was too strong for the ship to make any headway. Ten hours later she weighed anchor and proceeded upriver for twenty miles but was forced to drop anchor again to wait the turning of the tide. The following day was more of the same. The ship sailed against the current for four hours, managing to make only twenty more miles in that time, then anchored again, still forty miles from Calcutta. On September 23, she finally reached Calcutta, tying up just after supper to Berth 3 of the King William Docks.

On October 10, with the cargo loaded, the mooring lines were cast off and the *Jeremiah O'Brien* proceeded upstream to the oil dock for fueling. Continuing her struggle against the tides, she eventually arrived alongside the Burmah Oil Dock No. 4, fueled and proceeded back down the Hooghly River. She anchored to await a favorable tide, got underway just before noon the following day, and cleared the river that afternoon. Her cargo was listed as: general, army vehicles and gasoline; destination: Shanghai, China.

The leftovers of war, such as mines and uncharted wrecks, were still a serious hazard. Nearing the coast of China on October 27, eight minesweepers were spotted two miles off the port quarter. Two days later a U.S. Navy patrol vessel exchanged signals and escorted the *O'Brien* through the approaches to the Yangtze River. A pilot came aboard, guided the ship into the delta and ordered the anchor dropped.

The river delta was wide and shallow with sediment in many places. Ashore could be seen low, flat farmland. In the distance was the faint skyline of Shanghai. Because of the danger of pirates, sidearms were issued to the Armed Guard on watch. There were stories of junks silently coming alongside in the dead of night, pirates slipping aboard, overpowering a ship's crew, and stealing everything of value. The comic strip "Terry and the Pirates," popular at the time, was based on fact.

Shanghai was a considerable distance from the port but some of the crew were curious and wanted to see the city.

The next day the pilot came aboard, the anchor was raised and the ship proceeded up the Whangpoo River, the tributary to the Yangtze on which lies Shanghai. The *Jeremiah O'Brien* berthed at the military dock.

Charles Hord: "That was a pretty nice city. It was modern, like cities we were used to. The difference was really noticeable after Calcutta."

Stevedores unloaded the vehicles and the *O'Brien* then shifted to other docks to unload the general cargo. On November 3, she cast off her mooring lines to sail down river to a temporary berth at Holtz Dock, then shifted to the Hongkew Wharf to unload the fuel.

The next day the ship sailed at 1300 for Manila. Because of the danger of mines left over from the war a mine lookout watch was set up. This would continue until the ship arrived at Manila.

"Gearing down" orders continued piecemeal. On November 19, the Armed Guard crew received word to get rid of their ammunition. The Navy required that it be dumped in water more than 150 fathoms deep and more than ten miles from shore. Thousands of rounds were simply thrown over the side.

The *O'Brien* dropped anchor in Manila Bay on November 21. There was no cargo on board and the port of Manila was entered "for orders." On November 23, Capt. Gerdes was informed that they were sailing to Fremantle, Australia. The following day, when Lieutenant McGowan went ashore to report to the Port Director's Building, he learned that the ship would be placed on a maintenance status in regard to Armed Guard personnel and that the AGO [Armed Guard Officer] and twenty-four enlisted men would be detached from the ship. It was another step in the process of "getting back to normal" and many of the merchant crew probably welcomed the idea of having their ship returned to them. Symbolically, the departure of the gun crew meant a sure end to the war. The ship sailed for Fremantle, arriving on December 7.

Fremantle is an artificial harbor, built at the mouth of the Swan River. The river is geologically very old and consequently broad and sluggish. The harbor is virtually a tidal estuary, with brackish water backing as far upstream as Perth, twelve miles away. In the late 1800's a rock bar at the mouth of the river was blasted away, leaving a narrow entrance to the harbor, about one-fourth of a mile wide, and when the tide is on a strong ebb or flood a rapid current pours through the entrance. Great skill is required to maneuver a ship safely through the channel and Captain Gerdes was grateful to have a pilot familiar with the local waters guide him in. The *Jeremiah O'Brien* went straight into Victoria Quay on the south side of the harbor and tied up with her stern to the entrance.

Fremantle was a friendly port. The crew, feeling liberated from the strictly-enforced discipline of the war years, seemed to cast off all inhibitions.

Willis "Bud" Hitchcock recalled the people of Australia as being hospitable to seamen when he visited that port on the Liberty ship SS *Hiram S. Maxim.*

> I remember we docked very near the American submarine base and how proud we were to see one of our subs returning from patrol displaying a broom from its conning tower, denoting a "clean sweep" in Jap waters.
>
> The people of Fremantle and Perth were very kind to seamen at that time and brought to our ship "care" packages of fruit and knitted cold weather gear and clothing for us. We were also invited into their homes and treated with great hospitality. Everybody hated to leave this port to return to the winter gales of the high south latitudes.

The ship took on 4,005 tons of bunker fuel during her stay in Fremantle and loaded approximately 16,500 bales of wool and skins for discharge in California. But, before sailing, there was one more special cargo: War Brides.

War Brides were not uncommon in 1945. Wartime romances between U.S. servicemen and women they met while overseas occasionally resulted in marriages abroad. English, French, Australian and others and even ex-"enemy" German and Italian women were anxious to join their American husbands and begin a new life in the U.S. Americans often treated women more courteously than other nationalities did. Hector Miller, whose sister Brenda was one of the war brides scheduled for the *O'Brien*, explains how it happened.

> To start with, 98% of the population, which was just under 10 million, were of British descent (higher than Great Britain). You can imagine the cultural shock when nearly one million Americans, whose outlook was vastly different, more like that of people from

another planet, passed through Australia during '42 to '45. However, the girls thought they were marvelous, because they treated them so differently from Australian men. No Aussie, for example, would ever think of buying flowers for a girl, let alone be seen carrying them in public when going to collect a partner on a date, nor would he think of taking them in a taxi when Public Transport was available. When they did arrive at a dance or party they were abandoned at the door and he joined the other males, the girls being left in a separate group. The Americans did the opposite and treated them like people, not objects, and they loved it.

Thora Quackenbush:

I met my future husband, Jim, at the Embassy Ballroom. It was a very popular dance hall for the men and women from the services. At the time I was in the Australian Womens Army Service (AWAS). When I was told Jim's name, Quackenbush, I thought it was a joke. Who could have a name like Quackenbush?

Jim was a radio operator stationed in Kings Park, Perth. He was on the *Phoenix* at Pearl Harbor and had been sent to Western Australia for recuperation. We were married August 12th 1944 and Jim was sent to the Philippines shortly afterward.

Nine Australian War Brides, now Navy wives, and three children came aboard. They were lodged in the old gun crew quarters aft.

As sailing time approached on Saturday, December 15, the women and their families said their goodbyes. It was a sad time for many of them never expected to see Australia again. The brides' families — mothers and fathers, brothers, sisters, aunts, uncles — trudged down the gangway and stood on the dock waving. The women stood at the ship's rail waving, shouting last messages.

Thora Quackenbush: "The first time I saw the *SS Jeremiah O'Brien* at Fremantle Harbor was the day my family drove me up from Bunbury, which is 115 miles south of Perth, on the coast. I was surprised at the size of the ship, we expected a much larger ship, as we had seen newspaper pictures of war brides leaving from Sydney on larger passenger ships, and our quarters on board was my second shock."

They had plenty of time for Captain Gerdes waited two hours, but there was no sign of a pilot or tug to get the ship away from the wharf. Hector Miller watched from the dock. "It was a Saturday afternoon and weekends are sacrosanct in Australia, or at least they were at that time." Losing his patience, the captain unwisely decided to take the ship out himself. After raising the gangway, he ordered the bow lines taken in. The tide was running out and as he ordered the stern lines taken in the ship swung off the pier broadside to the current, moving sideways toward the harbor entrance. To gain steerageway he ordered full ahead on the engine so he could turn her bow toward the entrance.

Hector Miller saw what happened next.

> The result was she suddenly bolted straight across the harbor towards the North Wharf on the opposite shore, like a runaway horse. Anchored there, bow to stern, were three Dutch naval ships, a frigate and two destroyers, and a collision looked inevitable. You could hear the telegraph ringing for reversing the engines across the harbor, but she had too much way on her, so taking his only alternative the skipper dropped the anchor. This action averted the collision. Then using the anchor as a pivot, and his engines, he brought the bow around to the harbor mouth and eventually got under way.

The *O'Brien* was well out to sea before the captain finally let out a sigh of relief, thankful that the misadventure had not had serious consequences.

The captain's next decision was what to do about all the women on board. He issued an order to the crew: "No Fraternization."

Charles Hord: "They did have the after part of the ship off limits. The captain had the bosun paint a stripe across the ship

From left to right: Catherine Arthur, baby Maria Arthur, Grace Dexter and Thora Quackenbush. The other two brides are unknown. Thora Quackenbush.

between No. 4 and No. 5 hatch. One side of the line said 'USA' and the other side 'Australia' in white letters."

Ted Martin:

> There were nine women and three kids. They were all navy wives. Most of the guys, their husbands, worked in the fleet post office [in Fremantle]. There was no problem with them at all. Most of the time they ate in the gunners' mess with me and Swan. They kept them confined more or less from the merchant crew. It was my responsibility to keep them separate.
>
> They'd sunbathe while traveling. We weren't too much with them. They had the whole aft of the ship and they wouldn't come forward except to eat. We used to go out and talk to them on deck. The oldest was twenty-four or twenty-five. They were all young like we were. Once in awhile we sneaked them up on one of the guns to take a picture.

Thora Quackenbush: "The voyage to San Francisco was most enjoyable. Calm seas, beautiful blue waters and flying fish, which fascinated me as I hadn't seen them before."

Captain Gerdes' no fraternization rule wasn't strictly enforced. Thora Quackenbush: "We played cards, walked the decks for exercise, chatted amongst ourselves outside our quarters and also enjoyed the ship's company who joined us to pass the time of day."

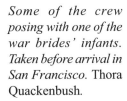

Some of the crew posing with one of the war brides' infants. Taken before arrival in San Francisco. Thora Quackenbush.

Initially, the port of arrival was scheduled to be San Pedro, but two days before arrival that was changed to San Francisco. Arriving on January 16, the vessel anchored overnight.

The final entry in the captain's night order book reads: "Check anchor bearings frequently. Have passengers called at 6:30 a.m. and be ready to dock at 8:00 a.m. Call me if it gets foggy."

The ship went alongside Pier 40 the morning of January 17, 1946. Matson Navigation Company served as agents. The passengers disembarked and the *Jeremiah O'Brien* began discharging what would be her last cargo.

Thora Quackenbush:

> In first seeing the U.S.A. I was so excited and greatly impressed going under the Golden Gate Bridge. It was in the evening. Many of the passengers and crew went out on the town for dinner and drinks the same night we berthed. My husband arrived the day after we berthed. It was the first time I had seen him in civilian clothes. He had a Homberg hat on. I nearly didn't recognize him. We took a train to his home in Shawnee, Oklahoma. During the trip I saw snow for the first time.

The *O'Brien* lay idle for a few days then the last two members of the Armed Guard were taken off on January 28 and she was taken to Richmond Yard No. 2 to prepare for lay-up. There simply weren't enough peacetime cargoes for all the leftover wartime tonnage. And the Libertys, at a maximum speed of 11 knots, were far down on the

Thora Quackenbush at one of the 3-inch 50 guns. Her radiant smile leaves no need for words. Thora Quackenbush.

"want list" when there were C-2s and C-3s that could carry the same or greater tonnages at speeds in excess of 15 knots.

Retired from service on February 7, 1946 the *Jeremiah O'Brien* entered the Reserve Fleet at Suisun Bay, California, a day later.

On February 8, 1946 the engineers rang Finished With Engines for the last time at 1153. The revolution counter showed 39,439,700 revolutions since the *Jeremiah O'Brien's* propeller was first turned over in Portland, Maine two-and-a-half years earlier.

Most of the crew departed with a last look around, remembering shipmates, ports and adventures. The messroom, once alive with the babble of conversation, was now ghostly silent. The main deck, once vibrating with the metallic clank of steam-spewing cargo winches, was serene. The ship itself became quiet, deathly quiet, as a lone engineer shut down the plant for the last time.

From the engineer's log:

> Shut down main engine at 1200 noon. Secured circulating pump and main injection valve at 1:30 p.m. Pumped up stbd setl from 6,900 gal to 13,000 gal. Secured aux. condenser, sea suction & discharge at 2:50 p.m. Shut off all fires in both boilers at 3:30 p.m. preparatory to cutting out plant. Put plant on atmospheric at 2:20 p.m. Drained main & aux condensers, hotwell and cleaned same at 3 p.m. Drained eccentric and

guide pans. Pumped bilges and shaft alley well at 3:15 p.m. Shut down fuel oil service pump, sanitary pump, feed pump and all sea suction and discharge valves at 4:00 p.m. Working steam off both boilers with the generators & atmospheric valve. Opened all drains on deck machinery. Both boilers dead at 10:00 p.m. All valves connected with same shut off and all drains open on boilers. First two rows of handhole plates opened on both boilers. Water-drum manhole and mud-drum plates opened. Plant dead and work finished at 12 midnight.

(signed)

1st Asst D.E. Kranich

Plant dead? Work finished? Not quite.

14

LAY-UP

What was believed to be the final page in the story of the *Jeremiah O'Brien's* active life started with a letter from the Maritime Commission's San Francisco Office to Washington, D.C., transferring title of the vessel.

March 22, 1946.

Mr. T. J. Kramer, Manager
Charters and Agreements Section
Operating Contracts Division
War Shipping Administration
Washington, 25, D.C.

Dear Mr. Kramer:

Subject: SS "JEREMIAH O'BRIEN"

The subject vessel has been placed in the Reserve Fleet at Anchorage 26, Suisun Bay (San Francisco Bay, California), and we attach hereto for your files and further disposition three copies each of certificates evidencing the redelivery by the General Agent to the War Shipping Administration and certificates evidencing the simultaneous delivery from our Operating Section to the Reserve Fleet Division of the War Shipping Administration.

Very truly yours,

(signed) L. M. Mauk, for
L. C. Fleming
Executive Assistant

The Reserve Fleet at Suisun Bay was one of eight such fleets in existence at the time. Located throughout the country, the eight fleets made up the National Defense Reserve Fleet, established so that in the next war the government wouldn't have to build shipyards from the ground up. They would have on hand a nucleus of ships that could provide the military a means of supply in any national emergency.

So many ships were laid up after World War II that not only was there an adequate emergency fleet of Liberty ships, but there was a sizeable surplus. The government spent several years putting that surplus to good use. At first, ships were sold to foreign countries including Greece, Taiwan and Panama to be used as the foundation of their post-war merchant marine. Others were sold into the U.S. fleet to companies such as Weyerhaeuser or CalMar, and modified with longer mid-bodies for enlarged cargo capacity. Later, Libertys were taken from the fleets and used for various government projects: remade into weather ships, missile trackers, picket ships, Navy supply ships or sunk off American coasts to become fish reefs.

The *Jeremiah O'Brien* was "in retention," tied up with several of her sisters, just one of the many that were "built by the mile and chopped off by the yard." Retention was the process by which ships were preserved so they would be ready for the next call-out. Inside, all the machinery, pumps, boilers, piping and equipment were opened. Cosmoline, a preservative grease that hardens into a thick protective film, was applied to boiler tubes, condensers, plumbing, valves, impellers, gears — any surface that might rust. The underwater hull was protected against electrolysis by graphite anodes hung on each row of ships. The outside of the ship was painted, dark red at first, and later gray. Portholes were left ajar to allow air circulation and prevent mildew.

The years passed and still the *Jeremiah O'Brien* sat, awaiting another call to duty. Eventually, the Libertys were no longer included in military plans for future wars. They were just too slow. Designed to last one voyage or, at the most, five years, the Liberty Ship had done her duty and outlived her purpose. Retention on the *O'Brien* was terminated in December of 1963 and the process of selling the Libertys out of the fleet for scrap began. One by one they disappeared.

The *Jeremiah O'Brien* languished, almost forgotten, her portholes and doors open to the wind, her superstructure providing a roost for pigeons and owls. In time, her gray paint scaled off, rust corroded her decks and ran down her hull.

But the *O'Brien's* luck was not all gone. Someone remembered her, someone with an idea, a vision and "A Plan."

15

RE-BIRTH

Enter Admiral Tom Patterson:

I came out here with MARAD, the Maritime Administration, in 1962. I was one of two captains and two chief engineers given the job of surveying 300 Liberty Ships. They were laid up in fleets at Olympia, Washington; Astoria, Oregon; and Suisun Bay, California. Some 500 other Liberty ships were to be surveyed at the same time on the East and Gulf Coasts."

Our task was to rank them in condition — best to worst. The government was going to sell them. That meant most of them would go to the scrapyard. Our orders were to hold the best to the last. The reason for the exercise with these vessels was that in 1962 the Navy had informed the Maritime Administration that Libertys would not be required in their future strategy. At ten knots, they were too slow.

The four of us 'walk-over surveyed' fifteen Liberty ships a day. We inspected the whole vessel, from the flying bridge to the engine room. We went down in every hold. Did the ship have wooden booms or steel booms? Had the ship been reinforced? What kind of ballast? Did she have any visible damage? What was the overall condition?

I had the strongest legs I ever had in my life. Up and Down. Fifteen a day ...

One ship stood out among all the others, the *Jeremiah O'Brien*. The original doors, furniture and linoleum tables were still in place and unmarked. Where normally bored crewmen carved their initials in table tops, these were unscarred. The forward gun tub still carried traces of Miss Jerry O'Brien, a bikinied pin-up painted there by the last crew. The ship was completely unaltered except that, like all others, her guns had been removed. All World War II equipment aboard was undisturbed. All the charts were there, from Normandy to the Pacific. The glass was intact in the license frames on the bulkhead. The wartime instructions were posted alongside the Mark XIV gyro. The station bill, signed by the captain, was in place. The captain's night order book at Normandy beach was in a desk drawer. There were only minor indents in the *Jeremiah O'Brien's* plating and little hull pitting. The blueprints of the ship were mounted in the passageway abaft the wheelhouse, intact. The oak joiner work throughout her quarters was beautiful to behold. She had been kept completely original. She was just like she'd come out of the builder's yard. She'd never been used for anything other than what she was designed to do — carry supplies to our forces — and she'd been kept in one piece. The ship was a time capsule. I didn't know whether some way to save her could be contrived, but something told me to try to hang on to her. We began a little exercise to keep her off the scrap list.

Some Libertys were sold for "non-transportation use" such as fish canneries, floating drydocks, crane barges. A few were towed out and sunk for fishing reefs. But most were cut up. The price they brought the government averaged $50,000.

We kept moving the *Jeremiah O'Brien* down the scrap list ... we kept shoving her back ... kept dropping her name down.

Harry Morgan, who became chief engineer for the project, recalled: "They kept moving that ship around because they were selling them off for scrap and she was in the best condition of them all. They kept putting her out of sight of the scrap dealers."

Admiral Patterson continues,

> There was another reason. A ship on 'scrap row' was subject to being raided by the Navy. With some logic, a ship that was going to be broken up was picked over for equipment and furniture that would enhance the still operational AGR's. The Navy had this access. So we kept the *Jeremiah O'Brien* in another row. The game went on for years. We kept her from being raided. We also protected her from vandalism.
>
> Finally, like the dwindling of the ten little Indians, *Jeremiah O'Brien* was the last one. The Maritime Administration said, 'You've got to do something with that ship.' They said they had no authorization to hold her for historical purposes.

It takes a unique combination of visionary, leader, arm-twister, supersalesman, money-raiser and motivator to conceive the idea of a living maritime museum, talk the government into giving up one of its ships, then convince business, industry and volunteers to contribute the time, labor and money to bring the dream to reality. Fortunately for the *Jeremiah O'Brien*, her champion was such a person.

Soon there was a nucleus of enthusiasts, other people who wanted to save a Liberty ship for posterity.

Admiral Patterson: "In 1977 I went back to Washington and met Captain Harry Allendorfer of the National Trust for Historic Preservation. He told us how to get the ship on the National Register. And he told us how to apply for a grant."

The National Liberty Ship Memorial (NLSM), a California non-profit corporation was formed in 1978.

The *O'Brien* was declared a National Monument and placed on the National Register as an historic object the same year.

This inside view of the wheelhouse is typical of the conditions the volunteers found themselves up against. National Liberty Ship Memorial.

Admiral Patterson:

So then Allendorfer advised us there would be a one-time grant for the fifty states. We asked for $550,000 for the *Jeremiah O'Brien* and explained what we were trying to do. That was in 1979. The catch was that we had to match it with funds, labor, services or material from the private sector. Barney Evans, who was then our secretary, was a big help in lining up these contributions. We made it!

The request was backed with a matching amount of more than $600,000 in services and materials from the volunteers and the maritime community.

Admiral Patterson:

Across the nation we came out #3. First was the USS *Constellation* in Baltimore. Second was the *Elissa* in Galveston. Third was the *Jeremiah O'Brien* in San Francisco. We got $436,512.

When we got word that we had the grant, it gave us more steam than ever before. Literally. We were up there looking the ship over, figuring how we would rig the towing bridle and Ernie Murdock says, 'Let's steam her down!'

One of the reasons we decided to get steam up in Suisun Bay was that a diver had gone down and inspected her intakes. They had not been blanked off. She had not gone to a drydock (where this was usually done) before being towed up San Pablo Bay and through Carquinez Strait. Her last wartime crew had steamed her into the Suisun Bay Reserve Fleet for lay-up. Grace Line was her general agent for MARAD back in those days and had maintained the ship properly during her wartime service.

The other reason was the challenge. No one had ever steamed up a dead ship that had lain there thirty-four years in a reserve fleet!

Now, the Maritime Administration had stopped all maintenance in 1963. The ship had been sixteen years with no preservation at all. But she was well preserved, just the same.

Chief Engineer Harry Morgan: "I was approached by Bob Blake in June of 1979. He asked me to come up to the fleet with him to help restore this Liberty ship. Captain Ernie Murdock was up there also. The ship was coated with cosmoline, all the pumps were open and the cylinder heads were off, and they asked me what I thought. They said, 'We're going to steam it down.'

"I said, "All right, I think you're nuts, but let's give it a try."

Robert Blake: "We went up to the fleet a couple of days later and went aboard the ship to look it over to see what we had to do. There were five of us — myself, a dispatcher from the mechanics union, Felix Childs from Farrell Lines, Harry Morgan from APL. We drove up every morning and came back every night."

Ernie Murdock: "Harry Morgan was very instrumental in getting the ship ready. We spent several weeks up there getting the boiler and the auxiliary equipment ready, the steering gear and so on."

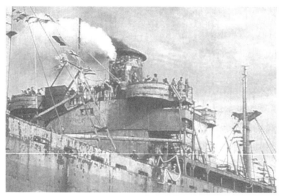

Loaded with passengers the Jeremiah O'Brien *steams in 1980 for the first time in thirty-three years.* George Lamuth.

Robert Blake: "People who are interested in ships are kind of crazy. It was a fun project. At lunchtime we'd all sit on deck and tell lies to each other, spin yarns. It was a labor of love."

Harry Morgan: "The fleet people were very cooperative. Anything we needed they'd go around to the other ships and get it. They located tools and brought us lube oil and even fuel oil. The crew up there was a great help."

It took three months in the fall of 1979 to reactivate the engine and auxiliaries.

More than 500 people boarded the ship for her historic ride down the bay. Among them was Captain James Nolan, who would become the master of the *Jeremiah O'Brien* in later years.

Full power — 76 rpms — from Suisun Bay to San Francisco. George Lamuth.

Just after haulout the crew inspects the underwater hull. Her condition was remarkably good after so many years of idleness. National Park Service.

On October 6, 1979 the *Jeremiah O'Brien* steamed out of the Reserve Fleet at Suisun Bay under her own power. For the first time since February 8, 1946 her engines were alive with fire and steam. Her machinery whirred and hummed. The entire hull once more vibrated and throbbed with life. Signal flags festooned the ship from stem to foremast to mainmast to bridge to aftermast to stern where the American flag proudly flew. Her decks were once again alive with people.

Ernie Murdock: "We proceeded on down without any tugboat assistance. We were met by the San Francisco fireboats and tugboats. It was a pretty good sight to see this rusty old ship sailing under her own power down the bay into the shipyard."

Admiral Patterson was thrilled. "To take a ship that's been idle for 33 years, eight months and revive it with volunteers and load 503 people on it and steam 40 miles was in keeping with the spirit of the Liberty Ship. She was built in six weeks and here she'd lasted for all these years."

At the shipyard, the lengthy process of reconditioning began. Harry Morgan: "The boiler tubes were good. In the yard we put a hydrotest on both boilers. We had to do some minor repairs on the brickwork, but nothing major."

The goal for getting the ship out of the yard was Maritime Day, May 21, 1980. Plans were made for a Seamen's Memorial Cruise on that day to honor the merchant seamen lost at sea since the beginning of World War II. As the May deadline approached, the numbers of volunteers increased.

Admiral Patterson: "The Liberty ship *Jeremiah O'Brien* blossomed once again in that Bethlehem yard — she came out of it looking like she did when she was launched. Or very close to it. We worked against a deadline of Maritime Day, 1980, and we made it."

The ship left the yard on that day and sailed into her place in history — the first surviving merchant marine ship of World War II to become a living museum.

16

THE
SECOND TIME AROUND

M ay 21, 1980. The *Jeremiah O'Brien* departed the shipyard at 0830 for the First Annual Seamen's Memorial Cruise. She sailed out the Golden Gate with 700 passengers and cut the engines. In a solemn ceremony wreaths were cast into the waters to commemorate the shipmates lost in so many wars on so many oceans. In silence the passengers watched the wreaths bob on the swells and, carried on the tide, gradually drift out to the open sea.

Admiral Tom Patterson:

> That day was declared National Liberty Ship Day by the White House. We got the ship underway and proceeded out the Gate for the ceremonies; Captain E. A. MacMichael was master. The Assistant Secretary of Commerce for Maritime Affairs, Samuel Nemirow, was on board to dedicate the ship in her new role, the National Liberty

Admiral Thomas J. Patterson, the man who made it all happen, at the podium during one of the many Seamen's Memorial Cruises. Don Watson.

Ship Memorial — a reminder of the largest fleet of oceangoing ships of a single type that this or any country has ever launched. Those 2710 Libertys were the cargo-carrying key to winning World War II and bringing peace and liberty to the world.

Harry Morgan, chief engineer, typically understated: "We put both boilers on the line and everything went all right."

One of the biggest challenges in the fledgling organization was keeping track of everything. What started as a fun project for a few friends and enthusiasts was quickly becoming a business with hundreds, and eventually thousands, of people involved.

Wreaths line the deck prior to departure on the morning of the Seamen's Memorial Cruise. They are cast into the Pacific in honor of America's merchant seamen who gave their lives answering the call of duty. Don Watson.

For the passengers, one of the more fascinating aspects of the annual cruise is passing under the Golden Gate Bridge. Most people drive over *it but few pass* under *it.* National Liberty Ship Memorial.

In 1982, 30,000 volunteer hours were contributed by 334 volunteers ranging in age from eighteen to seventy-eight.

Harry Morgan: "It was a fun job and we had excellent volunteers. Most of them had no previous experience. They'd do anything you'd ask them to. We'd just take everything apart and put it together again."

In June 1982 the first Women Shipbuilders Reunion Reception was held on board. "Rosie the Riveter" and "Wendy the Welder" were common nicknames in the group. Among them were the staunch women who made up a significant percentage of the workforce that built Libertys and other ships during the war. Long before the battle for "equal rights" they had proved their worth and won that battle.

Other maritime agencies and businesses began holding their gatherings on board in the spacious tween deck of No. 2 hold, which soon became a meeting room.

In the late 1980s additional cruises were added in October to coincide with San Francisco's "Fleet Week," a parade of vessels, from Navy ships to smaller craft that steam along the waterfront. The *Jeremiah O'Brien* occupies center stage under the U.S. Navy's Blue Angels, as they demonstrate their precision flying skills.

Visitors donate a small sum to see the ship but the cruises generate most of the ship's operating income and are the glamour event of the year. The *Jeremiah O'Brien* "shows" well — her brass polished, her woodwork gleaming, or, in the language of seafarers, "everything ship-shape in Bristol Fashion." Visitors are pleasantly surprised at "How good she looks."

It takes a lot of work to keep a ship looking good. Although the ship is open every day except Thanksgiving and Christmas, the public seldom sees what must be done to keep the *O'Brien* the showpiece she is. One day a week is set aside for the deck department, another for the engine department. This lets each group work on projects that need the labor of more than one

Ernie Murdock and crew working on main engine cylinder head. Mike Emery.

The completely restored engine room of the SS Jeremiah O'Brien, *taken from the fire room looking aft.* Russell Fraser.

person and keeps them out of each other's way. There is a traditional rivalry between the "deck" and "engine" departments on any ship and good-natured jibes come out at the slightest provocation.

Engineer: "You'd never get anywhere without us."

Mate: "You'd never know where you were without us."

The volunteers enjoy the time together and, as always, tell their sea stories, some of them true.

"I was on a ship one time..."

"You know, that Murmansk run was something..."

Tales of romance and adventure in strange lands abound.

"There was this girl in Valparaiso..."

Above, one of the 20 mms after restoration, as pristine as the day it was made and a tribute to the effort and skill of the volunteer crew. Right, although the O'Brien *was one of the few ships to have a 3-inch 50 at the stern, she now carries a 5-inch 38 in that location.* Above, Russell Fraser, right, Joanie Morgan.

Then coffeetime is over and the volunteers get back to the process of restoration and preservation that never ends. On any given day you will find volunteers chipping, painting, scraping, polishing, sweeping, cleaning. They are a resourceful group and often come up with creative and inventive ways to use what they can "scrounge up" to accomplish some project. The *Jeremiah O'Brien* presents a better appearance today than when she was launched because of the volunteers and their tireless energy and devotion.

"Steaming weekend" is a major event for the crew. Held on the third weekend of each month, it is devoted to the operation of the ship's main engine. Many volunteers show up on Friday night and sleep on board, all the better to get an early start in the morning. During the night the engineroom fires are lit and steam is raised. The galley crew sets out dinner prepared on the ship's coal-fired stove. In the morning everyone turns to and after a hearty breakfast prepared by the volunteer cooks, visitors are allowed on board and taken on tours of the engineroom. They see the massive gleaming piston rods of the ship's steam reciprocating engine powerfully pumping up and down. It is an impressive sight. Noise fills the air — the hiss of steam, the roar of fires in the boilers, pumps spinning, compressors building air. The more daring look in the shaft alley where the massive steel propeller shaft slowly turns. In the engineroom volunteers are oiling, cleaning, tending fires, watching gauges. They might range in age from an octogenarian chief engineer to a California Maritime Academy cadet in his late teens. Occasionally an engineer will climb to the main deck to get away from the constant heat, but soon returns to the "excitement" of the engineroom.

In another part of the ship the radio room will be open. Where radio operators once sent and received messages by Morse Code, they now communicate by ham radio. Occasionally a sea story comes out. "I was on a ship once..."

In the purser's office you may find someone on duty collecting and cataloging stories from Liberty Ship sailors who come on board. The *O'Brien's* files contain hundreds of adventures.

Saturday night dinners are the highlight of steaming weekend, something everyone looks forward to. The galley crew works most of the day keeping the big coal-fired stove stoked, preparing the meal. There may be up to half a dozen volunteers working in this small, hot space.

Cooking for up to sixty hard-working volunteers requires quantities of food and cooking equipment far larger than most people ever see. The mixer for the galley, located on the deck below, is industrial-sized, able to handle batter for a cake for a hundred people. The adjacent storerooms and refrigerated spaces hold meat by the hundredweight, canned goods by the car lot, eggs by the gross and produce by the case. Imagine stirring filé gumbo for sixty in a thirty-gallon pot with a paddle the size of an

A visiting Navy sailor demonstrates the technique of stoking the coal-fired stove in the galley. Coal and air-flow are the only temperature controls. National Liberty Ship Memorial.

oar. Envision making twelve large loaves of bread at once. A meal might include salad, roast ham, celery with pecans, corn on the cob, homemade bread and cherry pie. All done "from scratch" on a range whose only temperature control is the judicious balance of hot coals and ventilation. When the meal is ready — breakfast is served at 8 a.m., lunch at noon, dinner at 5:30 p.m. — a volunteer will take an old xylophone and go around the ship from engineroom to bridge deck, the melodious notes calling everyone to the galley.

"She's still a good feeder," is an appreciative remark often heard.

NOTE: The *Jeremiah O'Brien* cookbook, *Recipes From a Coal-Fired Stove,* contains recipes from meals served aboard the ship, including crew favorites, and the famed "Dinners for Eight;" menus from legendary ships and luxury liners; and traditional recipes from the Age of Sail, all adjusted for gas and electric stoves.

17

THE IMPOSSIBLE DREAM

C hief Engineer Ernie Murdock's suggestion had a simple title: "Proposed Anniversary Voyage of the SS *Jeremiah O'Brien*." It was an eight-page document suggesting that the ship take part in both the 500th anniversary of Columbus' landing in the Americas in 1992 and the 50th anniversary of D-Day at Normandy in 1994. He presented it to the Board of Directors of the National Liberty Ship Memorial (NLSM) on December 10, 1987.

The seed was actually planted in mid-1986. Marci Hooper, then the NLSM business manager, and Ernie sat talking in the gunners' mess one evening. Fundraising efforts for the centennial restoration of the Statue of Liberty were in the news, and while discussing that much-anticipated event, the notion of taking the *Jeremiah O'Brien* back to Normandy for the 50th Anniversary of D-Day came up. A fever of enthusiasm quickly burned and soon

Marci and Ernie were writing out names of potential crew members on paper napkins.

The proposal was thorough and well thought-out. It addressed financial planning, drydocking, logistics, supply, crewing, shoreside support, coordination with government agencies and myriad other details. But it involved taking the ship, almost fifty years old, on a voyage halfway around the world and back. Many thought it impractical, if not downright foolish, to even think of taking the vessel outside the Golden Gate, much less on an 18,000-mile voyage.

The proposal was tabled.

At the next board meeting, the proposal was raised again, and again tabled. And at the next one, and the next, for almost four years.

In November 1991 Marci Hooper was contacted by Professor Andre Delbecq of the University of Santa Clara. He was a member of a "sister city" association between San Jose and Rouen, France — home of *L'Armada de la Liberte*, a gathering of tall ships which was to take place in Rouen, in July 1994. It would be part of the celebrations commemorating the 50th anniversary of the liberation of France. At his request a meeting was called of the NLSM board members. In attendance were Rear Admiral Thomas J. Patterson, founder of the organization, Capt. Carl Otterberg, staff captain of the *O'Brien*, Robert Blake, Chairman of the Board, Capt. George Jahn, master of the *O'Brien*, Marci Hooper, and Donald Watson, medical officer. Mr. Delbecq brought books and posters depicting the previous Armada, *Les Voiles De La Liberte*, which took place in 1989. Passing the literature around, he said Rouen wanted the *Jeremiah O'Brien* to attend the 1994 gathering, and the ship would have a place of honor. He asked the critical question, "Do you want to go?"

And now, the years of patient lobbying finally bore fruit.

"Let's go around the table and see what everyone says," said Tom Patterson.

One by one, each person in the room was asked the question and, one by one, each agreed.

"The trip of a lifetime," was the almost universal reaction to the idea of the *Jeremiah O'Brien*'s return to Normandy. As the proposal evolved, plans were laid and ports of call suggested. Just hearing the names was thrilling — Panama, London, Edinburgh, Liverpool, Glasgow, Normandy.

Normandy! The name carried an almost electrical charge. It conjured a vision of thousands of ships covering the ocean from horizon to horizon, and the greatest maritime invasion in history.

Cardiff, Portland, Cristobal, Boston, Le Havre, Normandy. The volunteers

This World War I poster captures the spirit felt by the crew when the convoy was announced. Author's collection.

savored the names. New Orleans, Rouen, Cherbourg, Portsmouth, Normandy. It always came back to Normandy. Normandy and D-Day. Normandy and Operation Overlord. Normandy and the longest day in history. Normandy and the greatest gathering of ships since the beginning of time.

And the *Jeremiah O'Brien* had been there, and would be there again.

With the impetus of the interest on the part of Rouen and the *Armada* and the growing enthusiasm for what was being called "The Last Convoy,"[1] Marci Hooper went to ports in England and

---

[1] "The Last Convoy" would be the Liberty ship *John W. Brown*, the Victory ship *Lane Victory* and the *Jeremiah O'Brien* returning to Europe for the 50th Anniversary of D-Day.

France where she presented press kits to the authorities including ship photos, advertising brochures, histories, letters of commendation and certificates of merit for each of the three museum ships.

The effect was dramatic. To the British and the French, the proposed convoy was no longer an idea. Here was a real person, directly representing the *Jeremiah O'Brien* and the other ships, assuring them that three American World War II veteran ships were doing everything they could to attend the D-Day commemorations.

In December 1992 things really began happening. The *O'Brien* went into drydock. Among other things, it was time to have the tailshaft pulled for inspection. But as Ernie Murdock went through the ship with Coast Guard officials and American Bureau of Shipping (ABS) representatives, he was concentrating not only on this routine drydocking but on the one to come — the all-important drydocking that would take place just prior to sailing for Normandy sixteen months hence.

Retired Brigadier General R. C. Tripp, the *O'Brien*'s liaison with the Army, received a draft copy of the Army's concept plan for the D-Day ceremonies. Even a year-and-a-half before June 6, 1994, most of the final events for the ceremonies were already set. The theme was to be "A Grateful Nation Remembers — Honoring Those Who Served." The concept plan set out several key assumptions: the president would attend, as well as the Secretary of Defense, the Chairman, Joint Chiefs of Staff, the Secretaries

A GRATEFUL NATION REMEMBERS.

The United States of America commemorative logo for the 50th Anniversary of World War II features five stars symbolizing the five-star military leadership, five theaters of operations, participation of the five services and five commemorative decades. The laurel wreath symbolizes victory and peace.

The United States D-Day commemorative logo. Author's collection.

of the Army, Air Force, Navy and the Commandant of the Marines; veterans' groups and foreign dignitaries would take part.

The planning objectives were noteworthy in their simplicity and their focus. Key elements were: 1) Keep the World War II veterans central in all events, including planning and execution and, 2) make all events meaningful and dignified. Other sections dealt with logistics; timing and areas of responsibility.

Aboard the *O'Brien* a wide range of topics relative to the coming trip were discussed, many of them foreshadowing problems that could plague the endeavor throughout the voyage. Probably the most important was the budget. The bottomline figure of $2.6 million came as something of a shock. This was softened to a degree by the explanation that $1.6 milion was already on hand or would come "in kind."

One anticipated source of funds was the eagerly-awaited legislation that called for selling six scrap ships from the National Defense Reserve Fleet, two for each of the museum ships: *Jeremiah O'Brien, John W. Brown* and *Lane Victory*. The amount netted would depend on the demand for scrap steel and the value of the dollar on the world market, but many thought $750,000 was a realistic amount to expect from the sale for the use of each museum ship.

The concerns over funding were overriding. At this point the NLSM was almost broke. It barely had enough funds to meet the next few months' expenses, yet it was boldly planning to raise and spend another $2.6 million in the next eighteen months. Planning meetings went on for hours, with obsessive talk about (the lack of) money.

Other issues arose. Crew licenses and certificates: many of the volunteers had expired documents or never had documents to begin with. Would the Coast Guard waive requirements?

Bill Duncan, crew representative, expressed the concern on the part of the crew that outsiders and newcomers might be given precedence over the longtime volunteers. Adm. Patterson emphatically said, "It always has been and always will be the policy of this committee that the volunteer crew comes first."

Subsequent committee meetings covered an ever-expanding range of plans, problems, crises, logistics — and funding, funding, funding.

The *Jeremiah O'Brien* had to be drydocked in October 1993 if the Normandy voyage was to be made. At $500,000 it was the single most costly line item in the budget. Where would the money come from?

Everyone had ideas for fundraisers:

- maritime auctions.
- raffling an automobile.
- a crab feed.
- a late night infomercial.
- a video to solicit funds from corporations.
- "in kind" donations.
- selling vintage models of World War II ships, planes and jeeps.

And so it went — eventually every issue, proposal, problem came back to the question of funding.

Now, the ship began getting interest from overseas. The Last Convoy was becoming a reality in the minds of the British. From the British Ministry of Defence came a message addressed to Adm. Patterson, dated 26 March 1993:

> Dear Admiral:
> ### COMMEMORATION OF THE D DAY LANDINGS
> ### JUNE 1994
>
> During a recent visit to Washington LTG Kicklighter mentioned that it was hoped to refurbish and then sail two Liberty ships and a Victory ship across the Atlantic in time to take part in the ceremonies commemorating the 50th Anniversary of the D Day Landings.
>
> I have been appointed to lead the team responsible for the planning and coordination of the British Government's

commemorations for D Day and my team are now putting together an outline of the events proposed for June 1994.

One of the ideas being worked upon at present is the concept of a flotilla of ships sailing from Portsmouth and Southampton to the Normandy coast on June 5th 1994. The outline plan would be that the flotilla, consisting of a mixture of commercial vessels and warships would congregate first off Portsmouth and then, led by the Royal Yacht, sail across the Channel before dispersing to their various ports. While they were sailing across we would hope to fly the Royal Navy's and the Royal Air Force's Historic Flights overhead to add a little more atmosphere to the occasion.

Clearly, the addition of your ship to the flotilla would be most welcome and would add a touch of authenticity that would be much appreciated by all the veterans taking part.

Should you be able to take part I would be grateful if you would get in touch so that we could discuss the project in more detail.

I have also written to Mr Johnson [*Lane Victory*] and Mr Boylston [*John W. Brown*] concerning their vessels.

Yours Ever,
Tom Longland

Then came an important communication from France. Marci Hooper received a letter from Yves-Asseline, vice-president of *L'Armada de la Liberté.*

Dear Marci,
It was a pleasure to have you on the phone yesterday.
About the Liberty ship, we could propose you to be a "star" on the French TV on Saturday 9th or Sunday l0th July 1994.
We would like your ship arrives in the harbour of Rouen in the middle of the Armada.
Tall ships and moderne war ships could "welcome" the "*Jeremiah O'Brien*". All the event broadcast "LIVE ON TV", we

have a contract with the state TV channels covering all France. I think this sort of support could help you in finding sponsors.

Do you think possible to sign a contract between your association and the Armada in order to make these things sure.

Please be so kind to let me know your opinion on this and please give me your schedule.

Best Regards,

In July the Coast Guard issued inspection requirements for the three vessels of The Last Convoy. To comply with regulations, the ships would have to obtain: the Certificate of Inspection issued by the Coast Guard, a Loadline Certificate, issued by the ABS, an FCC (Federal Communications Commission) Radiotelephone certificate, an FCC Radio-telegraph certificate, a Safety Equipment Certificate, a Safety Construction Certificate and a SOLAS (Safety of Life at Sea) certificate.

Getting the certificates required inspections by various regulatory bodies, predominantly the Coast Guard, ABS and FCC. The ten page Coast Guard document further detailed the types of inspections and requirements: lifesaving equipment, fire protection equipment, operations, electrical systems, machinery, drydocking, manning, rules of the road, stability and general items.

For fifty-year-old ships staffed by seventy-year-old volunteers and funded by donations, these were major hurdles.

With the Coast Guard requirements and deadline approaching, a sense of urgency set in. To keep her appointment in Normandy, the *Jeremiah O'Brien* would have to leave San Francisco in April 1994. The volunteers began coming to work every day instead of a day or two a week. The chores multiplied and the social hours diminished.

Publicity was important and the NLSM was pleased to see their ship receive increasing attention in local newspapers and national maritime magazines.

Admiral Tom Patterson, Bob Blake and François Le Pendu, a French-speaking volunteer, went to France and England to gather official support, with stunning success.

The minister of France formally invited the *O'Brien* to France. Rouen wanted to make the *Jeremiah O'Brien* the centerpiece of the commemoration, at which they expected five million people. The *O'Brien* would hold the position of honor in the center of the line of tall ships from all over the world that would be there for the historic occasion.

In England the British Broadcasting Corporation (BBC) was very interested in covering the arrival of the *O'Brien* in London. The plan was for the *O'Brien* to come alongside HMS *Belfast*, moored in the Thames. Veterans from the British cruiser, which also served at D-Day, and ours would man their respective rails. It promised to be a dramatic event as the two ships tied up side by side; two survivors of the Normandy invasion fifty years past.

Patterson met Capt. Allan Swift of the Southampton Institute of Navigation. He confirmed the following itinerary: On arrival from New York, the *Jeremiah O'Brien* would come into Southampton. All the ships of the commemoration ceremony, including fifteen U.S. Navy ships, would assemble on the 4th of June at anchor. The Queen, in time-honored tradition, would review the gathered fleet from the Royal Yacht *Britannia*, traversing from Spithead into the Solent. On June 5 the ships would sail for Normandy, arriving the following morning. June 6 and 7 would be devoted to 50th Anniversary ceremonies which would be televised around the world.

The reports got better and better. Returning to London, the admiral met with the United States Naval Forces in Europe who promised to run interference for the *O'Brien*, help make advance arrangements and get her written into the operations order. This would ensure that the Navy included the *Jeremiah O'Brien* in their plans.

As the "Go-No Go" decision date drew closer, crew speculation increased. Will we? Won't we? Who? What? When? Adm.

Patterson put a stop to all the rumors.

Chief Engineer Dick Brannon:

> On November thirteenth at a big meeting in number two hold there was announced a special crew meeting, bring your family, bring your friends: there must have been about two hundred people there. Number two was jam-packed. Tom Patterson got up and addressed the crew. All during '93 it was, 'Are we going, if we're going, every coffee session, every bullshit session, are we going or aren't we. And November thirteenth Tom set it all to rest. He said, 'I want to announce to you now that the trip to Normandy is on, it's firm. It's no longer If we're going to go or When we're going to go, the trip is ON.

VOYAGE ITINERARY

The voyage itinerary given out at this time was:

April 14, 1994 depart San Francisco.

May 20, arrive Portsmouth.

June 4, arrive at Spithead anchorage.

June 5, depart for Normandy beachhead.

June 6, commemorations at Pointe du Hoc and Omaha Beach.

June 7, demonstrate loading cargo into DUKWs.

June 8, arrive at Chatham.

June 15, arrive in London.

June 22, arrive at Fowey, Cornwall.

July 2, arrive at Cherbourg.

July 10 arrive at Rouen.

July 17, arrive at Le Havre.

July 21, arrive at Londonderry, Northern Ireland.

July 25 depart for Portland, Maine.

August through September, visit ports on East and Gulf Coasts.

October 8, enter San Francisco Bay.

With the admiral's guarantee, preparations accelerated. For years the crew had stockpiled spare parts, unused equipment and replacement machinery in the *O'Brien*'s lower holds. They had become expert "scroungers," collecting no-longer-produced ship parts from wherever they could beg, borrow or steal, stockpiling them for future use. But now, most of the hoard had to be removed. The lower holds were needed to stow ballast and while it was perfectly fine to leave things sitting loose in the holds when the *O'Brien* cruised the protected waters of San Francisco Bay, the open seas encountered on an 18,000-mile trip were another matter.

And there were the countless other projects necessary to prepare the ship for the voyage.

    ... Prepare lifeboats for examination and inspection by USCG.

    ... Test air tanks

    ... Weight test boats and davits

    ... Prepare listings of any missing equipment, repairs or replacements required on air tanks, fuel tanks, and provision storage tanks.

    ... Remove all excess items from No. 3 Upper Tween Deck except spare shaft.

    ... Complete an updated ship's Emergency Plan and post as required.

    ... Strip and paint out No. 2 Hold Upper Tween Decks.

    ... Prepare listing of parts and supplies needed for 6 month voyage.

    ... Repair all required reach rods for remote activation of valves.

    ... Apply hydrostatic test pressures on the boilers and piping as requred by Coast Guard regulations.

    ... Prove proper operation of bilge system serving cargo spaces.

Interviews were already underway of volunteers wishing to make the Normandy trip. The word was out and eager future crew members burned up the telephone wires. The trip would be a major commitment for up to six months away from home and family with hard work and no pay. Most of the volunteers were retired and had the time, but problems of age and health had to be considered. The younger volunteers had jobs and other responsibilities. For married volunteers, the unqualified support of their wives was vital. Their families, too, would be making a major commitment. Yet, the inquires and applications flooded in.

Meanwhile, the preparations continued.

    … clean out the deep tanks.
    … install gaskets for all watertight doors.
    … backflush the bilges.
    … inspect and replace the hatch boards.
    … put the evaporators into service.
    … repair the feed water regulator.
    … determine license requirements for all hands.
    … install temporary radar mast.
    … prepare oil tanks.
    … clean No. 1 and No. 2 deep tanks.
    … remove and examine the anchor chain.
    … repair interior gussets and stays on the stack.
    … inspect boiler mountings.

Donations for everything from fuel oil to pilot ladders to toothpicks to brooms to stores to valves to satellite communications were sought.

    ... clean port and starboard potable water tanks.
    … inspect bilge piping.
    … repair valves on the No. 1 and No. 2 DC generator.
    … meggar all generators.
    … install two mast lights for canal passage.
    … install rudder angle indicators.
    … obtain a satellite navigation system, radar and weather fax.

Bill Bennett, left and Bob Burnett, center, removing hatch beams to give access to extra equipment going ashore for storage in Alameda. Bruce McMurtry.

Bill Duncan, crew chairman, pointed out that only eighty-four work days remained but just the projects already lined up totaled 373 man-days and the list did not include the unforeseen problems that would inevitably arise.

> … training programs including classes in cargo loading, lifesaving, lifeboat handling, firefighting, damage control and radar.
>
> … prepare the galley for major meal service.
>
> … inspect and clean port boiler.
>
> … navigation charts.
>
> … test general alarm.
>
> … lifeboat gear.
>
> … get spare piping, steel stock, threaded stock, boiler tubes.

Coast Guard requirements and SOLAS limit the number of the crew to the capacity of the lifeboats on one side of the ship. The *O'Brien* has four lifeboats, two on each side. The after boat is propelled by oars and rated to carry thirty-one. The forward one is a motor lifeboat. Since part of the space in the forward boat is taken up by the motor, it has a smaller capacity than the other, twenty-five. This set the size of the crew at a maximum of fifty-six.

There was a volunteer list of 200, plus applications from another 200, but some crewing problems were developing. Because some were taking leaves of absence from jobs or because of medical restrictions or financial considerations, many could not make the entire trip. Also, in consideration for age and the extreme temperatures in the engine room in the tropics, the engine department decided to stand three-hour watches instead of the traditional four-hour watch. This meant we would be carrying an additional watch of engineers, consisting of a licensed engineer, a fireman/watertender and an oiler. Where would they sleep? Someone had to start assigning cabins, bunks and lockers. Everyone agreed that, yes, someone should do that, then went on to other topics.

> … install washing machines.
> … renew gaskets.
> … run new piping to sanitary tank.
> … install wiring.
> … test oil-water separator.
> … repair lifeboat air tanks.
> … locate flags.
> … test refrigeration system.
> … run wiring and piping to generator.

In Maine, the following article appeared in the *Sunday Sun-Journal*:

> He was a Mainer and a Revolutionary War Hero. A Maine State Park at Machias is named for him, and his name lived in

The wheelhouse of the Jeremiah O'Brien. *The ARPA radar donated by American President Lines can be seen in the right background, just inside the door.* Author's collection.

the history of World War II. This year his name will live again in the 50th anniversary observance of the Allied liberation of France. He was Jeremiah O'Brien, and a ship bearing his name and built in Maine participated in the June 1944 Normandy invasion and is expected to return there this year. O'Brien was a staunch Revolutionary War patriot. He and other men of the Machias area won what is called "The First Naval Battle of the Revolution." They captured the British ship "Margaretta" in Machias Bay on June 12, 1775. O'Brien was chosen to supervise preparation of an earthen gun battery on the river below Machias in anticipation of British retaliation. The Machias men did not have long to wait. The month after the loss of their ship, the British sent the "Tatmagouch" and the "Diligence" to retake the captured ship. Without resisting, the vessels surrendered — to Capt. Jeremiah O'Brien. That was the start of O'Brien's trek through history.

Tom Patterson:

Every project that we took on became its own separate challenge. For example, the ballasting of the ship. We went all over trying to find the right kind of ballast. There were keel blocks from Hunter's Point Naval Shipyard, but they were too big. We had information about the Navy having surplus lead, and that took a couple of months to resolve. It took calling back to Washington, D.C., to the rear admiral in charge of Naval Sea Systems command, who was in charge of installation and logistics, to find out where the lead resided up in Puget Sound Naval Shipyard. Then we had to arrange for transportation down which we ultimately got from a Navy ship from Logistics Group One. That was another separate effort, to get the transportation …

A different problem concerned the generators. Alternating current was needed to operate the radars. The ship's obsolete system was set up for direct current.

- … drydock.
- … inspect fire and safety equipment, cargo handling equipment, cargo spaces, communications equipment, main propulsion, auxiliary equipment, fuel capacity, refueling points, water capacity, stewards stores.
- … determine officers' names and experience, number of junior officers, number of crew, rotation plan, other persons aboard.
- … decide on waivers, medical provisions, general specifications, cargo to be carried, where loading and discharge would take place, cargo plan, intended stevedores, emergency plans, watch, quarter & station bill, drills, towing plans, convoy plans, navigation and mooring plans, communications plan, stores and replenishment, agents, in-port security, lists of other agencies involved with the voyage.
- … obtain Certification from the Coast Guard, ABS and FCC.

Room assignments. Who would sleep where? There were seventy-seven bunks. Fifty-six people should fit into seventy-seven bunks. But it wasn't that simple. In some rooms the bunks were three and four high, designed during World War II when nimble kids of eighteen and nineteen manned the gun crew. But we had a not-so-nimble crew with an average age of seventy. Some assignments were obvious — the master had his own stateroom and office as did the chief engineer. The chief steward and the chief mate (the author) had individual office-room combinations and no one argued the point. But beyond that it got complicated.

> ... plan or expect crowds of 4,000 a day during ship's visit in European ports (one day we actually logged in more than 10,000 visitors)
> ... docents to explain the ship.
> ... brochures and inventory for the ship's store, which was set up in No. 3 tween deck and which we hoped would earn good revenues from sales.
> ... find and contract with vendors for scores of items from heavy sweaters embroidered with the ship's name and logo to commemorative Medals, caps, watches, flags, pencils, T-shirts, maps, books.

The NLSM office attended to thousands of details with two paid staff and a few volunteers. Making and answering phone calls, writing and responding to hundreds of letters, they were the nerve center linking the ship with agencies, government, donors, vendors, volunteers, news media, and many projects that did or did not work out. Their responsibility was enomous.

On February 18, 1994 the *Jeremiah O'Brien* shifted to San Francisco Drydock. It was a wet but calm day with intermittent rainsqualls and sunshine. After weeks of discharging excess equipment, loading new equipment and vans, with people swarming the decks and interiors, inspecting, visiting, checking, viewing, asking questions, wanting directions, it was relaxing to have the ship returned to us, even just for a few hours.

As always, there was something grand about being on a ship moving across the water. You feel at the center of the universe and

During the shift to drydock, Capt. Jahn, left, describes some of the finer points of piloting to Adm. Patterson. Mike Emery.

everything revolves around you. You become part of that great living being that is the ship, feeling the hum and vibration of throbbing machinery, as you watch the world pass.

The chief steward brought hot coffee and pastries to the bridge. For a few moments, all was at peace.

Then it was back to reality.

18

Normandy or Bust

O n March 1 the *Jeremiah O'Brien* was pushed by tugs into drydock. There, she was carefully positioned by the docking master over a series of keel and bilge blocks. The dock's ballast tanks were pumped out and the dock rose, the ship settling on the blocks, until the ship and the floor of the dock were out of the water.

To the crew, dry docking is a special event. It gives them the rare opportunity to walk under the hull and a chance to see the entire ship with its huge rudder and propeller exposed. Several volunteers came to see the ship out of the water.

Even before the hull was dry the Coast Guard and American Bureau of Shipping began inspecting the *Jeremiah O'Brien*. Whenever they came to a welding seam they scraped, probed and beat on it with pointed hammers and scratch awls. If they thought the seam weak, they marked it with a can of spray paint to indicate

After Coast Guard and ABS inspectors finished, the hull was striped like a cat. George Bonawit.

the area should be sandblasted and inspected further. By the following day the *O'Brien*'s hull looked like an abstract tiger. White and red paint marks were everywhere, even under the bottom.

After the hull is spray-painted the draft marks are put in by hand. Author's collection.

It was now the middle of March, only one month to departure date. Adm. Patterson said, "… it has gotten down to a seven-day-a-week job." Still, the tried-and-true volunteers showed up when they could, some every day.

The crew became resigned to the fact that each morning would present a new "crises *du jour*." The promised generator from Caterpillar hadn't materialized. Testing one of the lifeboats, a yard worker stepped into it, his weight causing the boat to tilt so that the test weights all shifted to one side and the boat sank.

Good things also happened. Capt. H.W. Simonsen generously donated a yacht to the ship which produced a handsome return in the form of a lease-purchase. The Foster Wheeler Corporation, a manufacturer of marine boilers (and the *Jeremiah O'Brien*'s boilers), donated $5,000. Thanks to negotiations by Art Haskell, the ABS waived the $12,000 in fees due for their inspections.

Tom Patterson: "One of the largest jobs that we faced was putting the vessel in class and obtaining the Coast Guard Certificate of Inspection. We recognized from the beginning that this was going to mean a tremendous amount of money. We had estimated our shipyard repairs plus the Coast Guard and ABS requirements at over nine hundred thousand dollars and ultimately it went over one point two million dollars."

The lifeboats were prepared for inspection and the ship readied for the inclining test. The purpose of the inclining experiment is to determine the height of the ship's center of gravity above

Ernie Murdock, right, and crew inspect rudder and propeller shortly after the ship is hauled out. George Bonawit.

Amidst all the turmoil this cartoon appeared in the crew messroom. It captured the indomitable spirit of the crew. Jean Yates.

This is how the main deck looked a few days before departure. George Bonawit

the keel. It is performed by moving a known weight a known distance across the deck, determining the angle of heel the vessel assumes and, with these values, solving for metacentric height. To measure the angle of heel a pendulum is hung in the lower hold. When the weight is shifted, the deflection of the pendulum is measured. This distance is then used in a trigonometric formula

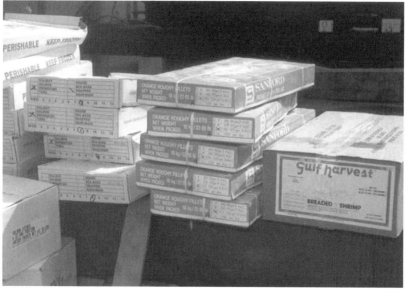

A small part of the food stores for the six months voyage: frozen fish. George Bonawit.

Above, frozen seafood being quickly removed from the pallets and taken below to the freezer boxes. Below, a shore crane lowers a pallet of beer, guided by a shipyard worker, onto the main deck. George Bonawit.

Coal, essential for the galley range, stowed on the boat deck in a crib used for potatoes during World War II. Author's collection.

to determine the ship's GM or metacentric height. From this, various calculations can be made to determine the ship's stability and, consequently, safety.

The inclining experiment is a surprisingly delicate procedure. Among other things, all the vessel's tanks must be either empty or full, otherwise as the ship starts to heel the center of gravity of the liquid would shift, causing exaggerated readings. The vessel must not have a list. The formula for calculating GM is based on a right triangle. If there is a list, the triangle is not right, hence inaccuracies. Balance is so delicate that Fred Kaufman, who was conducting the test, needed to know the weight of each person on board to include in his calculations and they had to all stand on the centerline of the ship while the test was being conducted.

The Coast Guard was aboard on almost a daily basis now, nosing into everything. The long hours and hard work were taking their toll.

Voyage 8 commenced at midnight on April 1. The deck log simply says, "0000 Begin Voyage 8." [Voyage 7 ended on February 8, 1946].

The ship swarmed with Coast Guard inspectors. The din increased and continued around the clock. On deck, welders' blue arcs flashed everywhere. The yard continued shifting ballast into the holds. The huge cranes traveled on their rails, lifting pallets of lead ballast and lowering them into the hatches where forklifts ran the heavy loads into corners and inaccessible underdeck areas, distributing the weight evenly. The decks were cluttered with lead ballast, pieces of pipe, hatch boards and beams. Miles of welding cable and air hose snaked over and under and around everything.

On top of it all came the stores — sacks of coal for the galley, sleeping cots for the tropics, bags of potatoes, boxes of bananas, onions, cases and pallets of canned goods — peaches, mayonnaise, tuna, fruit cocktail, prunes, juices, roasts, steaks, sausage, bacon, ice cream, flour, spices, yeast, fish, fresh fruit, toilet paper, soap, detergent, disinfectant, eggs, melons, apples, oranges, peanut butter, jelly, syrup, relish …

Otis Spunkmeyer donated a "ton" of frozen cookie dough — chocolate chip, sugar, ginger, vanilla — and a special oven in which to cook them.

The AC generator from Caterpillar arrived on the dock. This would provide the electricity to operate navigational, medical, lighting and other modern electronic equipment. It would provide the precisely controlled power required by today's integrated circuit electronics, and be fuel-efficient, clean-running and quiet.

Sea trials were run on April 10. Sea trials are to prove to the Coast Guard and the American Bureau of Shipping that all the systems work and, in particular, that the boilers can hold a sustained load for a period of time at full speed. One boiler was ready, the other wasn't. Nevertheless, the *O'Brien* crisscrossed San Francisco Bay at full speed (10 knots) for a couple of hours and was back alongside by 1130 with the traditional broom flying at the mast showing a clean sweep of all trials. Capt. Jahn did a masterful job of handling the ship and the crew felt that things were starting to settle in.

The media glare increased. The decks swarmed with TV crews, radio interviewers and newspaper reporters from local, national and foreign stations and papers. These in addition to the daily turmoil of welders, riggers, electricians, crew, ship chandlers, deliverymen, Coast Guard and American Bureau of Shipping inspectors and visitors.

From USA Today:

SAN FRANCISCO — A half-century after the D-Day invasion of Normandy, a crew of dream-driven old salts — average age 70 — has embarked on what some might call an assault on common sense. Their mission: to restore a ship that's 10 times older than its life expectancy and sail it halfway around the world through some of the roughest seas on Earth to join D-Day's 50th anniversary party June 6.

But $2.4 million and 500,000 volunteer hours later, here it sits in a shipyard berth, aswarm with crew members, yard workers, financial backers and Coast Guard inspectors — all working feverishly to ready the *O'Brien* for a voyage once considered impossible.

To arrive at Portsmouth, England, the beginning of festivities by June 3, the 12-knot-an-hour *O'Brien* must ship out this week. But it still hasn't passed inspection.

"There's nothing we want more than for this ship to get there," says Coast Guard Petty Officer Gary Openshaw. "It's part of history. But, unfortunately, there are still problems … We don't want any disasters."

Still to be done: loading and securing tons of lead weights as ballast to keep the *O'Brien* from capsizing. "Obviously, that's pivotal," says Openshaw. "But we do believe they can finish by the end of the week."

Not, however, without considerable mayhem and round-the-clock work schedules. These passageways bustle with sweaty-faced men in their 70s carrying boxes, huffing up ladders hauling tools, toiling in 130-degree heat below decks as they fire up the boilers.

The physical toll is substantial. "I guess three hours of sleep a night isn't enough," concedes Jim Wade, the *O'Brien*'s graying purser and chaplain, who was ordered to take the rest of the day off after growing dizzy. A half-hour later, he was back at work. "There's too much to do," he mumbles.

There are a few youngsters to help, two merchant marine cadets elated to go along but struggling with the complications of running a ship lacking computerized systems. "You have to do everything by hand," sighs Dirk Warren, 20. "It's going to be a long trip."

But the old-timers are untroubled by obstacles. For them, the *O'Brien* is precisely what a ship should be. "She's a fine ship," says Capt. George Jahn, 78, the *O'Brien*'s commander. "Old or not ... (she's) as seaworthy as they come."

April 14 arrived — the scheduled departure date. Instead, the ship returned to the San Francisco Dry Dock. Every moment was occupied trying to clear off the items on the Coast Guard 835s.[1]

Now, the Coast Guard inspectors, who earlier, had been bureaucratic and unbendingly "by-the-book," became easier to work with. It may have been a sense of mutual understanding; they respected how hard the crew was trying and the crew understood that they must answer to their superiors. There was also a sense of so much energy and momentum moving the ship forward that they were simply worn down by it. The inspectors began trying to help, rather than hinder us.

Almost everyone was living aboard, working almost around the clock. The crew began gathering in the messroom and the officers' saloon after dinner to talk and swap sea stories. A good sense of comaraderie was developing.

---

[1] Coast Guard form CG-835 is basically a "fix-it" ticket, describing something that needs to be repaired. Each one had to be cleared before sailing.

The sailing board set for departure. It shows the next port (country, in this case) and the date and time of sailing. "Call back" means the time everyone must return to the ship. Author's collection.

On April 17, the list of uncleared items was down to sixteen and many of those were partially complete.

On April 18, departure day came at last. We took on board several inspectors from the Coast Guard, FCC and ABS in addition to pilots, a compass adjuster, a Mackay radio technician and members of the press. Yachts and small boats milled around just off the pier, waiting to see us off. Just before noon, we let go the lines and slowly eased away from the dock. Whistles and horns blew. One boat had a small cannon on board which it fired several times. Picking up speed, the ship headed toward the Oakland-Bay Bridge. There were more whistles — the traditional three long blasts, answered by the *O'Brien*'s deep-throated, authoritative foghorn, then a short blast followed by our own short blast. As we passed under the bridge and crossed toward the Golden Gate, the San Francisco fire boat *Guardian* joined the cavalcade spouting gushers of red, white and blue water in arcing geysers that reflected rainbow prisms in their mist. A number of yachts came along, then helicopters from local television stations appeared, hovering first above the ship, then at wheelhouse level. The beautiful skyline of San Francisco passed on our port side, bright geometric blocks of glass and color.

Even while all this was going on, we continued working on those last 835s. Engineers welded the 'tween deck doors shut, showed the Coast Guard that each boiler, each system was working properly. On deck we broke out fire hoses and, with an inspector inside the 'tween deck, sprayed the hatches to prove their watertightness.

As the ship passed under the Golden Gate Bridge a thick fog set in. Suddenly the aircraft and small boats disappeared. Third Mate Pete Lyse began blowing the required fog signal, one long blast every two minutes. We were on our own except for the pilot boat following along to take off the inspectors, the media and the pilot. Up in the wheelhouse the radar was turned on. It didn't work. Well, no problem, we'll use the backup, a small yacht radar on the flying bridge. But it wasn't working either. At least we had the gyrocompass. The pilot knows the courses, he can get us out. Keeping a calm outward demeanor, we sent the nearby Coast Guard inspectors off with the bosun to check off another 835 item, one as far away from where we were as possible.

"Gyro's not working," said the pilot quietly, when everyone was out of earshot.

"How about the magnetic compass?" We both looked at the compass adjuster who was busily taking readings and making calculations. He shook his head 'no.'

Oh, Lord.

"Don't worry," said the pilot. "I'm on the radio to the pilot boat. He's got us on his radar. He'll guide us out."

With crossed fingers, we managed to distract the Coast Guard's attention from the problems on the bridge and quietly followed the pilot boat out through the fog.

Then the final moment came. The Coast Guard and ABS gave Capt. Jahn our certificates and agreed we could go. Guy

Therriault, of the Coast Guard, who had gone out of his way to help us, held out his hand, "All right, Mate. We're leaving," he said. We shook hands.

As the last pilot boat departed Capt. Jahn ordered a southerly course (the gyro, which takes more than an hour to warm up, was working now) and full ahead on the engines. At last, we were on our way.

19

A DOWNHILL RUN

And so, once again, to sea.

Now, the ship was ours. Gone, at last, were the Coast Guard, FCC and American Bureau of Shipping. Gone were the TV cameras and news photographers. Gone were the shipyard workers, deliverymen, inspectors, chandlers, officials and visitors.

Most of the electronic problems soon resolved themselves. The magnetic compasses were accurate by the time the compass adjuster left the ship. The gyro settled onto the correct heading by the time we cleared the pilot station. And the smaller of the two radars was working. That left the ARPA radar. It took another day to solve the electrical problems which caused it to receive the wrong amperage. It worked perfectly for the remainder of the trip. But for a while it was almost as if the old ship was protesting all the newfangled equipment.

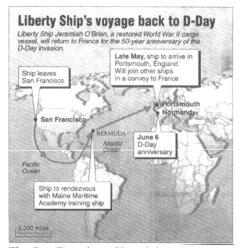

The San Francisco Chronicle*'s route map includes our rendezvous with the Maine Maritime Academy's training ship* State of Maine*, which crossed the Atlantic with the* O'Brien *to England.*

In the evening many of the crew repaired to No. 2 hold which became the theater. Five hundred videos and two television sets with built-in VCRs were loaned to the ship by the Norway House of San Francisco, a charitable organization that also provides newspapers, magazines, books and "home away from home" services to merchant ships. If two films were shown, the second would be in the officers' mess. As we got farther into the tropics, the movies moved out onto the deck. On this first screening "The Cruel Sea" was chosen.

April 20 was a beautiful sunny day with blue skies. The ship rolled gently to a moderate following sea. A large containership, American President Lines' *President Adams* was seen traveling north-bound. They called on the bridge-to-bridge radio and wished us well. The mate on watch knew all about our voyage, hoped we made good speed and said he wished he was there with us. Suddenly we realized the world had not seen an armed merchant ship in the open ocean since the late 1940s. We were a floating time capsule. Our voyage had received wide coverage, and we learned that it was being followed with avid interest and enthusiasm. The old-time camaraderie of the sea came back to the industry for this voyage. Modern maritime commerce has become a routine, undramatic, uninteresting business that all but ignores the old-time brotherhood of the sea. But mariners everywhere seemed to yearn for that lost camaraderie and all through the trip, ships of all types — cargo vessels, Navy ships,

LIFE ON A LIBERTY SHIP

It wasn't long before we realized there are actually some advantages to sailing an old Liberty Ship. Modern ships are air-conditioned and all the rooms, passageways and entrances have airtight doors. There are no smells outside your own room. On the *O'Brien*, the doors aren't sealed. They have louvers at the bottom and portholes are left open for ventilation and every time the cooks began working in the galley the smell of food permeated the ship. It was wonderful, the mixed smells of chocolate chip cookies, bacon, bread, pancakes, sausage, chicken, more cookies, roasts, potatoes, muffins and more cookies. Even the simple, pungent smell of coal burning somehow added to the feeling of traveling back in history to a better time.

Meals were a highpoint of the day. Breakfast consisted of juice, melon, toast, muffins, hot and cold cereal, bacon or sausage, scrambled eggs, hotcakes or French toast. Lunch was often chicken, pasta, or sandwiches with a vegetable such as cauliflower, or potato chips or coleslaw or a green salad, with cake and/or our famed Otis

One morning's baking by the galley crew and one reason for so many good smells throughout the ship. Bruce McMurtry.

Spunkmeyer cookies for dessert. Dinner could be salad with a choice of dressings, steak, fish, pork or lamb with potatoes, green beans or some other vegetable and cake or pudding and, again, cookies for dessert. No one ever got tired of cookies.

The atmosphere lulled the crew into reminiscent moods. Capt. Jahn talked about working for United Fruit Company just after the strike of '34. He was an AB on one of their ships. After the ship arrived in San Francisco and discharged its cargo of bananas, it was his job to sweep out the refrigeration compartments in which the bananas were stowed. They contained a few loose stalks and bits and pieces of dunnage. Because the bananas were refrigerated, the snakes and tarantulas that came along with them went dormant, most of the way. With the cargo off and the refrigeration shut down, these creatures slowly came back to life. Young George Jahn suddenly found his broom alive with slithery, crawly things. "I didn't stay there long," he said. "Those things gave me the willies."

After lunch those off-watch would sometimes go for a brief rest, drifting off to the mild sound and vibration of the engine's thump, thump, thump. It was a curiously soothing and quiet sound, so different from the harsh, mechanical, high-pitched whines and explosive roars of modern diesel engines. Everyone was pleasantly surprised to learn we made 12.4 knots for our first twenty-four hour run from noon to noon. We had cautiously projected nine knots for the trip.

boats, yachts, tankers — greeted us, blew their whistles in salute and took pictures, often changing course to do so.

The entry in the deck log simply read: "1135 Spoke the *President Adams*, northbound."

The ship steamed on, rolling gently on a slight swell. In the distance whales spouted. Nearby, porpoises playfully swam ahead of the ship, cutting back and forth in front of the bow.

We received welcome word that Norton, Lilly and Co., who would be our ship's agent in the Western hemisphere, had arranged to have some of the charges for going through the Canal waived in each direction, $3,750 worth of line handling, admeasurement, tug fees and other items. The fees for the transit itself could not be waived due to a treaty between Panama, Colombia and the United States that allows for such a contingency for Panamanian and Colombian warships only. The transit would now cost "only" $9,680.

The crew's news was written and dispatched daily by wireless to KFS, a marine radio station which generously donated all the official communication charges for the ship and their number was called scores of times each day by crew families and interested members of the public. Gary North became known as "The Voice of the *Jeremiah O'Brien*." Gary's speaking voice, rich, deep and expressive, couldn't have been better if we requested it from central casting. The first enthusiastic message went out on April 20 and read:

> This is the Voice of the *Jeremiah O'Brien*.
> Good evening San Francisco and greetings from the *Jeremiah O'Brien* — day three of our voyage back to the beaches of Normandy. Our vessel entered Mexican territorial waters at 0330 today and our noon position is 40 miles south of the port of Ensenada. Ship's speed the past 24 hours averaged 11.4 knots at 68 revolutions per minute. Chief engineer Dick Brannon is all smiles. When asked about the operation of his giant, triple-expansion steam engine, his response was just one word: "Excellent!"

By April 21 the ship was off the coast of Baja California and 800 miles into the voyage. The sky was overcast in the morning and cleared in the afternoon and the ship sailed on, surrounded by a calm blue sea. There was a growing feeling of bonhomie as everyone got more rest and fell into the routine of day-to-day ship operation.

We resumed the old tradition of ringing each half hour of time as the watch progressed. It was another pleasant reminder of the historic nature of our voyage.

One night the movie was "Action in the North Atlantic," with Humphrey Bogart. If ever there was a training film for the merchant marine, this is it. Made during World War II, it tells the story of the crew of a merchant ship sunk by a German submarine. They return to sea and sink a submarine in retaliation. It's the type of story that fires one with patriotism and makes one want to go out and fight Nazis, even fifty years after the fact.

The next night it was a double-feature, "Patton" and "Tora, Tora, Tora." The following night's double feature was aimed at submarine aficionados, "Das Boot," and "The Hunt for Red October." Our taste in movies certainly became predictable.

It appeared that everyone was getting younger. The seventy-year-old veterans walked with a bounce in their step. Animated chatter, laughter and jokes filled the messrooms. Good will abounded. Everyone seemed to be reliving his youth and the spirit was infectious.

The weather turned from comfortably beautiful to hot and beautiful. The sky was clear, the seas a flat, calm, deep blue. We passed Acapulco and entered the Gulf of Tehuantepec and the thermometer began to rise.

Journal entry for April 26: "Hot, hot, hot."

Heat permeated the old steel ship. Everyone outside was working in shorts and T-shirts or just shorts, The crew broke out the cots and began sleeping on top of the hatches and on the main deck.

If it was "hot, hot, hot" on deck, conditions in the engine room were hellish. Its only "air conditioning" was the adjustable cowl ventilators on the flying bridge and the open sky lights at the top of the fidley. Temperatures soared to 110°, 120°, even 130°.

On the night watch, distant faint flashes of heat lightning, too far away to hear, shimmered occasionally in a cloud bank hovering along the Mexican Coast. Around 2300, the lookout reported a ship's light forward. Then it rose, a dark orange ball of a full moon, directly ahead of the *O'Brien*. The night became bright with pale moonlight.

Here, Farley languishes for the "long sea voyage" he imagines we are enjoying on the O'Brien. Phil Frank and *San Francisco Chronicle.*

The sea ahead was a path of silver and gold. The masts and booms were outlined in moonlight and dark shadows. On deck, a few of the crew leaned on the rail, watching the silvery water; the orange glow of a cigarette arced into the sea. Behind them, someone tossed in their cot, a sheet billowing momentarily, ghostlike. A bird, a booby, landed on a light standard on the bow and, tucking its head under its wing, went to sleep.

Phil Frank's popular cartoon strip, Farley, runs daily in the *San Francisco Chronicle.* One of its main characters, Bruce, a talking raven, sophisticated far beyond his position on the evolutionary ladder, decided to join the *Jeremiah O'Brien* on its adventure. He immediately became the crew's alter ego. Copies of the strip (sent by fax) went up on the bulletin boards.

Bruce the Raven was not the only "reporter" on board. Carl Nolte, one of the *San Francisco Chronicle*'s top reporters, served as an A.B. aboard and filed frequent dispatches that were avidly read and collected by readers all over the state.

The Crew's News this day, sent by Bill Bennett to KFS and read by Gary North to an ever-expanding following of callers:

> This is the Voice of the *Jeremiah O'Brien.*
>
> Good evening San Francisco from the crew of the *Jeremiah O'Brien.*
>
> Day 10 of our voyage back to the Normandy coast. The past 24 hours we have traveled 284 miles. Our average speed was 11.8 knots. Sea water temperature is 82 degrees; on deck

Bruce leaves in pursuit of the O'Brien *and a chance to make a quick buck. Everyone on board adopted him as the ship's mascot.* Phil Frank and *San Francisco Chronicle.*

it is a toasty 90 degrees with about 95% relative humidity. We deck people are cool in comparison to the engineers. They must tolerate temperatures of 125 degrees plus, during their three hour watch. We are about to enter Nicaraguan waters today and ETA Panama is Saturday.

Jeremiah O'Brien -- out.

The movie another evening was "The Captain's Paradise." Long a favorite in maritime circles, it stars Alec Guinness as the

Entering the Canal Zone with the "Bridge of the Americas" just off the O'Brien*'s starboard bow.* Bruce McMurtry.

Bruce begins his quest. Would he make it to Panama on time? Would the crew want the brandy? For answers to these and other burning questions, read on. Phil Frank and *San Francisco Chronicle.*

master of a ship that runs a liner service between Gibraltar and Morocco. He has a wife in each port, one a staid, proper English lady, the other a firebrand. This old favorite drew one of the largest audiences of the voyage.

The morning of April 30 the *O'Brien* slowly eased her way into the harbor approaches to Balboa, on the Pacific side of the Canal, picked up the pilot and the customs and immigration officials. Then, with a tug as escort, she passed under the "Bridge of the Americas," the graceful, arching span that connects the continents of North and South America. Within a few minutes we were tied up to pier 2 South at Rodman Naval Base. The last time the *Jeremiah O'Brien* was in Panama was in 1944.

We dressed the ship, festooning it from stem to stern with brightly-colored signal flags strung together. Military Sealift

Miraflores Locks in the Panama Canal, taken in the early evening. Panama Canal Commission.

Miraflores Locks, the first set entered from the Pacific side. The ship in the background is going in the same direction as the O'Brien. *Jim Conwell.*

Command arranged a wonderful reception. Their band played rousing marches. The Navy sponsored a barbecue. It's surprising how good a hamburger tastes, grilled outdoors on a smoky fire, with the jungles of Panama providing background greenery. This enthusiastic welcome gave us the first hint of what might be in store for us. It was all quite exciting.

The sailing board was posted for Sunday, May 1, at 0600 "ship's time." The pilots came aboard, the four senior pilots on

A Panama Canal mule guides the Jeremiah O'Brien *carefully through the locks.* Author's collection.

Pedro Miguel Locks with a northbound bulk carrier headed toward Gaillard Cut. Panama Canal Commission.

the list. All were in the merchant marine during World War II, some on Liberty ships, and each wanted a chance to pilot the oldest American-flag ship through the Canal, generously donating their services.

Transiting the Canal is an experience that never pales, no matter how many times one does it. Every crew member not on watch was up on deck to see it all.

A member of the *Jeremiah O'Brien* crew transiting the Canal in 1994 would be hard pressed to see many differences from the 1944 transit. In the control tower, everything is computerized with the latest in operations systems. But, to the traveller the transit is very much the same (see p. 135). Watching the gates close, the locks fill up, the mules alongside (newer than in 1944,

Bruce arrives. Never let it be said that the ship's gunners don't have their priorities straight. Phil Frank and *San Francisco Chronicle*.

Looking astern toward Gatun Lake, the lock gates can be seen closing before the O'Brien *is lowered to the next lock.* Bruce McMurtry.

but not too much changed), the towers, Gatun Lake — it is almost a voyage back in time — a fascinating, never-ending marvel.

Arriving in Cristobal we tied up to Pier 16 and rang off Finished With Engines at 2020 (8:20 p.m.).

20

To England

Departing Panama at 2112 on May 2, the *Jeremiah O'Brien* turned on a course of 045°. There was no moon. The night was dark, the sea calm. To starboard was the coast of Panama, darker than the night, with an occasional weak light on shore flickering through the jungle. From time to time a brightly-lit freighter was seen in the distance, coming down from the American Gulf Coast, its running lights showing it was headed for the Canal. Overhead, the constellations were clear, pinpricks of light on black velvet. The Milky Way was a powdery blur across the heavens; the Southern Cross was visible low over Panama. The only wind was that caused by the ship moving at 11 knots through the water. The wake coming off the bow hissed, glowing green with phosphorescence as it ran past on either side. The propeller thump-thump-thumped through the water, like a healthy pulse. It was a good night to be back to sea.

Bosun Rich Reed applies a finish coat of grey paint to "Charley Noble," the galley smokestack. Bruce McMurtry.

Now began in earnest the task of preparing the ship for Portsmouth. We had twenty-one days in which to get the *Jeremiah O'Brien* shipshape.

The day started quietly with an overcast, grey sky and a short, choppy sea. Flying fish, bigger than those we saw in the Pacific, glided through the air in fan-shaped schools as they sensed our approach. Easing away from shore, the northeast trade winds, which were dead ahead, increased in strength and by the end of the day the deck log showed, "Wind NE [force] 5, Swell ENE 4. Vessel pitching to Mod NE'ly Sea & low short ENE'ly swell."[1]

The next day the winds were stronger, force six. The sea was a wild mix of color; frothy-white on the surface, but between the whitecaps, a sinister blue-grey, and, looking straight down close to the ship, bright blue. A swell coming from the wind direction had built to a height of ten feet. From any other direction this wouldn't be bad but with both the wind and the swell head-on, the bow and stern pitched up and down. When the stern rose, the propeller came out of the water and, without water to work against, raced in the air. Dishes, pots, pans and other loose items banged and shattered, a good reminder that things should be properly stowed.

By now, the cooks had mastered the intricacies of the coal-fired galley stove. They started each day about 4 a.m., cleaned the

---

[1] Wind force at sea is recorded according to the Beaufort scale rather than miles per hour. The "5" after "NE" refers to this scale.

Meanwhile, in the crow's nest ... Bruce enjoys the sea and — room service.
Phil Frank and *San Francisco Chronicle.*

ashes out, shoveled in new coal, and then lit the fire. It took a
while to get used to, especially the baking. In time they learned to
rotate the cakes and pies so they wouldn't be cooked on one side
and raw on the other. The saying, "an army travels on its stomach"
applies equally to travellers at sea. The bracing salt air whets the
appetite, and in the self-contained world on board ship, there is
little to provide distraction. This results in an inordinate interest in
mealtimes and food. The galley crew performed wonders on the
old, coal-fired stove, and were a major factor in the crew's high
morale. Russ Mosholder, the chief steward, planned the meals
and supervised the galley crew. Al Martino was the head cook,
responsible for preparing main courses. Jimmy Farras, who
attended the California Culinary Academy, was the second cook
and with Third Cook Eddie Pubill, prepared side dishes, breads,
pastries and desserts.

The halfway mark was passed on the 8-to-12 watch on May 7:
4,033 miles to San Francisco, 4,033 miles to Portsmouth.

Back in San Francisco, Farley is scooped by his raven, Bruce. Phil Frank and
San Francisco Chronicle.

Ever the opportunist, Bruce puts his brandy to good use. The crew appear to be spending all their time in the crow's nest. Phil Frank and *San Francisco Chronicle.*

The *Jeremiah O'Brien* theater continued its World War II retrospective with "Casablanca," "Run Silent, Run Deep," "The Longest Day" and a rerun of "Patton."

A ship at sea works on an around-the-clock routine. The deck watches change six times a day at 12, 4 and 8. Because the *O'Brien*'s engine department stood three-hour watches, they changed eight times daily at 12, 3, 6 and 9. Those who didn't stand watches (the cooks, the day workers) started every day at the same time — 4 or 5 a.m. for the cooks, 8 a.m. for the day workers. All was pleasant and low-key. The engines purred along. The black gang oiled bearings, watched fluid levels, checked steam gauges and changed oil burners. The deck department cleaned, slushed cargo gear, chipped and painted.

Unlike on regular merchant ships, where rank and duties keep the various departments separate, on the *O'Brien*, no artificial barriers separated the crew. The traditional respect for officers was there; orders were never questioned. Otherwise, from captain and admiral, deck department and engine department,

Jack Carraher, master of the dinner chime, in his element. Mike Emery.

Everyone on the ship, including Bruce, reads that which appeals to them the most. Phil Frank and *San Francisco Chronicle*.

ABs, OSs, oilers, wipers, messmen, it was a democracy — all volunteers without rank or station — bound together in the great adventure, "the trip of a lifetime."

At mealtime every day, messman Jack Carraher went throughout the ship beating a cheerful tune on an old, hand-held xylophone. He paused at each open door to announce what was being served. "Tonight we have poached salmon, baked potatoes, rice pudding and a bunch of other stuff I've forgotten." Then, with a demonic cackling laugh, he would continue pounding his chimes until he got to the next room where he repeated the menu.

As each day brought us closer to England, the excitement mounted, a growing undercurrent of pride and *esprit de corps*. We were doing what we set out to do. We were getting closer and closer to proving to the world that a fifty-year-old ship, manned by volunteers with an average age of seventy-something, carrying a cargo of American determination and know-how, could do exactly what it said it would — return to Normandy for the 50th Anniversary of the D-Day landings.

The ship was now in the North Atlantic and it looked and felt like it — constant grey, dismal rain and drizzle. The wind, from the south, had a bitter edge to it.

As the *O'Brien* neared Europe, a four-engine airplane buzzed the ship one morning on the 8-to-12 watch, appearing with a roar out of the mists astern and disappearing ahead almost before we knew what happened. A few minutes later the VHF came to life,

"Jeremy O'Brien, Jeremy O'Brien, thees es the Channel patrol. Come een pleese."

"*Jeremiah O'Brien*. Go ahead."

"You are arriving for the D-Day commemoration, no?"

"That's correct."

"Welcome to Europe. We weel see you in Normandy on June the seexth. Channel patrol out."

"Thank you. *Jeremiah O'Brien*, out."

In the early morning of May 21 the ship passed the Lizard, a famous landmark on the southwesternmost tip of England. The day broke grey and drizzly and continued that way to nightfall. But we were in the English Channel. As we skirted about ten miles off the south coast of England, mists occasionally cleared and we saw brown bluffs and rich, green forests and meadows.

Coming up the east coast of the Isle of Wight, the wind increased to gale force. Passing Nab Light, we saw the pilot boat approach. Soon Capt. Carnegie, a pleasant, cheerful pilot, was on board, skillfully guiding us into the harbor, at no cost to the ship.

"We weren't expecting you until Monday," he said. We'll have to put you at anchor." It was Saturday. We were two days ahead of schedule.

We had traveled 7,894 miles from San Francisco since April 18.

Our first contact with England, this helicopter hovered around the ship for half an hour, filming the deck department painting the primer-spotted decks during our approach to the Isle of Wight. Bruce McMurtry.

21

PRELUDE TO
THE COMMEMORATION

On Monday morning the English pilot boarded with representatives of BBC, ITC, Reuters and AP. Now, we began to get a good idea of the *O'Brien*'s status as a celebrity. Cameras whirred, reporters were all over the ship talking into hand-held recorders. Weighing anchor, we started toward the harbor entrance.

Crowds stood on the ramparts of Southsea castle at the entrance to Portsmouth, waving and cheering, some swinging American flags. Two people held a large banner, "W'come JOB. Well done."

The *Jeremiah O'Brien* was escorted to a berth on South Jetty. "This quay is usually reserved for the *Britannia*," our pilot said. The Royal Berth — this was an honor, indeed.

Officers of the Royal Navy were assigned to orient us with Portsmouth, the Navy Yard and the 50th Anniversary

Escorted by two tugs, the Jeremiah O'Brien *approaches the entrance to Portsmouth Harbor.* The Times *[London].*

Commemoration. Included was the calendar of events for the days ahead:

D-Day 50th Anniversary 1994
Programme of Events

28-30 May	World War II Military Vehicle Rally, over 1,000 vehicles from all over the world will be assembled on Southsea Common
28-30 May	Navy Days, Portsmouth Naval Base
31 May	Propaganda Film Evening, at 8.00 pm D-Day Museum, Southsea. Women & Work in World War II and British Propaganda in World War II.
31 May-3 June	Portsmouth 800 Pageant which will include a section on the war years in Portsmouth. Starting at 8.00 pm each evening at Southsea Castle and Castle Field.
2nd June	Anniversary concert, Anglican Cathedral, Old Portsmouth (City of Caen Orchestra), 7.30 pm.
3 June	D-Day Concert at Portsmouth Guildhall, featuring the BBC Concert Orchestra and H.M. Royal Marines Band plus guest soloist and narrator starting at 7:30 pm.
4 June	Garden Party, HMS Dryad, 3.00 pm (invited guests only) Beat Retreat, HMS Excellent, 5 pm (invited guests only) D-Day 50 Dinner, for

	Heads of State, Guildhall (invited guests only), French Market, City Centre.
5 June	Unveiling of statue of Roosevelt & Churchill, 10.50 am, Southsea Veterans' Drumhead Service, Naval Memorial, Southsea Common, 11.00 am. Flypast by historic U.S., British and French aircraft. 1.00 pm (approx.), Southsea Common. A flotilla of historic vessels and ships from the Allied Forces will sail past Southsea Common.
6 June	Veterans Parade, D-Day Memorial, Southsea. John Dunn Show live from the D-Day Museum, Southsea.

British hospitality knew no limits. Without fuss or fanfare, they organized everything from installing telephones to transportation to suggesting places to visit.

One of the first social events was an invitation for the officers and crew to have drinks and a buffet lunch at HMS *Nelson*. Known as a Stone Frigate, HMS *Nelson* carries the name of a ship but is actually a base ashore. The concept dates from an early Royal Navy ship that was used as a supply depot. The ship never sailed and eventually the nearby shoreline worked its way around it. Soon the ship was landlocked but still retained its seagoing name. The tradition has held and now most smaller Royal Navy bases are named HMS even if they are office buildings.

The building was large, extending several floors. Grand, museum-quality paintings of sailing ships hung on the wood-paneled walls; other art depicted the Battle of Trafalgar (of course) and there were several finely-crafted models of sailing ships in glass cases. In the wardroom the bartenders (actually, Royal Navy sailors) busily pulled drafts of the famed British beer and ale with both hands.

One of the officers proudly told us that this was "the premier wardroom of the Royal Navy." It was easy to see why. The food and drink were excellent, our hosts were warm and friendly.

Now, the *Jeremiah O'Brien*'s glorious time in the Royal berth was up. The queen would soon arrive for the anniversary ceremonies and the *Britannia* was due in her berth to take the queen aboard. We let go our lines and proceeded farther into the Portsmouth Naval Base to the Middle Slip Jetty. Our course took us past HMS *Victory*, Admiral Nelson's flagship. Although landlocked in a graving dock, she flew a large British ensign off her stern. As we sailed past, HMS *Victory* lowered her flag in the traditional maritime salute of one ship to another. The *Jeremiah O'Brien* answered by lowering her flag, then raising it and watching as *Victory* raised hers. It was a singular honor, the flagship of England's greatest Naval hero saluting an old steel American freighter.

As we tied up and got our gangways out, a sleek sedan drove up and parked alongside the ship. Four men got out. Each had blow-dried hair and wore a carefully-buttoned suit and an equally carefully-unbuttoned trench coat. They boarded and soon disappeared behind the closed door of the captain's office with Adm. Patterson and Capt. Jahn. Soon word got out. They were the Secret Service and the White House staff.

Tom Patterson: "We were surprised and elated that the White House Secret Service advance team was there and said the president had decided to accept our invitation. So we had to really put in a lot of time with them to inspect the entire ship, determine his route and also to make arrangements for how the president would come aboard out in this open seaway called the Solent."

We returned HMS *Nelson*'s courtesies of the past few days by throwing a party for them. No. 2 tween deck was a severe contrast to the elegant surroundings of their wardroom. Where their halls were decorated with gold-framed masterpieces on wood-paneled walls, our steel bulkheads were adorned with steamship company flags, a board of seamen's knots and an engine room telegraph. But the British seemed to enjoy the ambiance. A catering company was hired to bring in food, beer and wine. Amidst trays of hot and cold canapes, French wine and good British ale, we

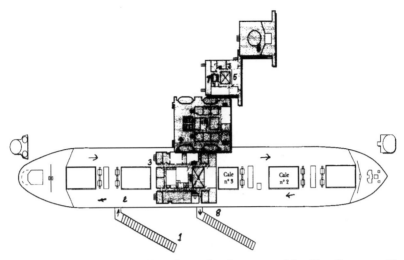

This exploded view of the ship shows the direction of the blue line tour. The numbers indicate key docent stations. National Liberty Ship Memorial.

mingled and talked, sharing the experiences and discoveries of the past few days. There was a general good feeling of Anglo-American camaraderie, a "special relationship."

May 28, the first day of Navy Days, was bleak and grey with a cool wind blowing. The *Jeremiah O'Brien* was the only merchant ship on hand. Navies of other countries were represented by the *U-19* (Germany), HNLMS *Zwaardvis* (Netherlands), BNS *Wandelaar* (Belgium), USS *Normandy* (United States), HMNorS *Utsira* (Norway), HMCS *Toronto* (Canada) and HMS *Active*, HMS *Illustrious* and HMS *Liverpool* (Great Britain).

Bruce has his own reaction to the crowds boarding the O'Brien. *Phil Frank and* San Francisco Chronicle.

Above, the Sea Cadets at attention before turning to for the day. Right, in a more relaxed pose. Jo Lawrence.

Thousands of visitors came aboard each day to see the ship and we were pleased that the self-guided tour seemed to be working. During the voyage, the crew had painted a blue line on the deck running to all the areas of the ship. Overlaid with a series of white arrows, it guided visitors to the aft house and guntub, then into the midships house, past the galley and crew messrooms, through the saloon, up two interior decks to the radio room and wheelhouse, up to the flying bridge, down the exterior of the midships house, forward to the bow guntub, back to No. 2, into No. 3 and the ship's store, then out the hatch to the main deck and off the ship.

We were assisted by young Sea Cadets from Tunbridge Wells and Whitestable who, dressed in crisp blue Naval cadet uniforms, marched to the ship in formation each morning and helped manage the visitors by handing out brochures and keeping them on the blue line. Only in their early teens, the cadets were refreshingly earnest and sincere. We all admired their professionalism and the disciplined way in which they conducted themselves.

Our English visitors were enthusiastic and, as one would expect of the British, very well-behaved. They especially enjoyed seeing the galley, the crew rooms, the engine room and the wheelhouse. They pointed out the coal stove to each other, looked or climbed down to the engine room to marvel at the old steam reciprocating engine and filed through the wheelhouse with interest taking in the combination of old-fashioned brass, World War II functionality and modern electronics.

The decks of the *Jeremiah O'Brien* are not very wide; the house, with its narrow passageways, and the hatches and equipment take up much of the space. There was not much room for anything like that number of people, but they squeezed by, good-humoredly, looking at everything with great interest, asking questions when they saw a docent or crew member. They were pleasant, orderly and appreciative.

But the interest of our visitors was not mere curiosity or coming to see a "celebrity." "It's an honor to be on board," people said. We must have heard the phrase a thousand times. The English observed the Commemoration very seriously, remembering the terrible days of half a century past. Many came very long distances to see the ship and shake our hands and thank us for coming. They remember the invasion vividly, and the ships that came to save England when all looked hopeless. They were very grateful to the U.S. then, and were vocal in expressing that gratitude to the crew, especially the veterans.

Everyone was impressed with the ship's state of preservation. And every day there were several old Liberty or "Sam" sailors (the British version of the Liberty carried the name Sam as a preface) with their discharge books and seaman's papers. Often they looked for "their room," the cabin they occupied on the Liberty ship they were on during or just after the war. Then it was,

Bruce recalls his European roots and his grandfather's tales of World War II.
Phil Frank and *San Francisco Chronicle.*

"Hasn't changed a bit. That's just where the sink was. I remember the bunk, exactly like that." They were all anxious to establish a sort of kinship, to share their experiences, to savor, once more, the thrill of being on a Liberty ship, and, for a few moments, like many of our crew, a chance to relive their youth.

The genuine friendliness of the British was humbling. None of us expected the emotion and gratitude displayed by the "reserved" English people.

Bill Bennett:

> The feeling that I got from the people of England, dozens and dozens of people who'd come up to me, and they talked about what we did for them during the war. And it got to the point where I started to tell the people no, you know, it's not what we did for you during the war. We produced goods, sent them over here, but you people sacrificed, you had your homes bombed all the time, you took the heat of the battle. We stayed home and lived in safety … I'm thanking *you* for what you did.

Bruce's ancestry goes back a long way, to both England and France, perhaps a form of Channel vision. Phil Frank and *San Francisco Chronicle.*

One of the events was a flying display by several types of aircraft. British tradition has it that flying shows take place over the oldest ship in the harbor and that was the *Jeremiah O'Brien*. Harrier jets hovered above our masts, the Red Arrows performed daring maneuvers as they trailed red, white and blue smoke from their gleaming red fuselages; helicopters flew sideways, backwards, and in almost every direction except forward; and large, low-flying cargo jets, Spitfires and Hurricanes passed overhead. The noise was deafening but it was a magnificent spectacle.

Marching bands were everywhere on the dock. The TS Unity Nautical Training Corps started and ended the day with a concert at the bandstand. The Herb Miller Orchestra played 40s music throughout the day. The Combined Bands of Tunbridge Wells and Whitestable marched along, their orchestrations of the calypso ballad "Jamaica Farewell" and the rock-and-roll classic "Wanderer" as marches, surprising everyone in their crisp execution and sound. The cheerful tinkling of bell lyres gave their music an unsurpassed, upbeat quality. At the end of the day, at 5:30 p.m., The Band of Her Majesty's Royal Marines Portsmouth beat retreat in precise formation.

Tom Patterson: "We entered into the spirit of their Navy Days which is kind of like our version of Fleet Week. The twenty-eighth, twenty-ninth and thirtieth we had a total of about twenty-four thousand visitors on board — one day nearly eleven thousand — all very happy English people from all generations, remembering what the ships like the *Jeremiah O'Brien* did for them in World War II."

The crew usually wore *Jeremiah O'Brien* crew jackets or polo shirts with the ship's baseball cap when they went ashore. It was like an identification badge. We were frequently stopped on the street and asked about the ship, treated to ales in the pubs, and often told, "No charge, mate. We're 'appy you made it over," when entering places that normally charged admission.

Now, the Sea Cadet corps would be leaving us. It was surprising how attached we became to them in such a short time. Everyone in the crew admired the cadets' discipline, their politeness, and the courteous yet firm way in which they handled the crowds. From the first few hours on board, we found them a wonderful help in keeping people from wandering off the blue line tour and preventing bottlenecks where the line came back on itself.

Being young, they were easy to semi-adopt, sneaking them Otis Spunkmeyer cookies from time to time, giving them breakfast, lunch and dinner if they were on board, making sure they had soft drinks or a place to sit if tired. The cadets were a particular bright spot even amidst the hoopla of the occasion and we knew we would miss them when they left. It was a surprisingly emotional farewell.

Southampton has a different maritime history than Portsmouth, but one perhaps closer to the heart of a merchant mariner. Our Southampton berth once saw the *Queen Mary, Queen Elizabeth, Titanic, Mauretania, Aquitania* and other blue riband leviathans board and debark passengers bound to and from America. Across the slip was the quay used by the SS *United States* in her glory days. Just a short distance farther into the port was the pier used by the *Jeremiah O'Brien* when she made her eleven trips to Normandy.

As in Portsmouth, hundreds of visitors came every day, including more former "Sam" ship sailors. Clutching their certification books and photos to "prove" it, they looked into the engine room, galley, wheelhouse and cabins, their eyes misting as they talked about memories of the war and their youth.

Ruth Robson, storekeeper:

> I don't think any of us in America know what those people went through. The people in England, the bombings, and the people in France, under the tyranny of occupation. I don't think we could fathom, we just don't realize what our being there did for those

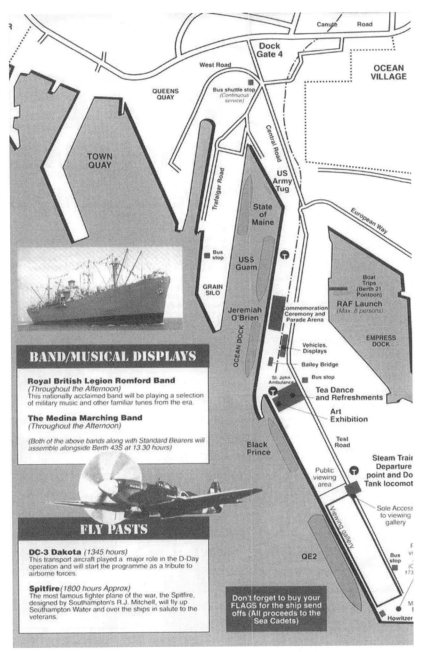

The official program shows the Jeremiah O'Brien's *berth next to the parade arena and gives the locations of the other ships in Southampton.* Association of British Ports.

people. It's an experience you have to live through to know and none of us ever did.

It was a very emotional experience. Our ship seems to have touched a lot of people, it really did, and even young folks, not just the men and women that were connected with Liberty ships when they were young, but the children of people that sailed. And mothers and fathers bringing their little children because grandpa sailed on one of these.

Those are things that you can't put into words, you have to experience their happening to you and see it yourself. Because there's a lot of emotion there that's hard to express in words. You saw the expressions on their faces and the tears in their eyes and heard the sound of their voices.

Friday, June 3 began with blustery winds and fast-moving clouds. D-Day weather, everyone called it. The media coverage for the "Commemoration," as it was called in England, was almost overwhelming now. The newspapers were filled with pictures of D-Day 1944. The great leaders of the war were gone, but interviews with veterans, many of whom had been young soldiers, evoked the awful, yet exciting event. "The invasion" was what Europeans called D-Day, and on both sides of the Channel, historic ceremonies were marking the greatest maritime operation that ever was, that changed the course of history. TV crews and big-name news anchors from the U.S. broadcast via satellite, even as their European counterparts filled the local airwaves with news, interviews, old war movies and film clips.

Amidst the tidal wave of information and pictures, the *Jeremiah O'Brien* held its own. Outdone in every department by newer, bigger, faster, more beautiful ships, none could approach her unique historic presence and the "ugly duckling" basked in the special limelight.

The officers and crew of the *O'Brien* were treated with warm hospitality everywhere we went. Capt. Lomax, a former Liberty ship officer, brought aboard the June issue of *Shipping Today and Yesterday*, which was devoted entirely to Normandy, June 1944, and featured the *Jeremiah O'Brien* as its centerfold. The crew went out and bought up all the copies they could find.

The *QE2* came alongside the adjacent berth. The *O'Brien* was keeping fine company, indeed. The wind was howling at gale force and our ship was surging at her moorings but the large, majestic liner eased her way alongside so skillfully it looked easy.

Now the real countdown to the Commemoration — D-Day plus 50 years — began. All ship movements in the harbor had been carefully calculated weeks earlier. Each vessel was to sail at an assigned time so that visitors could see them pass out of Southampton toward the Solent. The *Jeremiah O'Brien*'s scheduled departure time was 5:30 p.m.

In the afternoon the admiral and the chief mate went to HMS *Illustrious* on behalf of Capt. Jahn for a briefing of events. Capt. Lomax drove us in his Rover so we arrived in style, were piped aboard, and escorted to the wardroom where coffee and cookies were set out. In attendance were the commanding officers and staff of all the ships of the nations scheduled to attend the queen's review and the ceremonies at Normandy — Australia, Belgium, Canada, Czech State, France, Greece, Luxembourg, Netherlands, New Zealand, Norway, Poland, Slovakia, the United Kingdom and the U.S.A. There was a reception after the briefing. It was a unique opportunity to meet our counterparts from many nations.

England was swarming with distinguished and other visitors now and events came one on the heels of the other — a D-Day Concert at the Portsmouth Guildhall, featuring the BBC Concert Orchestra and H.M. Royal Marines Band, a Garden Party at Southwick House (the headquarters from which General Eisenhower issued the final order to launch the invasion), attended by 1,000 veterans and the heads of state, Beating Retreat at HMS *Excellence.*

The Beating Retreat ceremony, now symbolic, stems from the time when soldiers were called back to their barracks from nearby towns to prepare for battle. It marked the end of peacetime activities and the beginning of war. In this case it symbolized the embarkation of the invasion force. Five thousand veterans, heads of state, the Queen Mother and Princess Anne were on hand for the occasion. Military bands from the U.K., U.S.A., Canada and France, and the Queen's Colour Squadron of the Royal Air Force marched in perfect step, each making a separate appearance on the grassy green field dressed in uniforms of red, blue and khaki. The music was inspiring and professional, military and precise. But the biggest round of applause went to the Band of the United States Air Force in Europe. As they played Glenn Miller's "In the Mood," two members broke ranks and jitterbugged, then chased each other through their fellow musicians who swung and swayed in time with the music. It was the hit of the Retreat. Even the Queen Mother was seen smiling delightedly and clapping her hands. All the bands came on the field for the finale which included the traditional "manning the mast," British sailors climbing in step to the top of the ship's mast and yards at the far end of the field.

The evening was capped by a banquet in the Portsmouth City Guildhall with the heads of state of Australia, Belgium, Czech State, Greece, New Zealand, Norway, Poland, Slovakia and the United States as invited guests.

Despite the persistent drizzle, the pier area alongside the ship had a festive air. Vintage steam trains chugged back and forth along the length of the quay. Veterans in uniform mingled with soldiers and sailors. Bands played and marched.

We sailed at 1730. It was cold and wet. We began casting off the lines, not knowing that this routine departure would be one of those transcendent moments, an epiphany, a memory to last a lifetime. British Standard Bearers were gathered on the pier in formation. As the lines fell, the band on the quay played "The Star-Spangled Banner" and "God Save the Queen." Then the last line was gone and the tugs backed us slowly out of the berth. The final notes of the music faded. In the silence that fell, Paul Dunellon, the head of security for

Just before departure at Southampton (note the raised gangway), from the pier looking up toward the ship. Author's collection.

One of the bands at Southampton marching past shortly before we left the dock for the anchorage. Jo Lawrence.

Associated British Ports, came forward on the dock and shouted, "Thank you for 1944."

In that moment, the events that had brought us here — beginning in 1944, throughout the voyage, our recent experiences with the English people — suddenly came together in an almost overwhelming wave. On the bridge Adm. Patterson wiped away a tear. Capt. Jahn was misty eyed. All over the ship, the crew above decks stood silently in the rain, looking across the widening water to the veterans standing in salute, the bands and the people on the pier. It was a moment of grace, never to be forgotten.

We backed into the channel and turned toward the Solent. As we got up speed and let go the tugs we passed the *QE2*. Her whistle sounded the three long blasts of the traditional maritime salute. As we continued down the channel a single Spitfire came out of the clouds and rain, like a ghost of the past, and flew overhead, leading the way out of Southampton, then disappeared in the drizzle.

View of the anchorage in the Solent taken from the flying bridge of the Jeremiah O'Brien *on the morning of June 5.* Author's collection.

There was a lot of talk of "D-Day weather" from those who were in the invasion but the following day looked more promising. Dawn came with a clear and fine sky. A slight breeze was on the water. During the night more ships came in to the anchorage. We were now in the company of the USS *George Washington*, the *QE2*, the *State of Maine*, the *Vistafjord*, the USS *Guam*, the *Canberra* and others, some thirty ships in all. It was probably the last time in history so many historic and famous ships would be gathered in one place.

Ashore, the major event of the Commemoration was the Drumhead service. It was held in front of the Naval War Memorial on Southsea Common with 7,500 people attending.

The Drumhead ceremony is one of the most solemn in the long tradition of the English military. It signifies "The Forces Committed," the point at which there is no turning back. Guards of Honor from the Royal Marines and the U.S. Marine Corps took part. The Archbishop of Canterbury presided, speaking over an

Yachts, tour boats, ferries and small craft toured the Solent in the morning hours before the Queen's review. Here, the Waverly, *a famous British paddle wheeler, passes as the* O'Brien *crew waves.* Marty Wefald.

Front cover, left, and center, below, of the official program for the Queen's Review. The Jeremiah O'Brien *was in good company and part of what probably would be the last time in history for such a gathering of ships.* The Queen's Harbor Master, Portsmouth.

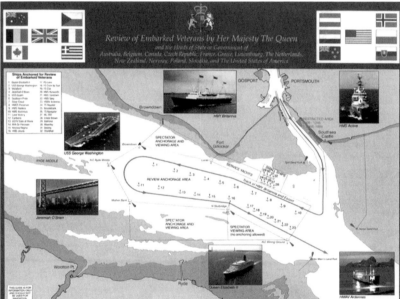

altar which was an upturned drum covered by flags. "We gather here to remember with pride and thanksgiving and, yes, even with cheers, those who gave everything for freedom fifty years ago and who in our hearts we have never forgotten."

The *Britannia* was scheduled to leave her berth at 1230 on June 5. Shortly after 1230 we saw the Trinity House vessel *Patricia* come out of the entrance to Portsmouth Harbor. Trinity

The Britannia *passes, escorted and followed by so many boats that their wakes churned the Solent white.* Elizabeth Wade.

House was once responsible for all maritime piloting and aids to navigation in England. The *Patricia* is the only vessel allowed to precede the Royal Yacht in review. Then came the *Britannia*, sleek and elegant with her white superstructure and deep blue

The Queen's Review made a splash in the next day's newspapers. Daily Telegraph.

hull. President and Mrs. Clinton were aboard as were other heads of state. As she rounded the outer Spit Buoy, turning west to begin the review of anchored ships, small boats of every size and description converged on her like drones to a queen bee. Motor boats, sailing yachts, steam boats — there were so many small boats around the royal yacht that they literally churned the Solent white. At the same moment planes appeared in the sky, passing down the Solent and over the fleet. First came historic planes, Royal Navy Swordfish and a Firefly, followed by a Lancaster bomber escorted by fighters — a Spitfire and a Hurricane. With them was a B-17 and a TBM Avenger. Then came a formation of more Spitfires with a Sea Fury, an F4U Corsair, a P-38 Lightning, a P-51 Mustang and a P-47 Thunderbolt. The fourth flight was a group of planes formed up to spell out the number "50." These were followed by sleek modern jet fighters and bombers from all the gathered nations. The entire air formation was twenty miles long.

President and Mrs. Clinton with Capt. Jahn and Adm. Patterson. Note the excellent taste the president and first lady display in baseball caps and sweaters. Mike Emery.

For the crew of the *Jeremiah O'Brien* the highlight of the event took place shortly afterward when President and Mrs. Clinton came aboard. We saw a fleet of small white boats approaching. Despite our best intentions of maintaining decorum, everyone clamored to the railing. Mrs. Clinton stepped out to the float, and then the president, himself. At that moment the presidential flag was raised on our halyard, the first time in history a presidential flag was flown on a U.S. merchant ship.

Tom Patterson: "They were brought over in the captain's gig from the *George Washington* and with this perfect lee they were able to come right aboard and walk up the gangway. The captain and I met them at the head of the accommodation ladder, saluted the president, welcomed them aboard and took them into the officers' saloon."

There were gifts for the presidential party, including sweaters and baseball caps with the ship's logo on them.

The president and the first lady meet the crew of the Jeremiah O'Brien. *Note the press corps on top of the hatch (left) and beside the guntub, right.* Marty Wefald.

Clinton Visits Crew on Jeremiah O'Brien

In San Francisco, the visit by President and Mrs. Clinton rated a front page photo in the San Francisco Chronicle. San Francisco Chronicle.

Soon Adm. Patterson and Capt. Jahn escorted President and Mrs. Clinton onto the main deck. The president was wearing one of our baseball caps and sweaters. Mrs. Clinton also had on one of the caps. As Admiral Patterson introduced each crew member to the president, they shook hands, exchanged a few words and went on. "This is a great day for the merchant marine," "I'm proud to be on board," "You have a fine ship."

Capt. Jahn and Mrs. Clinton followed but the first lady began to lag farther and farther behind as each member of the crew seemed to want to talk with her more. Her smile was dazzling, her manner relaxed and friendly.

They finished the foredeck, then went aft and shook hands with everyone there. Before leaving, President and Mrs. Clinton returned to the foredeck, he saluted, waved and said, "Thank you. Thank you for what you've done."

Someone shouted, "Three cheers for the president of the United States. Hip, hip, hip,"

"HOORAY," everyone shouted. There were no Democrats or Republicans, just Americans, feeling proud and patriotic.

The president and the first lady went down the gangway and, smiling, turned and waved, then got in the boat. Soon they were on their way to the USS *George Washington* where they would stay for the next few days.

Tom Patterson:

> It was the greatest day of my life; a wonderful event. First of all, for the SS *Jeremiah O'Brien* to have the president and first lady on board to recognize our Commemoration Voyage. It was a great tribute to the ship and to the crew. And, second, no president in anybody's knowledge had ever been aboard a United States-flag merchant ship. To have our Maritime Administrator and our president and the head of the AFL-CIO be there to witness this was a great day for the U.S. Merchant Marine.

Capt. Jahn, a reticent man, didn't say much, but as he walked about his ship, he looked both pleased and proud.

Now, a continuous stream of ships sailed out of Portsmouth Harbor bound for Normandy. Heading this international flotilla were a force of eleven warships from the United Kingdom, the United States, the Netherlands, France, Canada, Poland, Greece, Belgium and Norway led by the flagship HMS *Edinburgh*. These were followed by the royal yacht, more Naval ships, passenger liners, small boats and vessels carrying the veterans of 50 years past. *Britannia* passed down the center as each ship cast a wreath in the Commemorative Act of International Maritime Forces. A Lancaster bomber flew over the *Canberra* releasing two million poppies. The flowers hung for a second, then fluttered downward to make a carpet of red on the waves before sinking into the choppy seas.

After dark, the warships slipped in and anchored off the famous beaches and invasion sites — Arromanches, Ouistreham,

Omaha, Utah, Sword, Juno, Gold and Pointe du Hoc, awaiting D-Day Plus 50 Years.

A dozen Hercules C130 aircraft from the U.S. Air Force dropped 560 paratroopers from the 101st and 82nd Airborne Divisions, along with thirty-eight veterans aged 68 to 83, at St. Mère Église.

Shortly afterward, twelve RAF, three French and three Royal Canadian Air Force C130s dropped 1,300 paratroopers at Pegasus Bridge near Caen. These were followed by historic and modern planes which were to take part in ceremonies at Arromanches and Omaha Beach.

The *Jeremiah O'Brien* sailed on in a southerly direction. Ahead and astern were other ships bound for the same destination. Overhead, planes flew on the same course. It was early evening, Sunday, June 5, 1994 and the *O'Brien* was bound for her appointment in Normandy.

DECK LOG of the S.S. / M.V. JEREMIAH O'BRIEN from _____ to _____ **Date** JUNE 5, 1994 SUNDAY

OWNED BY UNITED STATES OF AMERICA

VOYAGE NUMBER — ZONE DESCRIPTION

DECK LOG—REMARKS

0001 - Vessel at anchor ...

0400 AT ANCHOR 50-45.8U 1-01.2 W 12 FTM UNDER KEEL
0730 SHORTEN ANCHOR TO 5 SHOTS
0800 VESSEL SECURE
0915 ...
1200 ...

1340 ...
1410 ...
1435 PRESIDENT PARTY AWAY.

1515 - COMMENCE HEAVING ANCHOR. 1530- SEE & STOP 1555- ANCHOR AWEIGH
1627- No Men's Land Boat Aboard. 1652- SOUTHAMPTON PILOT RETURNING BY
DEEP SEA PILOT CAPT C.R. LUKE HURST AND AWAY. ...
SOUTHAMPTON. ...

2000 VESSEL STEAM

2130 APPROACHING POINT ...

22

RETURN TO NORMANDY

From the deck log, SS *Jeremiah O'Brien*:

> June 6, 1994.
> 0000 Approaching anchorage at Point Du Hoc — Arrival.
> 0118 Let go stbd. anchor — 4 shots on deck.
> 0130 FWE. Riding to moderate strain on 4 shots of chain
>   in 14 meters of water. Point Du Hoc [bearing] 212°T,
>   0.8 miles.

The first American ceremony, to honor the memory of those lost in battle, took place at sunrise aboard the USS *George Washington*.

It was wet, with a cold wind that whipped across the carrier's flight deck. American and Allied warships could hardly be seen through the fog.

265

DECK LOG of the SS/MV __Jeremiah O'Brien__ OWNED BY UNITED STATES OF AMERICA from __Southampton, England__ to __Point Du Hoc__ Date __June 6, 1994__ ZONE DESCRIPTION __-1__ VOYAGE NUMBER __8__

WEATHER OBSERVATIONS

HOURS	COURSE					WIND		VISIBILITY (MILES)	BAROMETER (INCHES)	TEMPERATURE			WAVES			SWELL	
						DIRECTION	FORCE			DRY BULB	WET BULB	SEA WATER	DIRECTION	HEIGHT (FEET)		DIRECTION	HEIGHT

DECK LOG—REMARKS

0000 – Approaching at Point Du Hoc – Anchored
0118 – Let go Stbd Anchor – 4 shots on deck
0130 – Full away. Proceed to Wigwam Stern Channel
Meters at Wheel. Point Du Hoc 0212°T, 0.8 miles

D & Ho. Boats away with crew members

0800 Vessel secure at anchor

1200 Vessel at anchor, center by GPS

1830 & 0070°

2000 Vessel steady
2200 S/b OBS coming
2400 Pilot Capt.
2400 Securing

On the *O'Brien* many of the crew tuned their personal radios to the BBC which was full of reminiscences of the invasion and recordings of some of the original newscasts. The darkness slowly faded revealing naval vessels at anchor with us, giving some sense of what it was like fifty years before, when the *O'Brien*, carrying hundreds of American troops, rode at anchor in the Solent, awaiting orders to begin the first of her eleven landings on "Omaha" and "Utah" beachheads. Through binoculars we saw the shoreline, Pointe du Hoc itself, a low brown bluff capped with green. Set slightly back was a pavilion with a white roof and flag standards. To one side of the pavilion was a field with several helicopters at rest, their drooping blades making them look sad and reverent. People walked along the cliffs, heads bowed or gazing seaward.

Except for necessary watches, and the galley crew, of course, all work was suspended for that day. The *Jeremiah O'Brien* rested easily in the choppy seas. The mood aboard was quiet.

We spent the morning studying the chart and coastline. Using binoculars, for we were anchored off away from the coast, we searched the shoreline until we found the historic beaches — Omaha, Utah, Gold, Sword.

Ashore, tens of thousands of veterans fulfilled their pilgrimage to Normandy on the beaches and in the cemeteries. At the American Cemetery in Colleville, President Clinton, accompanied by other heads of state, paid homage to those who lay buried there. In one of his finest speeches, he said,

> In these last days of ceremonies, we have heard wonderful words of tribute. Now we come to this hallowed place that speaks, more than anything else, in silence. Here on this quiet plateau, on this small piece of American soil, we honor those who gave their lives for us fifty crowded years ago.
>
> Today, the beaches of Normandy are calm. If you walk these shores on a summer's day, all you might hear is the laughter of children playing on the sand, or the cry of sea gulls overhead, or

Phil Frank and *San Francisco Chronicle.*

perhaps the ringing of a distant church bell. The simple sounds of freedom barely breaking the silence. Peaceful sounds. Ordinary sounds. But June 6, 1944, was the least ordinary day of the 20th century. On that chill dawn, these beaches echoed with the sounds of staccato gunfire, the roar of aircraft, the thunder of bombardment. And through the wind and the waves came the soldiers, out of their landing craft and into the war, away from their youth and toward a savage place many of them would, sadly, never leave.

They had come to free a continent — the Americans, the British, the Canadians, the Poles, the French Resistance, the Norwegians and others. They had all come to stop one of the greatest forces of evil the world has ever known.

As news of the invasion broke, back home in America, people held their breath. In Boston, commuters stood reading the news on the electric sign at South Station; in New York, the Statue of Liberty, its torch blacked out since Pearl Harbor, was lit at sunset for fifteen minutes; and in Newcastle, Pennsylvania, a young mother named Polly Elliot wrote to her husband, Frank, a corporal in the Army, "D-Day had arrived. The first thought of all of us was a prayer."

Below us are the beaches where Corporal Elliot's battalion and so many other Americans landed — Omaha and Utah, proud names from America's heartland, part of the biggest gamble of the war, the greatest crusade, yes, the longest day.

During those first hours on bloody Omaha, nothing seemed to go right. Landing craft were ripped apart by mines and shells, tanks sent to protect them had sunk, drowning their crews; enemy fire raked the invaders as they stepped into chest-high water and waded past the floating bodies of their comrades. And as the stunned survivors of the

The front page of the Stars and Stripes *commemorative edition carried a photo of the 1944 invasion.* Author's collection.

The back page of the Stars and Stripes *commemorative edition was a reproduction of their issue fifty years earlier.* Author's collection.

first wave huddled behind the seawall, it seemed the invasion might fail.

Hitler and his followers had bet on it. They were sure the Allied soldiers were soft, weakened by liberty and leisure, by the mingling of races and religion. They were sure their totalitarian youth had more discipline and zeal. But then something happened.

Although many of the American troops found themselves without officers on unfamiliar ground next to soldiers they didn't know, one by one they got up. They inched forward and together, in groups of threes and fives and tens, the sons of democracy improvised and mounted their own attacks.

At that exact moment, on these beaches, the forces of freedom turned the tide of the 20th century. These soldiers knew that staying put meant certain death. But they were also driven by the voice of free will and responsibility nurtured in Sunday schools, town halls and sandlot ball games — the voice that told them to stand up and move forward, saying "You can do it. And if you don't, no one else will." And as Captain Joe Damson led his company up this bluff, and as others followed his lead, they secured a foothold for freedom.

Today, many of them are here among us. Oh, they may walk with a little less spring in their step and their ranks are growing thinner. But let us never forget — when they were young, these men saved the world. And so let us now ask them, all the veterans of the Normandy campaign, to stand if they can and be recognized. The freedom they fought for was no abstract concept. It was the stuff of their daily lives.

Well, millions of our GIs did return home from that war to build up our nations and enjoy life's sweet pleasures, but on this field there are 9,386 who did not — 33 pairs of brothers, a father and his son, 11 men from tiny Bedford, Virginia, and Corporal Frank Elliot, killed near these bluffs by a German shell on D-Day.

They were the fathers we never knew, the uncles we never met, the friends who never returned, the heroes we can never repay. They gave us our world. And those simple sounds of freedom we hear today are their voices speaking to us across the years.

At this place, let us honor all the Americans who lost their lives in World War II. Let us remember as well that over 40 million human beings from every side perished — soldiers on the field of battle, Jews in the ghettos and death camps, civilians ravaged by shell fire and famine. May God give rest to all their souls.

Fifty years later, what a different world we live in. Germany, Japan and Italy, liberated by our victory, now stand among our closest allies and the staunchest defenders of freedom. Russia, decimated during the war and frozen afterward in communism and Cold War, has been reborn in democracy. And as freedom rings from Prague to Kiev, the liberation of this continent is nearly complete.

Now the question falls to our generation. How will we build upon the sacrifice of D-Day's heroes? Like the soldiers of Omaha Beach, we cannot stand still. We cannot stay safe by doing so. Avoiding today's problems would be our own generation's appeasement, for just as freedom has a price, it also has a purpose, and its name is progress.

Today our mission is to expand freedom's reach farther, to tap the full potential of each of our own citizens, to strengthen our families, our faith and our communities, to fight indifference and intolerance, to keep our nation strong and to light the lives of those still dwelling in the darkness of undemocratic rule.

Our parents did that, and more. We must do nothing less. They struggled in war so that we might strive in peace. We know that progress is not inevitable, but neither was victory upon these beaches. Now, as then, the inner voice tells us to stand up and move forward. Now, as then, free people must choose.

Fifty years ago, the first Allied soldiers to land here in Normandy came not from the sea but from the sky. They were called pathfinders, the first paratroopers to make the jump. Deep in the darkness, they descended upon these fields to light beacons for the airborne assault that would soon follow. Now, near the dawn of a new century, the job of lighting those beacons falls to our hands. To you who brought us here, I promise we will be the new pathfinders, for we are the children of your sacrifice.

Thank you, and God bless you all.

Fifty years ago, on a beach not far from this ground, an event took place that changed the world forever. It happened during a great war. It happened in a place called...

NORMANDY

23

ON THE MEDWAY

C hatham Dockyard started out as a safe harbor for British warships in the reign of Henry VIII. Here, his vessels were protected from winter storms and could be refitted from a storehouse located just off Dock Road in an area later called Gun Wharf. In addition, the ships were conveniently situated near London, should the King take time from pursuing his successive wives to examine them.

When Elizabeth I took the throne in 1558, she decided the cozy, well-hidden location at Chatham was ideal for her new dockyard — a perfect place to build ships for the fighting fleet. In 1585 a huge chain was put across the Medway as a defense against a Spanish invasion. The first ship built at Chatham, the *Sunne*, was launched in 1586 and in 1588 she joined the "grand fleet" of the Medway which sailed out to assist Sir Francis Drake in defeating the Spanish Armada.

Approaching Chatham the Jeremiah O'Brien *steamed past a fallen sister, the Liberty ship* Richard Montgomery, *which went down in 1944 with 7,000 tons of bombs on board.* R.L. Ratcliffe.

In 1765 Britain's most famous warship, HMS *Victory*, was launched at Chatham. Twelve years later, the twelve-year-old Horatio Nelson came through Chatham as a young midshipman on his way to his uncle's ship, *Raisonnable*. He got lost and in the course of his wanderings caught a glimpse of his brilliant future in the form of the *Victory* at anchor in the Medway.

The basin at Chatham was a perfect reflecting pool. Author's collection.

Chatham was a busy dockyard during both World Wars, building submarines and sloops and refitting 1,360 other ships. But in 1984 the yard closed.

Rather than let the area languish, the yards became a museum complex with an adjacent real estate development and industrial park. *Jeremiah O'Brien* was the centerpiece at the grand opening of the industrial park, a living monument that evoked the yard's past while pointing toward its future.

The morning of June 9 hit us like a hammer — school kids all over the place playing with the telegraph, blowing the whistle, ringing the general alarm, opening closed doors, flipping switches, touching, feeling, prodding and pulling. Their harried teachers tried to keep them in order but, like kids everywhere, they had to try everything. Eventually we got the telegraph locked in position, the foghorn tied off, doors locked and our British and crew docents in place.

The Jeremiah O'Brien *was the center of attraction for Chatham Maritime as evidenced by this poster. It was a unique honor in an equally unique location.* Chatham Maritime.

Once the children left we settled down for another day as a tourist attraction.

Their Worships, the Lord Mayors of the three cities that shared the industrial park — Rochester, Gillingham and Chatham — visited the exhibit and the ship with their staffs. Resplendent with their chains of office draped about their shoulders, they toured the ship from bow to fantail and wheelhouse to engine room.

Dick Brannon, our chief engineer, took great pride in showing visitors around, the engine room clean and neat and well swept down and everything looking beautiful. He showed them the engines, the boilers. One person asked in absolute sincerity,

The reception and cabaret were one of many highlights of our stay in Chatham. Chatham Maritime.

"Where are the boilers that you used to steam across the ocean, that you came across in, that you steamed the ship with? These are on display, yes, but where's the real boilers.? And Dick said, "These are the boilers. This is the engine and these are the boilers."

From the moment we docked at Chatham, it was clear this visit would not be a weak anticlimax to the events of previous weeks.

A special D-Day display was housed in a large white tent just a few yards away from the ship. It was an evocative exhibit of life in Britain during the war. Inside the tent, the visitor walked through an Anderson Shelter. Made of corrugated metal it contained benches, an air raid shelter lamp and sandbags. There was a wartime kitchen complete with furniture, utensils, gas

Gunner's Mate Otto Sommerauer demonstrates the forward gun for a fascinated young admirer. Mike Emery.

masks, utility radio, ration books, recipes and an actress playing a wartime mother. Nearby was a D-Day exhibition of newspaper headlines, maps of the landings, photos and letters to the forces from General Dwight D. Eisenhower. The favorite of the *O'Brien* crew was the display of Liberty ships featuring ship models, plans and photographs.

On June 10 a special D-Day 50th Anniversary commemoration was held aboard the ship in No.2. This was followed by a cabaret — a series of skits and songs provided by an amateur troop, the Phoenix Players, whose professionalism was astounding. Dressed in wartime uniforms, they sang World War II songs and kept everyone entertained. The next evening the cities of Rochester and Gillingham threw a party on the *O'Brien* and the entire crew was invited. A well-stocked bar and a well-set buffet were laid out, followed by another performance by the "Cabaret."

The entertainments continued, as did commemorative services for those lost during the war. The two types of events were never far apart, a paradox. We celebrated life while remembering the dead.

We were continually surprised and touched at the depth of gratitude the British felt toward America for helping them during World War II. Our ship seemed to symbolize all Liberty ships which in turn symbolized all that America did to help. We frequently heard remarks like, "You saved our bacon. America saved us. We would have lost the war without the Yanks." Even more amazing to us was that this history was taught in the schools and was part of the education of even the youngest children. A cute little blond-headed boy, no more than five or six years old, came to a crew member and said, "During the war the Germans were bombing us and the *Jeremiah O'Brien* came over and brought us food when we were starving."

More than 15,000 people came to see the *O'Brien* in Chatham. The sailing board was posted for June 15. Next port: London.

A Rochester town crier, resplendent in black hat and red uniform, took up a position at the foot of the gangway. Ringing his bell, he periodically announced the departure of the ship. As we prepared to pull in the accommodation ladder, one of the crew suggested he come along. He hesitated a moment, looked around, and bounded up the gangway.

The pilot skillfully guided the ship out, across the outer basin and into the tidal locks. As the gates opened and we exited into the river, a lone Scottish piper, in full highland dress, marched in time step across the face of the dock. The music from his bagpipes echoed across the hull of the *Jeremiah O'Brien*.

We blew three long blasts of the whistle in farewell to Chatham and proceeded down the Medway, the notes of "Scotland the Brave" fading behind us.

Right, Bosun Rich Reed at the anchor windlass for departure. Jo Lawrence.

Left, the Rochester town crier at the foot of our gangway announcing the ship's departure. Jo Lawrence.

24

LONDON

Clearing the River Medway, the con was turned over to a Thames River pilot. The ride up the Thames was spectacular. As the ship snaked her way upriver the vista changed from flat, lush green countryside to gritty industrial areas then to the magnificent urban skyline of London, every ship and barge along the way saluting with its whistle. Late in the afternoon we went through the Thames River Barrier, truly a wonder of the modern world. Opened in 1984, it is a series of

The futuristic looking towers of the Thames River Barrier. Author's collection.

Changing pilots. Because of the distance involved, we used three pilots going up the Thames. Marty Wefald.

futuristic towers planted across the river which raise a man-made barrier from the river bottom to prevent flooding from the North Sea. The pilot guided the ship past the Royal Naval College, where we were honored by the salute of a midshipman in full dress uniform standing at the wrought iron riverside gate. The *O'Brien* dipped her ensign in answer. In the distance, jutting above the trees, we saw the Royal Observatory at Greenwich and, soon, the *Cutty Sark*, elegantly resting in her graving dock.

On both sides of the river, people came out from their apartments, pubs and office

Passing the Royal Naval College at Greenwich. Marty Wefald.

buildings at the sound of our whistle, shouting and waving flags, toasting with pints of ale and cheering our passage. The air was charged with a holiday spirit.

The *O'Brien* approached central London and the great Tower Bridge. Motor traffic on both sides of the river stopped. The twin spans slowly opened. The old ship, proudly decorated with vividly colored signal flags from stem to stern, corporate flags aloft and our largest American flag on the steaming gaff at the mizzen mast, passed slowly through into the heart of London. The crowd on the bridge, above and below, waved and cheered. We waved and cheered back.

Crew's News for June 15:

> Good evening, San Francisco.
>
> This is the Voice of the *Jeremiah O'Brien*. *Jeremiah O'Brien* departed Chatham Dockyard today and proceeded up the Thames River to London. Returning the whistle blasts from several passing vessels with the *O'Brien*'s steam whistle brought hundreds of citizens onto their shoreside sundecks. Upon seeing our ship arms waved and cheers were heard. We

The Jeremiah O'Brien *approaching Tower Bridge in London.* Author's collection.

Tower Bridge opens, the first time in history for a Liberty ship. Marty Wefald.

We arrive at "The Pool of London." Don Maskell.

Capt. Jahn, left, and Adm. Patterson spent most of their first days in London on courtesy calls. Here, they enjoy a sherry with representatives of Trinity House. Mike Emery.

passed through the Tower Bridge at 1940 and moored alongside HMS *Belfast.* This well maintained ship served in the entire period of World War II. She acted as the Royal Navy's Naval Bombardment Command vessel for the three beaches assaulted by British and American forces at Normandy. It is midnight now and the view of Tower Bridge and other buildings in the area is a sight to behold; and we have the honor of being right in the middle of it.

  Jeremiah O'Brien — out.

It was a great honor to have Tower Bridge open for our old ship, and to be berthed in the Pool of London, in the very heart of the city.

Tom Patterson: "This was the first time in history that a Liberty ship had actually sailed under Tower Bridge.

During our London stay, Pat McCafferty brings aboard, appropriately, a case of Liberty Ale. Mike Emery.

The ship opened to visitors at 1000 the following morning. We had 698 people on board, many of them old "Sam" sailors looking for "my old room," and complimenting the engine crew on how good the engine room looked. Many others wanted to be part of the historic event and we hosted special groups and private tours. Even the famed shipping line, P&O, rented No.2 tween deck for a private catered party.

There was a private tour of the engine room on the *O'Brien* for the Foster-Wheeler company, manufacturer of our ship's boilers in 1943. Our engineers showed the boilers off, and the Foster-Wheeler people observed, both with justifiable pride. Then followed a party on HMS *Belfast*.

Once again, we listened to the people who had a story to tell about a Liberty ship when they were young. They would unfold their papers and, with tears in their eyes, say something like, "I went to Long Beach at sixteen years old and lived in a hotel for two weeks while they painted my ship to bring it back to the U.K."

To the mariner, Historic Maritime Greenwich is the equivalent of St. Peter's to Roman Catholics, Mecca to Muslims, Jerusalem to Christians and Jews, or Disneyland to children. Greenwich is *the* center for navigation, history and the romance of the sea for all English-speaking cultures. The museum friends' group had been aboard the *O'Brien* for a tour in Portsmouth and they kindly provided passes to Historic Maritime Greenwich for all the crew. We spent hours looking at intricate ship models, grand paintings of historic sea battles and video presentations of modern ships at sea. Two things stood out: an exhibit on pirates that was both enchanting and realistic, and an excellent model of a Liberty ship. After a lunch of fish and chips at the museum cafeteria, the author went to the Royal Observatory and realized a lifelong dream to stand astride the Greenwich Meridian, at zero degrees longitude — one foot in the Western hemisphere, the other in the Eastern.

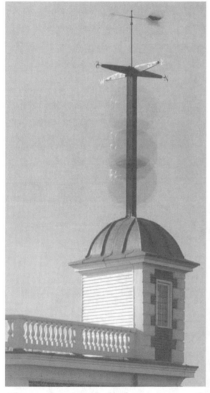

Above, the time ball drops at exactly 1300 each day. Above right, children straddling the Greenwich Meridian. Right, the Meridian at night, looking south. Historic Maritime Greenwich.

The Cutty Sark, *one of the finest tea clippers ever built, in her graving dock at Greenwich.* Historic Maritime Greenwich.

Greenwich, the seat of maritime history for the English-speaking world. This scene was painted in 1750 and comes from their brochure. Compared to the photo on page 282, we see little change. Author's collection.

Inside were the Harrison clocks (responsible for the establishment of longitude) a refracting telescope, and a well-documented history of the observatory building. Outside, the grass was thick and green, the trees were in full foliage, birds fluttered, people strolled around. It was an oasis of beauty and serenity surrounded by the noise and hustle of greater London.

Many went to the usual tourist spots in London. Here Pat Jahn, left, and Nell Otterberg have their picture taken with a Beefeater at the Tower of London. Jo Lawrence.

Approaching the *Cutty Sark*, one gets a sense of how near to perfection the design of clipper ships came. The rigging and hull blended harmoniously in a sleek, graceful presence that captivates the imagination. Her lines are lovely, her presence, majestic. Standing on the quarterdeck, one could almost relive her races from China and Australia through the Roaring Forties, around the Cape of Good Hope and up the Channel. Looking up from her main deck, the masts seem to touch the sky as if seeking "a star to steer her by."

From the beginning there was the feeling that the ship should charge admission. We had incurred tremendous expenses to make the voyage and there would be more before the trip was over. Also, probably unique among the museum ships and training ships of the world, we were not sponsored by any government organization except for the onetime sale of the scrap ships. Although everyone was an unpaid volunteer, the costs of fuel, food, parts, supplies, insurance, postage and countless other items added to the costs of operating the ship. Pilotage, tugs, berths, water, electricity, garbage collection — were provided free. Nevertheless, the ship still accumulated $3,000 a day in expenses whether at sea or in port.

In London it was agreed with the authorities that any admissions to HMS *Belfast* that were over and above what that ship normally received would be shared with the *O'Brien* on a fifty-fifty basis. It wasn't much, but it was a beginning.

The river traffic was a source of unending fascination. It was constant — workboats, tugs and barges chugged past, tour boats with two and three decks of people coasted by. We could hear the guides announcing on the public address system, "… the grey-hulled ship made fast to the *Belfast* is a Liberty ship, the *Jeremiah O'Brien*. She has come all the way from San Francisco and is operated by a crew made up entirely of World War II veterans. She has just returned from Normandy, where she was the center of attention and will be with us …" In the evenings sleek, modern dinner cruise boats slowly navigated the river as their patrons dined by candlelight, And at all hours harbor police, sailing yachts, motorboats and an occasional jet-ski passed by.

Probably the most memorable event of the stay in London was a Beating Retreat ceremony held at the Tower of London on June 20. The invitation was limited to the captain and three officers. Capt. Jahn, Adm. Patterson, Capt. Otterberg and the author donned dress blue uniforms. A car and driver were provided which drove us across Tower Bridge to the Tower of London. The first sight that caught our attention were the ravens. Sleek, black and well-fed, they looked almost as big as turkeys. We were met at the entrance and escorted into the White Tower where drinks and a finger buffet were provided. A large group of important guests was at the reception, friendly, courteous and polite, as always. Surrounded by glass cases of medieval weapons and suits of armor, we talked and sipped champagne. Then we were seated around the square outside the White Tower with Capt. Jahn in a position of honor on the dais. The resident Governor, Major General C. Tyler, CB, welcomed everyone: "It is my pleasure to welcome you to Her Majesty's Palace and

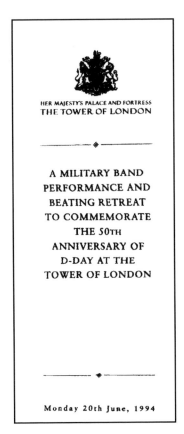

HER MAJESTY'S PALACE AND FORTRESS
THE TOWER OF LONDON

A MILITARY BAND
PERFORMANCE AND
BEATING RETREAT
TO COMMEMORATE
THE 50TH
ANNIVERSARY OF
D-DAY AT THE
TOWER OF LONDON

Monday 20th June, 1994

Fortress, The Tower of London, to mark the 50th anniversary of the D-Day landings ..."

The Drums and Pipes of the London Regiment, a Territorial Army consisting of companies of the Princess of Wales Royal Regiment, the Royal Regiment of Fusiliers and the London Scottish and London Irish Rifles, gave a stunning marching exhibition, coming in at a diagonal from one corner of the square and marching across and back again to the sound of pipes and flutes. This was followed by a reenactment of the Ceremony of Constable's Dues. Based on an ancient Custom dating back to the 14th century, the ceremony represents the paying of dues on the part of any ship moored in the Pool of London and coming under the protection of the Tower. Payment was in the form of a barrel of wine, strung beneath a spar and ceremoniously carried under escort to The Tower to be received by the Constable or his representative. A contingent from HMS *London* did the honors this evening with the recipients being the Resident Governor, the Chief Yeoman Warder, Yeoman Gaoler and Yeoman Warders. A group of sailors from HMS *London* marched across the square, a barrel of wine hanging on ropes swinging from side to side under the oars from which it was hung. On arriving at the Resident Governor's platform, the officer saluted with his sword. The general returned the salute, the sailors set down the keg, aboutfaced and marched off.

Next was the Ceremony of Beating Retreat, performed by the Band of the Adjutant General's Corps. Their instruments included bagpipes and they gave a stirring performance, marching in close formation.

The finale of the evening was presented by the combined bands which played several marches, "The Star Spangled Banner," and ended with "God Save the Queen."

It was a memorable ending to a visit that had been one long celebration of goodwill, helpfulness, warm hospitality, and comrades-across-the-sea.

25

CHERBOURG AND THE
BEACHES OF NORMANDY

J une 23, 1994.

Now, once again, the *Jeremiah O'Brien* sailed to the Normandy coast, heading for Cherbourg, a port at which she last called on September 23, 1944. The Channel was calm, sparkling under sunny skies. The cool air, damp with the sea, carried with it the earthy smell of land. Where warships and liners tossed and sailed on choppy seas in the historic event just two weeks past, today the white sails of private yachts dotted the bright blue waters. Here and there the distant silhouette of a passing freighter was seen on the horizon. In the early afternoon, the low hills of coastal France showed darkly in the distance. As the ship drew closer, the red rooftops and white buildings of the city itself materialized.

Once again we were early, so the pilot kept the engine at slow ahead as the *O'Brien* glided through the western entrance to the breakwater. Three castle-like fortifications, now abandoned, were built into the ends and center of the rock wall. The pilot told us that the breakwater protecting the harbor was begun by Louis XVI in 1776 and was built over the years with the labor of British prisoners captured in the many wars between England and France. It was completed during the Second Empire of Napoleon III (1846), giving France a sheltered roadstead as large as the British Royal Navy's in the Solent. During World War II, Germany further fortified the breakwater with pillboxes containing gun emplacements. On this golden afternoon, however, it was not a forbidding fortress of war, but a welcoming haven into the harbor of Cherbourg.

The *Jeremiah O'Brien* moored at the *Quai de France*, the terminal for the magnificent trans-Atlantic liners of years gone by. Ordering a tug made fast on the stern, the pilot turned the ship and backed her toward the berth. A large crowd was gathered on the pier and as the first lines went out they applauded. The ship drew alongside and a military band, wearing dark blue uniforms with the can-shaped de Gaulle hats struck up "The Star Spangled Banner." We secured the lines and rang off Finished With Engines. It was 8 p.m. but the sun was still high. We were on French double summer time and it wouldn't get dark until after ten.

The *O'Brien*'s accommodation ladders are permanently rigged on the starboard side. Because we were port side to, we needed gangways from shore. These were lowered into place by a shore crane and the band came aboard, set up on the flying bridge and played marches.

Tom Patterson: "We arrived in Cherbourg on the twenty-third of June and started a two week period which none of us will ever, ever forget. Our arrival was timed to coincide with the fiftieth anniversary of their liberation from the Nazis, the twenty-sixth of June."

Friday, June 24, and daylight came well before six a.m., a clear, warm day with blue skies and a slight breeze. The first sights that greeted us were several fleets of sailboats scattered around the harbor. Each group consisted of seven or eight one-person boats propelled by a single sail. Within each group were several small boats manned by school children and a larger one, equipped with sail and motor, operated by their teacher. Several times each day during our stay we saw the larger boats towing their "flock" of smaller boats, tied bow to stern, to and from the center of the harbor — like mother ducks with their progeny. Sailing was a required course in the local school system.

From the ship, the crew surveyed this first French port, eagerly anticipating the chance to go ashore and practice the phrases they had studiously memorized. François Le Pendu, our French-born fireman/watertender, had given them some useful phrases including "*Un biere s'il vous plait*" meaning "one beer please."

A large passenger terminal dominated the pier. Once bustling with travelers from luxury liners such as the *Queen Mary*, the *France*, the *United States*, now the cavernous rooms with rows of dark kiosks, empty perfume counters, and dusty snack bars sat silent on dry, pale wood floors that had not seen a coat of wax for decades. In an adjacent room, equally large and dank, stretched two wooden tables, hundreds of feet long. One could envision the customs officials opening and examining the luggage of impatient travelers. Rail lines, rusty and weed-grown with disuse, led to platforms under a vast barn-like steel-and-glass canopy, evoking images of shrilly-whistling black steam trains loading passengers for far away cities on the Continent.

Capt. Jahn and Adm. Patterson were soon off to make courtesy calls on the local French Naval commander, the Captain of the Port, the Mayor and others. Wearing dress blue uniforms they were chauffeured in a private car donated by the ship's agent in France, Worms Services Maritime. Our dignitaries were followed in very short order by the off-duty crew going ashore for *their* courtesy calls on the shops, bars and restaurants of Cherbourg.

On the opposite side of the pier from the *Jeremiah O'Brien* was another waterway, the entrance to the inner harbor of Cherbourg. A yacht harbor colorfully marked its opposite shore leading past floating public piers through a small draw bridge to an inner harbor in the center of town. It was a short walk from the ship across this bridge directly into downtown Cherbourg's narrow, cobblestoned streets lined with shops, bistros, sidewalk cafes and creperies. Shopping in this old part of town meant walking through streets suffused with heavenly aromas — the scent of fresh-baked bread from the boulangeries, their windows piled high with loaves, round, long, seeded — coffee, chocolate, fresh fruits and flowers. Patés, sausages, cheeses, pastries and wines were gaily displayed in the windows of charcuteries, fromageries, patisseries and wine shops.

Tables and chairs under colorful awnings lined the sidewalks of many restaurants, especially those fronting the harbor. Tuesday, Thursday and Saturday were market days with farmers' stands set up in the Place de Gaulle in and around the main theater and fountain — kaleidoscopes of fresh-cut flowers, fish, produce, sausages, fresh bread and rolls, cheeses, cakes and croissants. The crew was ecstatic and spent much of their free time wandering the streets sampling the color — and the food. For those interested in history there was the statue of Napoleon overlooking the harbor and the nearby Trinity Basilica dating from the 11th century.

Cherbourg is a major ferry port and every day we saw several of these massive ships entering and leaving the harbor, each as large as an ocean liner. Their bow doors began opening even before the ship was alongside, great massive hinged mouths that yawned at the front of the ship to allow cars to drive off and on. In the evening, the blue and white P&O ferries arrived from England, nosing into a berth closer to town. After a few hours they departed, returning again the following evening. Less frequent was the boat from Ireland, green and white with a shamrock on its stack, tying up across the harbor. Occasionally, a grander P&O ship, but a ferry nonetheless, arrived from Bilbao.

Saturday was cooler with a somber overcast sky and a slight wind blowing. As it was a weekend we were inundated with visitors, with more than 5,300 aboard. We still weren't charging admission but we had our donation barrel strategically placed at the gangway.

France definitely presented a different culture. The children were much more free-spirited than the British, running, shouting, nosing into everything. And their parents were far more curious, opening doors, looking in portholes and wandering off the blue line tour. One surprising discovery was how attached they are to their pets. Many French people brought dogs on board, as often as not carrying the animal the entire time they were on the ship. On several occasions we saw women carrying baskets and shopping bags with a small dog inside, its head sticking out as it viewed the surroundings.

There were a few French-speaking people on board including François Le Pendu from the engine room and their talents were constantly needed to translate for the many French people who came on board to thank us. As they had in

NATIONAL LIBERTY SHIP MEMORIAL

JEREMIAH O'BRIEN

50ème ANNIVERSAIRE DU DEBARQUEMENT
DE NORMANDIE 1944-1994

ports d'escale

ANGLETERRE
Portsmouth
Southampton
Chatham
Londres

FRANCE
Cherbourg
Rouen
Le Havre

**Présentation du navire
&
plan de la visite**

The French version of the self-guided tour brochure. It was translated for us by Lee Curtis of The Wordmill, Queensland, Australia.

England, with quavering voices and tears in their eyes, our visitors told stories of the occupation, showed us old photographs and newspaper clippings, and expressed their gratitude to America for liberating them. This was another revelation. In England, the thanks were for our help and for saving them from the threat of Nazi domination. But the French had actually lived and suffered from the Nazi oppression and, even fifty years later, their gratitude to the United States for liberating them was heartfelt and sincere. The crew, unready for such an outpouring, did not know how to react. Such emotional displays were outside the American experience. In time we learned to accept them with understanding and empathy.

Mike Emery:

> I think one of the unexpected things was the response that we got from the British and the French, the old sailors who pointed out their fo'c's'le and their seat in the mess and where they slept. And to see the look of gratitude and the real feeling of nostalgia on the faces of the French and British sailors who had spent time on Liberty ships, and then taking them down to the ship's store and finding the history of their ship in one of our books.[1]

Sunday, June 26, was the 50th anniversary of the liberation of Cherbourg. To commemorate the event we began preparation for something planned many months earlier by Jean-Paul Caron, owner of the DUKW that came over as our deck cargo. In 1944 the normal port facilities for handling cargo were unusable after Allied bombing and German sabotage. Because Cherbourg was the only deep water port in Allied hands as the armies advanced, it was essential to find a way to get food, stores and ammunition off the ships and onto trucks. The answer was the DUKW, the amphibious version of the GMC 2½ ton truck. A "merry-go-round" was established, with DUKWs travelling out to Liberty ships anchored outside the harbor, accepting a cargo lowered by the ship's booms and travelling back to improvised ramps where they clambered out onto dry land and were unloaded by mobile cranes, or even other DUKWs fitted with A-frames. This final trans-shipment took place on the town foreshore near the statue of Napoleon and the area became known to irreverent American servicemen as "Nap and the Ducks."

---

[1] After World War II, the United States sold hundreds of laid up Libertys to foreign countries. These became the foundation of the burgeoning maritime industry of Russia, Greece, England, France and other countries.

This photo of our recreation of "Nap and the Ducks," looks like it was taken in 1944 rather than 1994. Author's collection.

One of the DUKW crew members, Dewane J. Englerth, was a veteran of the Cherbourg liberation. He recalled what it was like in 1944:

> About two weeks later [after the landing at Omaha] we came back to the beach to run amphibious boats that we called 'ducks.' They could haul about five to seven tons of cargo. There were two twelve-hour shifts and I had the night shift. We were bombed and shot at by Germans about twice each night for three months. We ate 'K' rations and had little time to clean up or rest. We each dug a hole or a trench in the ground about a foot deep and that's where we slept.

The view from the DUKW toward the O'Brien. Messman Chuck Jennings is on the left facing the camera. Jean Yates.

One morning when I got back to my trench, there was a hole through my blankets. I looked to see what had made the hole and found a piece of shrapnel about a foot long and an inch thick. It had gone all the way through my bedding and into the ground. I dug it out and carried it with me for a while, but finally threw it away. I was sure glad that I'd been working nights!

About three months after the invasion the armed forces took over the boat docks from the Germans in Cherbourg. I think that this was the first dock opened, which meant that the big boats could come in and dock to unload. We didn't need to operate the 'ducks' anymore. By this time the Allied Forces were almost to Germany.

In the city of Cherbourg, *Jeremiah O'Brien* veterans who served in World War II, including Art Taber, Bill Williams, Richard Hill and Wes Masterson, were marching as an honored contingent in a big civic parade. The streets were lined with enthusiastic citizens cheering and waving flags at each passing group.

The streets were decorated with flags, bunting and large photographs taken during the actual liberation in 1944. It was the liberation all over again with crowds in the streets, people waving and cheering from windows and accompanying tears of joy. And it wasn't just the French. We, too, got caught up in the realization

The Jeremiah O'Brien *veterans march past the statue of Napoleon in Cherbourg. Our crew drew the largest ovation.* Mike Emery.

The parade in Cherbourg was a moving experience. Note the difference in expressions between, left to right, Art Taber, Jean Yates and the French soldier. Mike Emery.

of what the liberation meant to France, even fifty years later, and understood a little more how important it was that we had come. The common bond of understanding linked us and the language barrier fell as we all wept and rejoiced together, just as we had in Southampton.

KFS' *Jeremiah O'Brien* line was busier than ever.

Crews News
June 25, 1994
This is the Voice of the *Jeremiah O'Brien*.
Good evening, San Francisco.
Almost 6,000 citizens of the Cherbourg area visited *Jeremiah O'Brien* today. Some of these good people were part of the hundreds that attempted to visit the ship as late as 10:30 PM last evening. We reluctantly explained that visiting hours ended at 9 PM and that in order to inspect the ship they must return today; and they did, in most satisfying numbers. Ron

Robson reported that the ship's store had a very good day with purchases inclined towards the *O'Brien* coffee mugs and especially the "Back to the Beaches" tee shirts depicting the landing on the Normandy beaches fifty years ago.

Ron Robson, gift shop manager:

I had some very moving experiences in Cherbourg on the night of the fiftieth anniversary of their liberation. It was 11 p.m. and the church bells started ringing. Then people began coming out of their shuttered houses in twos and threes, walking down these narrow old cobblestoned streets to the common area where there was a fireworks display. To hear the church bells and to hear the sound system playing, mostly American music was memorable.

The Jeremiah O'Brien *story in French. Gérald Guétat did a remarkable job of telling our story in this book which was sold in the ship's store.* Author's collection.

While the people of Cherbourg were visiting the *O'Brien*, the *O'Brien*'s crew was visiting Cherbourg. Every day and night, the off-duty crew was out exploring and enjoying the attractions of the city. Starting just across the swing bridge at the tourist office they branched out into Old Town to window shop or enjoy the restaurants overlooking the harbor or the theater and town square. Others stopped for coffee, beer, pastries, cakes and croissants. Many brought back Normandy cheeses and Calvados, the apple brandy for which the region is famous.

Everyone was looking forward to visiting the Normandy battle scenes. Our whole voyage was a "Return to Normandy" but, so far, all we had seen was a distant bluff from our offshore anchorage on June 6. Tours were donated by the local tourbus company.

We boarded the bus after breakfast, settling into the comfortable red and blue velvet seats. The vehicle was comfortable, had large windows and contained a restroom. Soon we were on our way though the streets of Cherbourg and out into the countryside of Normandy.

The first stop was Utah Beach and the war museum, a modern, sandy-colored building with sloping roofs that fit well with the low sand hills fronting the beach. At the entrance were tanks and cannon left over from the war. Inside, we saw that the foundation of the museum was the top of a former German gun emplacement. Photographs, displays and artifacts evoked that "longest day" fifty years earlier. Outside, several of the crew walked down to the beach, a long, gently-sloping expanse of hard-packed sand. It was low tide and in the distant surfline we saw tractors pulling in fishermen's nets. Closer to shore, a horse and sulky trotted, working out in the fresh sea air. It was difficult to imagine that this had been the scene of part of the greatest military landing in history.

Then it was off to the village of St. Mère Église. A picturesque town, with narrow cobblestoned streets, its two and three story homes and shops are set around a large square. Our first stop was the church in the center of the square on whose steeple American

Sainte-Mère-Église

L'équipage du Jeremiah O'Brien en visite à Utah et à Sainte-Mère

Le contre-amiral Thomas J. Patterson et son équipage sont en escale à Cherbourg, à bord du Liberty Ship, le Jeremiah O'Brien.

L'équipage devant la borne 0

Ils sont venus et revenus en Normandie pour les cérémonies du cinquantenaire et le bateau-musée ouvert au public est reparti hier en direction de Rouen, puis Le Havre, et rentrera à San Francisco, son quartier général.

Ce navire a été construit en 1943 à Portland dans le Maine (USA), en 96 jours (longueur 135 mètres, largeur 18 mètres). Le liberty-ship, le Jeremiah O'Brien a participé à de nombreux convois entre la côte Est des USA et la Grande-Bretagne avec des cargaisons de munitions, céréales et divers. En juin 1944, il effectua entre l'Angleterre et les plages d'Utha Beach, onze navettes avec des chargements de munitions, vivres et matériel.

Sur 2 710 liberty-ship construits entre 1941 et 1945, il n'y eut que deux « rescapés », le John W. Bron et le Jeremiah O'Brien, qui furent plus tard déclarés « monuments historiques » et exposés au musée de San Francisco. Il y a une douzaine d'années, le contre-amiral Thomas J. Patterson, président de la commis-

sion de marine marchande a décidé de remettre en état ce bateau-musée ouvert au public.

Ainsi, pour le cinquantenaire, ils ont fait le voyage, une partie de l'équipage ayant navigué à bord du Jeremiah, en 1944. Ce bateau a navigué seulement trois ans, jusqu'en 1946, puis il est resté 35 ans dans la baie de San Francisco.

A Saint-Marie-du-Mont (Utah Beach), comme à Sainte-Mère-Église, l'équipage a été reçu par le maire de la commune. A Utah, comme à Sainte-Mère, ils ont eu le plaisir de découvrir une maquette du liberty-ship, confectionné par des maquettistes passionnés. A Utah, c'est Yves Osmont qui a offert la maquette au musée d'Utah, à l'occasion du cinquantenaire et à Sainte-Mère-Église, c'est M. Dupuis qui l'a offert, il est exposé à la mairie et s'appelle le « Sainte-Mère ».

L'équipage a été ému devant ces petits liberty-ship ai bien reproduits. Après la réception à la mairie, ils ont visité le musée de Sainte-Mère-Église, ils font ainsi le tour des plages du débarquement.

RAVENOVILLE

Méchoui du comité des fêtes

Le comité des fêtes de Ravenoville que préside Michel Bertin organise un méchoui (dansant sous chapiteau (avec orchestre) à la salle de la plage.

dimanche 17 juillet à 12 h 30.

Pour les réservations, vous pouvez appeler le 33.21.02.34 et le 33.41.33.26.

Les vétérans dans les jardins du musée

The French newspapers carried an article with pictures of the crew at our visit to Omaha and St. Mère Église. La Presse de la Manche.

paratrooper Private Steele hung by his parachute for two hours playing dead the night of the first Normandy landings. We were surprised to see a mannequin hanging by parachute from exactly the same spot. Inside, the church's stained glass windows depicted parachutists descending from the sky. St. Mère Église was the first French village liberated on June 6, 1944 and their gratitude to the 82nd Airborne has never dimmed. Nearby was a large museum filled with mementos of the war: a glider, a cargo plane, mannequins in uniform, clothing, munitions, weapons, posters, photographs and, outside, tanks, half-tracks and other vehicles. In the nearby shops and stores were postcards, books, wine, scarves, hats and countless other souvenirs depicting the liberation.

In the Hotel De Ville, the city hall, was a model of the Liberty ship *St. Mère Église*. Most French Liberty ships were named after cities and towns in Normandy where World War II battles took place.

Back on the bus the guide had the driver pause at a pasture. Beside the road was a marker. " At one time," explained the guide, "there were 6,000 American soldiers buried in this field. They have all been moved to Colleville. During June 1944 each kilometer of countryside gained cost one life." It was a sobering thought. Fifty years earlier, American soldiers died on foreign soil so that others might enjoy the fruits of liberty and freedom. In that moment, our understanding of the gratitude of the French, so often expressed by visitors to our ship, so sincerely felt, deepened. Again, we were grateful for the privilege of making the voyage to Normandy, and very glad we had come to honor those who lived — and died — in the battle of Normandy. For all the dramatic events and official ceremonies of the D-Day + 50 Years commemorations, it was these experiences with the ordinary people that really brought home to us just how important it was for the *Jeremiah O'Brien* to return to Normandy and share the memories and ceremonies with them.

Back at Cherbourg, a beautiful French three-masted bark, the *Belem*, arrived, giving us our first view of what lay ahead at the tall ships gathering at Rouen. She gracefully slid across the harbor, tying directly astern of the *O'Brien*.

The *Belem* was black-hulled with white trim and her masts and spars glowed with varnish. Her brass was highly pol-ished and glittered in the sun. The wooden decks were buffed white. Built in 1896 by A. Dubigeon in Nantes, France as the *Giorgio Cini*, she was

The French training vessel Belem *was the first indication of what was to come in Rouen.* La Presse de la Manche.

originally a cargo ship. After two name changes, several owners and many years, she became a museum ship. Her steel hull measures 173 feet overall with a breadth of 29 feet and a depth of 11 feet. In addition to sails she is powered by an auxiliary diesel engine. Although technically not a clipper, she rivaled many such a vessel in her trim lines, fine bow and the graceful way in which she sat in the water. We spent much time admiring her. Interestingly, our old steel ship seemed of equal interest to her crew and we looked across at our counterparts looking at us.

Another sailing ship arrived in the afternoon, the *Cuauhtémoc*, also bound for the tall ships gathering in Rouen. A beautiful white-hulled bark with green trim, she coasted across the harbor like a ghost from the past. At almost 300 feet overall she was much larger than the *Belem*.

On July 4th, the *Jeremiah O'Brien* hosted a barbecue for all the people who had helped us during our stay — including the mayor, port officials, the owner of the tourbus company and officers from the Naval base.

The crew of the Mexican training vessel Cuauhtémoc *at ease in Cherbourg.* La Presse de la Manche.

The following day, we went to Pointe du Hoc, walking across a bomb-cratered landscape overgrown with grass to the cliff, marked by a stone monument, a granite pylon atop a concrete bunker with inscriptions in both French and English at its base. We looked out over the calm blue waters trying to envision the stormy Channel fifty years earlier when the 2nd Ranger Battalion attacked, scaled the one hundred-foot cliff under heavy fire and, after great losses, succeeded in capturing, then defending the area against German counterattacks. The sheer drop to the ocean looked impossible. A few feet back from the cliff were the remains of the German gun emplacements, fearsome-looking even in ruin. The remaining guns were twisted and rusty. The calm summer day, the butterflies fluttering about and birds singing made it difficult to imagine the great battles that took place on D-Day.

The next stop was the Normandy Cemetery at Colleville-sur-Mer, overlooking Omaha Beach. One month earlier, President Clinton stood in this cemetery along with heads of the Allied Nations gathered to remember and honor the thousands of American soldiers who lie there. On this day we were met by Sgt. Hooker, retired from the U.S. Army and now an employee of the American Government in France.

The Normandy Cemetery is actually American territory, given to the United States by the French government in gratitude for

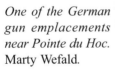

One of the German gun emplacements near Pointe du Hoc.
Marty Wefald.

The perfect rows of grave markers at Colleville inspired deep emotion and reflection. Marty Wefald.

American sacrifices during the liberation of France. Sgt. Hooker escorted us along gravel paths through immaculately manicured lawns to the memorial. There was a natural reverence to the surroundings that caused us all to unconsciously speak softly. We brought a wreath from the ship. For the first time, a memorial wreath would be laid for the fourteen merchant mariners who lost their lives at Normandy and are buried in Colleville.

The memorial is a semicircle of colonnades, open to the sky, with shrines at each end depicting the D-Day landings engraved in stone and embellished with colored enamel. In the center is the bronze statue, "Spirit of American Youth," a tribute to those who gave their lives. Around its base is the inscription "MINE EYES HAVE SEEN THE GLORY OF THE COMING OF THE LORD." Symmetrically arranged, row upon row of white markers indicated the resting places of our countrymen.

At the edge of the cemetery was a parapet overlooking the landing beaches of Omaha. We stood there quietly, looking at "bloody Omaha," the site of the fiercest of all the D-Day battles, waves of emotions flooding over us.

Our final stop was Arromanches, at the heart of Gold Beach during Operation Overlord. A small coastal village, it contains a museum dedicated to the British landings that freed the area of Nazi domination. Inside the museum were glass-cased dioramas depicting the events surrounding D-Day, a theater showing a short film of the landings, and displays of artifacts, uniforms, weapons, ammunition, posters, letters, insignia and military equipment. We were all wearing crew jackets and, as we entered the museum, the curator announced over the public address system that we were from the Liberty ship *Jeremiah O'Brien* and we had brought the ship from the United States to help commemorate the liberation of France. The room burst into thunderous applause. We were stunned. We simply didn't know what to do. The people shook hands with us, asked for autographs and even delivered a few hugs and the French custom of kisses on both cheeks. It was an overwhelming experience.

We returned to the ship in the evening, tired, yet uplifted, humbled, with a number of other indescribable emotions coursing through us, and, above all, deeply moved at the gratitude of the French people.

Tom Patterson:

On the sixth of July I drove to Rouen with Maud Paléologue, the French communications expert assigned to us and paid for by the NLSM to meet with Mr. Patrick Herr the president of the organization that was putting on the *L'Armada de la Liberté*. The way it was set up we wouldn't be able to charge any admission to the ship and we desperately needed money at that time. I carefully explained our whole ship's program to him and what we had done and where we were and why we needed some money and the whole thing, and asked if we could charge ten francs [$2] per person admission to the ship. We knew that the other forty-six ships there were not charging admission as they were all government ships sent by their countries.

I explained to him we were a museum and that we were operated by volunteers, not supported by our government, and we simply had to have this money. I said if he would allow us to do this we would make up the appropriate sign and explain to the French people why they're being asked to give us ten francs. At that point he said, "I think you've made a very reasonable request. I agree with it. I will let you do it. Let us make up the sign and we'll post it for you." And he said, "Is there anything else?" And I said, "Yes, we would also like to cruise down the river and we would like to take 500 guests and we would like to charge them 1,000 francs per person," [the equivalent of about $200 per person]. We explained that to him and he agreed that was fair and reasonable and he would help us in any way he could.

On Thursday, July 7, the *Jeremiah O'Brien* sailed from Cherbourg. At a dockside ceremony we thanked the organizations that had supported us — the French Rotary and Lions Clubs, the tourbus company that gave us the tours — presenting each one with a *Jeremiah O'Brien* plaque.

The navigation gear was tested. At 2135 the deep sea pilot and the harbor pilot were aboard. Shortly before 2200 the dockside crane hooked on to the first gangway and took it ashore. Then the longshoremen hooked up the second gangway. The gangway went ashore. The weather, which early in the day was grey and overcast, turned to drizzle. As we began throwing the lines off fore and aft, the pilot asked for whistles. We blew a prolonged blast as the last line went ashore. Then, as we moved away from the dock, three long blasts. The small crowd remaining on the pier applauded. Three more long blasts in farewell to Cherbourg and, with the engines slow ahead, the *O'Brien* pointed her bow toward the breakwater.

Once outside the harbor, the local pilot left on the pilot boat. It blew three whistle blasts as it turned back toward the harbor. We returned the salute, rang off departure and headed into the night.

26

L'ARMADA DE LA LIBERTÉ

It was a short run to Le Havre at the mouth of the Seine. At 0800 the next morning the *O'Brien* circled the harbor buoy, waiting for the pilot to arrive. Suddenly, we were transported back a hundred and fifty years, to a busy harbor filled with beautiful, tall, graceful windjammers. To starboard was a sleek, white-hulled sailing ship. Her seamen lined the foremast yardarms, clawing at billowing buff-colored canvas as they furled the sails. Farther aft sailors climbed the ratlines on either side of the main and mizzen masts. On the quarterdeck stood the master, calmly giving orders to the mate who relayed them through a speaking trumpet. Aft of the brass and wood binnacle two seamen handled the spokes of the ship's wheel, their legs spread wide to hold the deck.

A couple of miles astern another tall ship, a three-masted bark, black-hulled, under full sail, was heading our way with a bone in her teeth. Her sails were snow-white and swelled tightly as she sleekly knifed her way through the water. Ahead were two other tall ships, their auxiliary engines pushing them toward the entrance to the Seine under bare masts. Even without sails they looked splendid, their lines hard and straight in a symmetry that was both aesthetically pleasing and spirit-lifting. Images of the great days of sail came to mind — the gathering of tea clippers on the coast of China; Donald McKay's ships rounding the Horn, each cutting the time of its predecessor; the homeward-bound ceremony of the last load on the nitrate clippers in Chile; the wool clippers from Australia; legendary names such as *Cutty Sark, Rainbow, Sovereign of the Seas, Flying Cloud* and *Sea Witch*; images of bucko mates, King Neptune and pirates. It was a thrilling beginning to the great event that awaited sixty miles upriver.

We fell back to reality at the sight of the pilot boat in the distance, a billow of dirty grey smoke pouring from its exhausts. The harsh sound of its diesel engines pierced the silence and grew louder. Then the orange and black-hulled craft with "PILOT" painted in large white letters was alongside. Capt. LeMalet climbed quickly to the *O'Brien*'s bridge and pointed her up the Seine toward Rouen, sixty miles away, the closest port to Paris navigable by ocean-going vessels.

The weather was mild, the blue sky partly covered with white patches of clouds. The flying bridge, high on the ship, with open views, was an ideal navigation — and sight-seeing — platform. The ship passed under the Normandy Bridge, its suspension cables fanning out geometrically from two towers like the beginnings of a massive spider web. Now, the delta of the river narrowed. To starboard were low hills covered with green grass and oak forests, pastures with brown cattle grazing and small houses with white stucco walls, red tile roofs and large flower gardens. To port was a wide, low, flat green marsh.

Capt. LeMalet was full of enthusiasm at being aboard the last active veteran of Normandy and the last Liberty ship in Europe and asked if he could steer it himself. Soon AB Jim Conwell was standing to one side as the pilot handled the wood spokes of the ship's wheel. A barge came down river and saluted with its whistle. The deep answering bellow of the *O'Brien*'s foghorn echoed off the starboard bank and rolled across the flatlands to port. Capt. LeMalet was in ecstasy. He hadn't realized we

One of the more distinctive small castles seen on the ride up the Seine. John Linderman.

had a real, bellowing, steam-powered fog horn and, once aware, he was at the whistle pull himself, saluting each ship, barge, boat, ferry crossing, town and chateau along the way. Between steering and blowing the whistle he had a grand time taking us up the river. His enthusiasm was infectious and we enjoyed his enjoyment.

The banks of the river drew closer and the terrain changed. Low-lying hills on each side were covered with green grass or vineyards. Occasionally, a small castle was seen atop a nearby cliff or peak, its turrets and parapets commanding the surrounding countryside. We passed small villages with bustling shops, busy market places, town squares lined with open-air cafes and always a church, its spire the tallest structure in sight. Capt. LeMalet was still steering and whistling and at the sound of our foghorn people appeared in the windows of their homes, waving. They looked up from their gardening, their farming, their walks along the river banks, their shopping, to wave and cheer at the sight of the old Liberty ship steaming up the Seine.

Just after lunch and before the Brotonne Bridge and the town of Ville du Clare, about thirty miles up river, we changed pilots. Capt. Tilly took the con with Capt. LeMalet reluctantly going ashore. Now the river closed in. White chalk cliffs and white marble quarries punctuated long stretches of beautiful rolling green countryside. We saw old houses, half-timbered stucco with thatched or slate roofs, elegant chateaux and villas. Small boats, barges and an occasional freighter came downstream. The people we passed on the banks of the river waved and cheered. Capt. Tilly was equally enamored of our old steam whistle and blew it diligently and the people applauded each volley delightedly.

In mid-afternoon we entered the river valley in which Rouen resides. Here, the grasslands and forests of the country, the villages and chateaux, gave way to hard, flat industrial piers, grain elevators and faceless concrete warehouses and factories. The *Jeremiah O'Brien*'s berth was to be in the very heart of the city. At this point, the low *Pont Guillaume le Conquérant* (Bridge of William the Conqueror) prevents navigation farther up river by all but low-profile barges. This area of the river, which contained the berths for all the ships gathering for *L'Armada de la Liberté* was lined on each side with a modern quay.

We tied starboard side to on the face of a long concrete wharf or quay, the *Rive Droite* (right bank), that stretched downstream more than a mile from the bridge of William the Conqueror. On the opposite side was the *Rive Gauche* (left bank), not quite so long but equally well-laid-out. The area adjacent to where the Armada ships would moor was a broad esplanade about 100 feet wide. Brick buildings and white tents of various sizes housed the Armada's souvenir stands, snack bars, bistros, wine bars, exhibits, a post office, first aid tents and a bank branch.

The official souvenir stands featured every item imaginable with the logo of *L'Armada* on it: post cards, posters, insignia,

The logo of L'Armada was everywhere. Here, a large banner dresses the top of a nearby building. Bob Black.

umbrellas, baseball caps, T-shirts, jumpers, blouses, jackets, and the favorite novelty item of the crew, *L'Armada* condom in a small white box with red and blue logo.

Larger tents were set up as open-air restaurants with a stage for evening entertainment and a kitchen in back. The smaller ones offered such treats as American-style fast foods — hot dogs and hamburgers with *pommes frites* (french fries), sandwiches, crepes, Haagen Dazs ice cream, pastries, cakes, soft drinks, beer and wine. There were also tent-shops offering paintings, ship models, brassware, prints, clothing, jewelry and the opportunity to join the French Navy. Just beyond the tents, adjacent

One of the many brochures advertising L'Armada. *Author's collection.*

to the ship, the crew quickly discovered a bar that immediately became a popular hangout. For the duration of *L'Armada* it featured a nightly wet T-shirt contest.

Tom Patterson:

> Rouen is probably the only port in the world that has a river with berths on both sides and a bridge at the end of it and you can display

This brochure features a photo from the previous Armada. Author's collection.

all these beautiful, wonderful ships. And you can see them all together. Any angle you look at it you're seeing beautiful ships and over 2,000 sailors from these ships. It was an unbelievable spectacle, and *Jeremiah* was right in the middle of it as the guest of honor, being the only original ship from World War II.

Just on the other side of the William the Conqueror bridge was the center of Rouen with its Old Town, university, cathedral, shops and restaurants. Here, narrow, cobblestoned streets wound through blocks of half-timbered houses, many dating back hundreds of years. The centerpiece of the Old Town is the Great Clock, or Gros-Horloge, on the street of the same name. The Great Clock itself is housed in a Renaissance structure which spans the street, open to pedestrian traffic only, like a gate. The clock's large gilt face can be seen from either side, its single hand showing the hour.

The cathedral, dating from the 1100s, is delicately-spired and stands tall and majestic in a large square in the center of town. There was always musical entertainment of some type going on in the square: a brass band from one of the Russian ships, a bagpipe band from the Omani ship, folk-singers, blues musicians. In another part of town, a cross marks the spot where the English burned Jeanne d' Arc — France's greatest national heroine — at the stake in 1431. Next to it was a modern, futuristic church, its architecture evoking the feel of waves and the sea. Inside are stained glass windows dating from the early 1500s that were saved from St. Vincent's church and sheltered from bombing during World War II by hiding them in nearby cellars. This church is set incongruously next to a fish market, providing its worshipers with an odd assortment of sights and smells.

The Armada wouldn't start for two days but some of the ships were already there — across the way the *Lobelia*, a Belgian minesweeper; the *Kaskelot*, a British three-masted bark; the *Moen*, a Danish minesweeper; the *Sagres II*, a Portuguese three-masted bark. On our side of the river were the *Gloria*, a

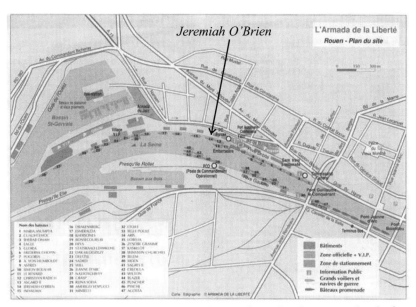

This map from the official program shows where the ships were berthed in Rouen. The Jeremiah O'Brien *is at No. 14.* Author's collection.

Newspaper photo of the A. Von Humboldt from Germany. Paris Normandie.

Colombian three-masted bark; the *A. Von Humboldt*, a German three-masted bark; the *Jeanne d'Arc*, a French helicopter carrier and flagship of the French Navy; and the *Dar Mlodziezy*, a Polish three-masted ship.

Newspaper photo of the Polish training ship Dar Mlodziezy *arriving in Rouen.* Paris Normandie.

The *L'Armada* organization had scheduled events for the *O'Brien* crew, volunteer docents to help with crowd control and a cruise down the Seine at the end of *L'Armada,* a wonderful opportunity to raise funds.

We constantly reviewed the blue line tour, analyzing bottlenecks and problem areas. The crowds on the quays and the visitors on the ships far surpassed even the best turnouts in England. Never had we seen so many people. We were to learn that more than five million people came to see *L'Armada* in the nine days it was open.

The close contact with the French people continued to touch us emotionally. Each day brought new stories of white-haired veterans, former seamen and civilians coming aboard and, with heartfelt emotion, saying again and again, "Merci, thank you," expressing their gratitude for our coming and bringing the ship to France. More and more we understood how the French and English felt about the United States and the ships symbolized by the *Jeremiah O'Brien,* yet we were constantly surprised and moved at the depth of emotion and feeling.

More beautiful, tall-masted sailing ships arrived. The Mexican *Cuauhtémoc* motored past, a huge red, white and green flag flying from the stem. Her cadets manned the yards in traditional style, standing atop them, their bright uniform jerseys standing out against the clear blue sky. Then came the U.S. Coast

Our old friend from Cherbourg, the Cuauhtémoc *arrived shortly after the* O'Brien. *L'Armada de la Liberté.*

The Italian Amerigo Vespucci *at sea before arrival. Author's collection.*

Guard training ship, *Eagle*, white-hulled with a broad diagonal orange stripe across the bow, her crew likewise aloft. By far the most colorful and dramatic-looking ship to arrive was the *Amerigo Vespucci*, the three-masted full-rigged ship from Italy. She was massive, with an extreme length of 331 feet, breadth of 50 feet and a draft of 21 feet. Built in 1931, her black steel hull with horizontal white stripes displaces 3,550 tons. Her cadets, too, stood on the yards amidst flags and bunting, making a truly grand entrance.

Although *L'Armada* hadn't officially opened, people thronged the walkway next to the ships. As the day progressed, more and more people came and soon the whole esplanade was a mass of colorfully-dressed humanity, ebbing and flowing past the ships.

One of the most popular items for sale was a full-color program. Inside were listings of events and historical descriptions. Each ship in the Armada was given a page of its own with a color photograph of the ship and a place for the "ship's stamp."

Someone on the dock gestured up at one of our crew leaning on the rail watching the crowd. He went down and learned she wanted her program stamped. Bringing the program up, he then heard other people asking the same thing. We quickly realized this was going to be a very popular memento of the Armada and set up a card table and chair at the foot of the gangway. Suddenly, there was a long line of people waiting to have their programs

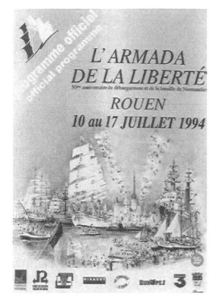

Left, the cover of L'Armada *official program, probably the most popular item for sale. Right, the* O'Brien*'s page from the program which kept the crew busy signing autographs day and night.* Author's collection.

L'Armada de la Liberté *with Rouen in the background. Note the crowds of people on the esplanade alongside the ships and the* Jeremiah O'Brien *in the center.* Author's collection.

stamped. Then they began asking for autographs. We brought out another chair and another crewman to autograph while the first stamped. This went on nonstop from mid-afternoon, through the supper hour and into the night.

Sunday, July 10, the first day of *L'Armada*, broke fine, clear and calm. The quays were lined with large and small tall-masted sailing ships, some moored two and three abreast. In the crowds on the pier we saw the uniformed officers, midshipmen and sailors of a dozen countries, enjoying the open-air cafes or walking arm-in-arm with beautiful young French girls. Excitement was in the air. This was a gathering of ships to end all gatherings of ships and the *O'Brien* was right in the middle of it. We had brought our ticket booth with us from San Francisco and now set it on the dock at the foot of the entrance gangway with a sign explaining in French why we charged admission.

There were French-speaking docent-volunteers in the ticket booth, at the top of the gangway, in the engine room, on all three levels of the midships house, at the forward guntub and in the ship's store. Crewmembers were stationed at the ticket booth, in the wheelhouse, in the radio shack, at the exit gangway, on the flying bridge and in the guntubs.

This sign explained to our visitors why we were the only ship at L'Armada *to charge admission. It says, "In June 1944 the* Jeremiah O'Brien *was at Omaha Beach. She is the sole survivor of the debarquement. She has returned to Normandy for the 50th Anniversary. This Liberty ship is a museum unique in the world. It is run by an association of volunteer veterans. Your donations will help them in the return to the U.S.A. Thank you."* Author's collection.

At ten o'clock we opened the gangway and immediately lost any sense of "our" ship. It became like a ride at an amusement park and we were suddenly in the business of moving people. The crowd swarmed aboard and lines formed outside the after main deck house, at the aft entrance to the midships house on the port side, throughout the interior passageways inside the ship and at the staging area for the engine room tours, starboard side, main deck, aft of the midships house. The docents acted as traffic cops, holding the line up to let a few dozen pass in one direction, then the other.

People also came aboard to see the captain or the admiral on business. It

It was summer, most of France was on vacation, and most vacationers came to L'Armada. *Newspaper photo from* Paris Normandie.

Crowds were incessant. Millions of people from all over Europe came to see the Armada. Newspaper photo from Paris Normandie.

took half an hour to work our way against traffic up to the captain's office. The warm day turned hot, then blistering. Our valiant volunteers did their best but needed brief breaks. When a crew member assigned to the exit gangway left to eat lunch, some of the mob on the dock made a rush up to the main deck. The after deck became packed with the unmoving line running back down to the quay.

We were all worn out with the heat, the unending crowds, and the strain of trying to be friendly and hospitable, answer questions, and yet keep the line moving. The narrow interior corridors were jammed and every inch of the ship was packed with people. There was a line of people four wide extending from midships to the bow on the dock. Many had waited more than an hour in the heat. When we finally closed for the day, we tallied 4,960 visitors aboard.

Tom Patterson:

> When we got to Rouen the ship was just besieged with French people trying to get on board, and this became our single biggest challenge. The weather that week was gorgeous, but it was up in the high 90's most of the time. In France people take vacations in July so the quay by the side of the ship, which was about a hundred feet wide, was completely jammed with people. There were six million people reported to be in Rouen to see this Armada.

It didn't get dark until after ten and the nightly fireworks displays started just before midnight. Looking across the river we

Even Bruce the raven got into the act, inspired, no doubt by the enthusiasm on the part of the French for all things American. Phil Frank and *San Francisco Chronicle.*

This serene evening view from the river belies the intense activity on the esplanade alongside the ships. The Jeremiah O'Brien *is left center.* Author's collection.

saw the first colorful balls of yellow sparkle shooting off in all directions somewhere behind the ships. Then came puffs of red, green, blue and white climbing higher and higher and coming more and more frequently. Some of the fireworks exploded with a cannon roar, delayed by the distance from the harbor, others fizzled and crackled, like water on a hot stove. The display ended with a crescendo of multicolored sparkling balls of light and thunderous explosions. When it was over everyone in the harbor cheered and applauded, their ovations echoing across the water from ship to ship.

The parade on the dock continued with revelers stopping at the tent-cafes for a late

Fireworks were a nightly climax to the day's festivities. Newspaper photo from Paris Normandie.

night snack and live entertainment. Slowly, then, the crowd thinned, until by two a.m. the quay was empty, the ghostly yellow light of the tall lamps shining dispiritedly on scraps of paper and empty soda cans.

The following morning we awoke to the shrill piping of boatswain's whistles as the various Navy ships piped morning colors for their crews. Then came the morning announcements over ships' public address systems in a polyglot of languages, one on top of the other, through the still, smoky air in the harbor. Thirty-four tall ships were part of *L'Armada*, plus eighteen Naval ships of various nations and twenty-five assorted brigs, pinnaces, yawls and catches — and one fifty-one-year-old Liberty ship in its center.

Over the course of the following days, we developed more efficient ways of deploying the volunteers and cooked up other tactics to facilitate the movement of the torrent of visitors through the ship. Most of the volunteers were French youngsters in their late teens and twenties, bright and eager to work. Some developed such loyalty to the *O'Brien* that they followed her to Le Havre and worked there, too, A number of retired French merchant mariners, some who had served on Liberty ships, volunteered, as well. One day, there were eight retired ship captains on duty directing the human traffic on board.

Darwin Curtis, a retired State Department official who spoke fluent French, was of inestimable help, arranging, organizing, running interference, smoothing the way.

> My most indelible memories of this experience will be the visitors to the ship. No one associated with the *O'Brien* had any idea of the emotions she would evoke in France. She had revived the memories of older Normans about that cataclysmic time of their liberation so long ago. Liberty ships, hundreds of them, had suddenly appeared off the battered coast of France with all the means necessary to rid the country of its plague and begin its reconstruction. To their minds she was a symbol of deliverance.

Countless times, I looked down into the moist eyes of old faces and heard a whispered, '*merci*.' Most would then turn away, overcome. Some would dig in a pocket or purse for old, dog-eared photos of Liberty ships moored at rubble-strewn quays, or produce some other memento they wanted to share with a veteran.

Almost every crew member had similar experiences, repeated scores of times over the nine days of the Armada. The gratitude of the French people was overwhelming. Again and again, as it did through the whole trip, we were made to feel that all the effort to bring the ship over was worth more to the people than we could ever understand.

Throughout the days and well into the early hours of each following morning, the walkway alongside the ships was a river of people, ebbing and flowing in a colorful mass. At the foot of the gangway to each ship a logjam formed as visitors waited to board or grouped around the sailors stamping and autographing programs. During open hours the line waiting to come aboard was four, six and even eight wide and as long as the ship itself.

It was a carnival atmosphere with white tents from one end of the quay to the other. Everything was open until ten or eleven at night, some until one or two in the morning. You could sit down to a full dinner or snack your way the length of the esplanade.

The party atmosphere seldom let up. Around 3 a.m. one morning we heard the beat drums and the clanging sounds of metal. The din came from a mob moving along the pierside from town in our direction, pounding on conga drums, pots, pans, garbage can lids, sticks and anything else that made noise. The drums set an underlying samba beat but that was all but drowned out by the accompaniment. The mob moved to the *Simon Bolivar*, two ships away, then stopped, although the noise continued. Three or four sailors separated themselves, dropped their "instruments," waved and staggered aboard. The mass of people moved again, toward the *Christian Radich* tied up behind us. Now, individuals took shape. There were sailors from *Jeanne d'*

This newspaper photo shows the crew of the Colombian training ship Gloria *manning the yards as the ship arrives at Rouen.* Paris Normandie.

Arc, their pom-pommed hats askew, sailors in white T-shirts from the *Inhauma*, a Brazilian frigate tied farther up the dock, crew from the Ukrainian ship ahead of us — in other words, about fifty "drunken sailors" returning from a night on the town, having the time of their lives and making as much noise as possible. A couple of sailors weaved their way aboard the Norwegian square-rigger and the mob continued toward the *Jeremiah O'Brien*, drums pounding, pans and tin cans clattering, sticks beating. As they neared our gangway a police car appeared in the distance and sped up the dock, blue lights flashing, its claxon all but drowned by the noise. A police van came into view following the car. The mob finally became aware of them and the "music" stopped. The car and van slowed, detoured around the sailors and continued on to the gangway of a ship farther down the river. The band struck up again and continued on its way.

The high level of excitement was constant. Day or night there was always *something* going on. The instant one stepped out on deck one was in the middle of, and part of, one of the greatest maritime spectacles of all time. The great, majestic sailing ships with their tall masts, the warships' monumental masses, the uniformed sailors, the crowds — it was all one great, big, colorful kaleidoscope of shapes, color, movement and enthusiasm.

Early each morning, many of us got up on deck, steaming mugs of coffee in our hands, trying to take in our surroundings. Forward of our bow a line of tall ships and Naval vessels led in a gentle arc against the bank down river. First was the Ukrainian square-rigger *Kershones*, white hulled with gold trim. Ahead of her, the *Esmeralda*, the Chilean four-masted schooner, then the *Dar Mlodziezy*, a Polish three-masted tall ship, then a mix of warships and tall ships from all over the world — South Africa, Brazil, Denmark, Italy and Russia — a forest of masts cutting through the smoky morning air. Astern of the *Jeremiah O'Brien* was the *Christian Radich*, the three-masted Norwegian square-rigger, next to her the *Asgard II*, an Irish brig, then the *Simon Bolivar*, the *Astrid*, the *A. Von Humboldt*, the *Pogoria*, the

Frederyk Chopin, the *Gloria*, the *Eagle*, the *Shebab Oman*, the *Cuauhtémoc* and the *Maria Asumpta*, tall ships all. On the opposite bank of the river lay the *Amerigo Vespucci, Belem, Winston Churchill*, and a grand mix of warships and sailing ships. "There will never be a gathering of ships like this again," said Capt. Jahn.

Thursday, July 14, was Bastille Day, France's national day, equivalent to our Independence Day. Morning began with the usual sound of boatswains' whistles skirling through the harbor, then the announcements over the various shipboard public address systems. But today, the *Jeanne d'Arc* fired her deck cannons — twenty-one volleys in honor of French Independence.

Our World War II veterans were very much in the forefront of peoples' interest. Capt. Jahn, Adm. Patterson, Ed Lingenfield, Bill Duncan, Russ Mosholder, Jim Wade, Phil Sinnott, Dick Brannon, Jean Yates, Bill Rowlands, Bob Gisslow, Carl Kreidler, Ed Smith, François Le Pendu, Jim Miller, Rich Hill and Wes Masterson were constantly in demand because of their status as World War II veterans. In the Bastille Day parade, they received the greatest applause from the onlookers.

Our crew of veteran mariners received the strongest ovation from the crowd in the Bastille Day parade. Paris Normandie.

Top, the Jeremiah O'Brien *with the Rouen Cathedral in the background. Bottom a similar photo showing the Coast Guard's bark* Eagle. Top, National Liberty Ship Memorial; bottom, newspaper photo, *Paris Normandie.*

Bastille Day was our best day yet with almost 5,300 visitors on board.

The gratitude of the French people seemed inexhaustible, often as touching as it was surprising. Darwin Curtis:

> One day, a tiny old lady, beautifully dressed, came up the accommodation ladder, saw the collection box and put in twenty francs. Then she came over and handed me a plastic envelope. Inside was the 8 June 1944 edition of a Rouen newspaper. The front page was covered with stories of the allied invasion, the devastating German counterattack and the confidence expressed by the German General Staff in Berlin that the invaders would soon be hurled back into the sea. At the top, in pencil, she had written in English, "For the Liberty ship *Jeremiah O'Brien* for whole veterans crew with gratitude Armada Liberte Rouen — 10 July 1994." She had treasured it for fifty years but now she wanted the captain to have it. I asked for her name and she demurred, she preferred to remain anonymous.
>
> Officers and crew from other ships came aboard frequently. Some acted as though it was a shrine. "You are welcome aboard," I said to a smart French Navy commander from the *Jeanne d'Arc*. "It is an honor to be here," he answered.

The *Jeremiah O'Brien* and *Jeanne d'Arc*, flagship of the French Navy, vied for first place with the visitors to *L'Armada*.

In all about 35,000 people visited the *O'Brien* at Rouen. The gate receipts and store sales providing enough to continue the voyage.

It had already been decided that to reward our French volunteers for all their help, we would let them ride down the Seine with us. It would be small enough thanks for all they had done. The *Jeanne d'Arc* graciously lent us 500 lifejackets for the cruise.

July 17 came, the day scheduled for *L'Armada de la Liberté* to sail down the Seine to Le Havre. We woke to an overcast and — finally — cool day with very mixed feelings. It had been a hectic, frantic, nerve-frazzling nine days; we were worn out from the heat, the strain of coping in a foreign language with thousands of people, exhausted from days that began at 6 a.m. and ended with noise, fireworks and samba bands at 2 a.m. And yet it had been the most exciting, most remarkable nine days of all our lives. In a trip filled with highlights, memorable events, emotional upwellings and nostalgia, *L'Armada de la Liberté* would stand out as the highest highlight, the most memorable event, the pinnacle of our once-in-a-lifetime voyage. "Never again will there be a gathering of ships like this," we told ourselves, and each other, over and over. With great regret we prepared to bid farewell to Rouen.

Passengers and volunteers boarded at 0730. It was a day of celebration, with cannon fire from the Naval vessels and the sound of ships' whistles echoing across the harbor. At 0820, the *Maria Asumpta*, a British brig, departed, followed every five minutes by another ship for the 60-mile run down the Seine to Le Havre. The *Jeremiah O'Brien* was scheduled to leave at 0930. The last ship, the *Iskra*, would depart at 1135. Helicopters hovered above the harbor as the procession got underway.

The official parade route down the Seine as provided by L'Armada de la Liberté.

Crowds line the river and villages were packed with people. John Linderman.

Crowds were gathered on the pier cheering each ship as she sailed slowly by. As our turn came, we singled up, then threw off the last line. The people applauded as we slowly moved out to midstream. Ahead was the USS *Grasp*, a U.S. Navy underwater recovery ship. The *Minbelli*, an Italian destroyer, soon pulled up astern. As the *Jeremiah O'Brien* passed ships that were still tied up awaiting their turn, we received flag and whistle salutes. On some ships the officers and sailors, in formation at their ship's rail, hand-saluted.

Both banks of the Seine were lined with people, from Rouen sixty miles to its mouth at Le Havre. The French newspapers the following day would report an estimate of six to eight million. They were waving and cheering, waving American and French flags. As we returned their salutes with the ship's whistle they shouted and applauded even louder. It was an unforgettable experience — an unsurpassable cap to the whole glorious Armada.

Sailing down river, we recognized the chateaux, thatched roof cottages, castles on hills, towns and villages we had seen just two weeks before. Looking beyond the crowds, the view was peaceful and serene, like a Monet painting, fields or hills, small towns and villages. The sky was hazy with an occasional grey plume of smoke rising from a chimney. From time to time we even smelled the wood fires burning. But these sights were overshadowed by the unbelievable crowd gathered to see *L'Armada de la Liberté* pass into history. Up and down the river were the great sailing ships, their masts probing the sky, in a tableau from centuries

Kershones, trois-mâts
ukrainien : la voile
traditionnelle sur
coque d'acier.

Basé à Saint-Malo, le côtre-
hunier Le Renard appartient
un certain Robert Surcouf : ç
ne s'invente pas !

Jeremiah O'Brien :
comme à Rouen, le
liberty-ship rivalisera,
au Havre, en nombre de
visiteurs, avec la Jeanne.

Press coverage was phenomenal. This article is from Paris Normandie.

past. The whole scene was mind-boggling — the *Jeremiah O'Brien* sailing down the Seine in the midst of a fleet of tall ships, millions of people clustered on the banks — literally, sixty *miles* of people — behind them, chateaux-covered hills or small French villages. Bands in some of the towns we passed played "The Star-Spangled Banner" or "Battle Hymn of the Republic."

A fraction of the six million people that lined the banks of the Seine River for the departure of L'Armada de la Liberté. *Newspaper photo from* Paris Normandie.

Chile's Esmeralda *clearing the Bridge of Normandy, bound for Le Havre. Newspaper photo from* Paris Normandie.

The Simon Bolívar, *Venezuela's traning vessel, outbound from the festivities.*
Author's collection.

In the excitement, Tom Patterson armed himself with a battery-operated megaphone and went from one side of the flying bridge to the other, shouting to the people lining the banks, "*Merci, merci beaucoup. Vive la France.* From Jeremy O'Brien. *Merci Beaucoup.*" He did this for hours and when his voice gave out he handed the megaphone to our chaplain, Jim Wade, who took up the chant.

L'Armada ended at Le Havre, where the *Jeremiah O'Brien* was open for a few days.

July 22 was her last day in Europe. Five pilots came on board, one to guide the ship out, four to take a last ride on what would probably be the last Liberty ship in French waters in history. The tugs *Abielle No. 7* and *Abielle Le Havre* were made fast fore and aft. The gangways were taken ashore and we started singling up the mooring lines.

We blew the traditional three whistle blasts to the crowd. They applauded and cheered, waving. Some dabbed at their eyes with handkerchiefs. Offshore, a large tug-fireboat spouted water in white, frothy, arcing spumes as the other tugs spun the *O'Brien* around and pointed her toward the harbor entrance.

The program announcing the parade to Le Havre, the official termination of L'Armada. Author's collection.

Motorboats and yachts escorted us out the harbor, horns and whistles blowing. When we reached the sea buoy, the five pilots got off, climbing down the Jacob's ladder. The deck crew pulled the ladder on deck, rolled it up and tied it behind a mast house. The pilot boat blew three blasts, we returned the salute. Capt. Jahn ordered "full ahead" and the *Jeremiah O'Brien* was on her way home.

27

PORTLAND, MAINE

After fifty-one years, the *Jeremiah O'Brien* came home. Maine is where she was born and Maine is the home state of Jeremiah O'Brien, the Revolutionary War hero for whom she was named. His hometown, Machias, is just a short distance up the coast from Portland. It was there, in 1775, that Jeremiah O'Brien led a group of patriots armed only with a few shotguns, some axes, and thirty pitchforks, and captured the British man-of-war *Margaretta* in the first naval engagement of the War for Independence. We were doubly proud to be returning.

The sky was clear, the sun was out and a brisk breeze blew from shore carrying with it the land smells of evergreens and New England vegetation. Grey and white seagulls glided astern of the ship, looking for scraps. The rugged Maine shoreline, a mosaic of green, blue and brown, grew larger, then her rocky coves and inlets became distinctive, each one begging exploration, promising adventure.

'She's coming home'

Greeted by a ferry, the Jeremiah O'Brien *passes the Bug Light at Portland, Maine, entering the harbor for the first time in fifty-one years.* Maine Sunday Telegram.

Within each inlet and cove solid New England brick, masonry and wood houses, many surrounded by trees, faced the ocean, the morning sun reflecting off their windows.

The *Jeremiah O'Brien* approached the Portland Head Light, the oldest light house in the United States, built on the orders of George Washington and first lighted on Jan. 10, 1791. We were in our finery, the deck officers in dress blues, the ship with signal flags from bow to stem, corporate sponsors' flags on the triatic stay, our large American ensign on the steaming gaff. A great mass of people lined the shore.

More than 1,500 people were on hand for our arrival at Portland. Ed Langlois.

The view from the water, the Jeremiah O'Brien *with "a bone in her teeth," approaching Portland harbor.* Ed Langlois.

As we passed the light, the pilot asked us to blow the whistle. Three times the *Jeremiah O'Brien*'s foghorn bellowed out into the crisp morning air. The crowd waved and cheered. The American Legion Militia honored the *O'Brien* with a twenty-one cannon salute[1] and the Civil War re-enactors fired their twenty-one gun salute at Spring Point Light at nearby Fort Preble. Bob Crocker, who was in the ship's original Armed Guard gun crew on voyages 5 and 6, came up from Florida and, from the shore near Portland Head Light, watched the ship come in. "To see my old ship come in after all these years was one of the most moving experiences of my life. There were a couple of minutes there I couldn't say anything."

Passing the Head Light we were joined by yachts, motorboats, excursion boats and a fire boat, her nozzles sending glistening arcs of water into the blue sky, creating misty rainbows in the morning sun.

In England and France, we were surprised and moved by the deep emotions the sight of our old ship, and her old crew, stirred in so many people. We came to understand the feelings expressed by so many and treasured the experiences as among the most memorable in our lives. But we didn't expect the deep emotional response that our

---

[1] We later learned it was actually a twenty-three gun salute. The Militia had some black powder left over and rather than take it home they fired twice more.

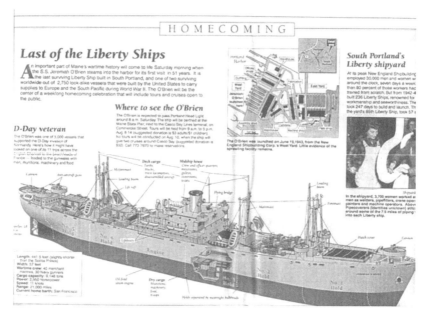

The Portland Press Telegram *did a fine job of creating interest with this piece on the* Jeremiah O'Brien*'s homecoming.*

ship would evoke in our own country. The difference this time was, in Portland, the ship brought back memories of youth and a sense of important contribution to the country.

Thousands of people who worked in the New England Shipbuilding Corporation's yard during the war, including several of the *O'Brien*'s old crewmembers, visited the ship. There was always somebody pointing out the weld they laid in, or the wiring they installed, or explaining the difficulties of connecting piping in the bowels of the ship, or pointing out the bunk they slept in, or explaining what it was like living aboard the ship.

Most of them claimed to have worked on the *Jeremiah O'Brien* herself, but most likely they only worked in the yard at the time the ship was built. New England Shipbuilding constructed more than 200 Liberty ships and most of the workers wouldn't have been aware of the name of any particular ship they worked on. Each one was just another of those ships "built by the mile and chopped off by the yard." The Libertys were designed to be simple, uncomplicated ships that could be "built faster than they were sunk," and in yards around the country, 2710 were stamped out of the same giant ship cutter and sent across the oceans. But, maybe, in a sense, those thousands *did* work on the *O'Brien* and could now come to see her one more time with tears in their eyes and nostalgia in their souls as they touched a welding seam with shaking fingers or ran their wrinkled hands over a rail. For the *Jeremiah O'Brien* embodies all those that went before her or came after, a living symbol of all Liberty ships.

Capt. & Mrs. Jahn on the flying bridge of the Jeremiah O'Brien. *Ed Langlois.*

In Portland, we also understood better the universal human desire that transcends culture and language — the need to share important memories of events that are bigger than daily life. Just as they had in Europe, visitors came up to crew members, showing long-kept badges, treasured papers and keepsakes of their youth. We were learning that it wasn't just those who suffered in a great war who are forever marked by it. Here, in Portland, it was people who worked in a great cause, and who, too, were forever changed by it. At the tall ship armada in Rouen, we talked about the brotherhood of the sea. Now, we were realizing the brotherhood of man.

The day of our departure, Monday, August 15, opened with blue skies behind thick, fast-moving clouds. After the good-byes, we took a quick departure. Our pilot, Capt. Granville Smith, shook hands with everyone on the flying bridge and said, "God bless you for bringing the ship to Portland."

At 0830 the *Jeremiah O'Brien* departed buoy "P" into a moderate head sea. It was a "straight shot" to the Cape Cod Canal with no course changes. We could see the New England coast to our right, and an occasional fishing boat, pulling its lobster pots.

28

Ships Passing ...

Two thousand seven hundred and ten Liberty ships were built in the 1940s during America's greatest shipbuilding era. Of them, only two remain operational, the *Jeremiah O'Brien* and the *John W. Brown*. The *O'Brien* is the only unaltered Liberty in the world, looking exactly as she did fifty years ago, inside and out. The *Brown* is modified from her original configuration, but she is still an active ship. The *Brown* was to have been part of "The Last Convoy" to Normandy (together with the *Lane Victory* and the *Jeremiah O'Brien*), but the high cost of replacing too many rivets prevented the trip, to the disappointment of her crew. She observed the 50th Anniversary by sailing from her home port of Baltimore to visit ports on the East Coast.

We received word that the *John W. Brown* was sailing from Baltimore, bound for Halifax, Nova Scotia and as we departed

The John W. Brown *approaches.* Author's collection.

Portland, our radio operator "Sparks" (Bob Gisslow) received word that the *Brown* was scheduled to transit the Cape Cod Canal at noon.[1] A rendezvous was set for 1530.

The sky was clear, the ocean a calm blue, a picture-book setting for the meeting of the last two Liberty ships in the world.

Just after 1500 hours the *Brown* was sighted on the horizon, slightly on the port bow. Every pair of binoculars on the bridge was in use. Steaming closer, we saw a freshly-painted grey hull and superstructure and the familiar Liberty silhouette. The differences were minor — her boot-topping was red where ours was black and her after machine guns were on raised platforms above her after gun, while ours were on the same level as our after gun. Otherwise, it was almost like seeing a reflection of ourselves. Capt. Jahn brought the *O'Brien* to the left to give us a better view while the *Brown*'s master, Capt. Esbensen, did the same. We both kept turning left, left, to get closer and closer.

At exactly 1532 Eastern Daylight Time (1932 Universal Coordinate Time)[2] on August 15, 1994, the Liberty ship *Jeremiah O'Brien* and the Liberty ship *John W. Brown* passed port side to port side one-quarter of a mile apart. The traditional three-whistle

---

[1] By tradition, all radio operators in the merchant marine are called Sparks because the early marine wireless sets were prone to throwing off electrical sparks; just as all ship's carpenters are called "Chips" because that is the by-product of their labors.

[2] Formerly known as Greenwich Mean Time.

The John W. Brown, *looking "ship shape in Bristol fashion" passed on her way to Halifax, Nova Scotia.* Author's collection.

salute and short answer were exchanged and flags were dipped.

It was a poignant occasion — the last time in history that two Liberty ships would meet and pass on the open ocean. On both ships everybody waved, then each vessel continued on its way.

At 1800 that day the *Jeremiah O'Brien* transited the Cape Cod Canal. Then it was on to the U.S. Merchant Marine Academy

A historic meeting. The John W. Brown *and the* Jeremiah O'Brien *pass — the last meeting of two Liberty ships at sea.* Denys Lomax.

at Kings Point, New York, alma mater for some of the officers on board. Anchoring off the campus overnight, the voyage continued the following day: New York City; Baltimore, Maryland; Jacksonville, Florida then once more through the Panama Canal.

29

STORMY WEATHER

Normally, the coastwise route up Central America and Mexico would consist of a series of straight lines laid down between points two to five miles abeam of major headlands. Because the coast itself is not straight but made up of bays, harbors, lagoons and other indentations, such routing would keep these areas generally out of sight. Also, the ship would be bucking the Japanese Current, running down the Pacific toward the equator. But Capt. Jahn knew these waters. His first trip on this coast was on a tug in 1933 and he had been in every port, down to Chile. He ordered a track drawn on the chart that paralleled the coast two miles off. This kept the ship close to shore, causing us to travel more miles to get where we were going, but also giving better scenery, and the captain thought there was a good chance of picking up a countercurrent close inshore for greater speed and more than making up for the straight line approach.

We began to see more and more marine life. A school of tuna passed, large fish, flashing silver and grey as they jumped playfully out of the water and splashed their way along. Flocks of black and white birds with long, pointed bills dived in the water around the ship. As each one surfaced it swallowed an anchovy or two, then flapped its way into the air, circled and dived again.

One evening, we had front seats at a most spectacular sound-and-light show over the shore as we passed the Costa Rican coast. The sky to seaward was perfectly clear with stars showing but on shore large areas of light grey clouds glowed yellow and seemed to vibrate with each thunderclap. From time to time a startling yellow-white flash of multi-forked lightning shot from the base of the thunderheads to the ground. Otherwise, it was a dark night with no moon and the only other lights were those of coastal fishing boats bobbing peacefully on the sea as we passed.

The next day started with thick clouds and drizzly rain but soon cleared to a blue sky and flat calm sea. To starboard we saw the lush green coast of Costa Rica, thick with jungle vegetation and occasional barren brown outcroppings where the coastal hills dropped into the Pacific. Small, colorful fishing boats worked offshore, the fishermen waving as we passed. Schools of light-grey dolphin came leaping out of the water toward the ship. They followed for a while, riding the pressure wave at the bow, then disappeared as quickly as they came. Black and white birds with angular wings and long sharp beaks dove at flying fish, frightening them out of the water in delicate fan-shaped formations as they glided through the air, trying to escape.

The sea water temperature was in the high eighties making the engine room all but intolerable. The black gang often came up out of their 120° "hellhole" drenched with sweat and looking like they had been through a wringer.

In the evening as we coasted past the town of Champerico, Guatemala, there was another pyrotechnic display. Large grey billowing thunderheads covered most of the shoreline. We heard the thunder and saw the clouds flash brightly in the distance. As

Bruce gets into the spirit of life at sea. Phil Frank and *San Francisco Chronicle.*

it got darker, the entire cloud mass above the coast was brilliantly lit with forked lightning that shot horizontally from cloud to cloud creating an electric grid of white flashes filling almost a quarter of the sky. Then, thick white columns of electricity shot straight to the land, backlighting the clouds in eerie, pale yellow-grey light. It was an awesome, spectacular show.

As we approached the Gulf of Tehuantepec we received a weather warning for high winds within 120 miles of the Gulf. Many a ship has been caught in a "Tehuantepecer," the violent winds blowing off the Mexican coast in this area, and suffered severe damage or loss. The prescribed maneuver in such a case is to hug the coastline. Capt. Jahn prudently ordered a course change, a dogleg up into the gulf that would take us away from the center of the potential storm.

The pyrotechnics were even more awesome that night. The coast was spotted with great towering thunderheads that threw off spectacular lightning storms; yet, between these massive storm systems, the sky was clear with stars showing. As we steamed along at ten knots, a thunder cloud slowly moved out from shore toward us, throwing off sheets, bolts and chains of lightning in all directions. It was like a living creature, a huge swirling mass of dark grey cloud angrily throwing off electricity at anything that might be in its path. Another storm cloud appeared ahead to port, equally tall, equally threatening. It was as if the two cloud masses were giant beasts on a forlorn planet, rolling out into an arena, threatening, displaying, challenging each other with their might and power. And we were caught between them.

The wind came up, blowing strongly from ever-changing directions. The cloud storms attacked in counter-point, the one ahead dropping bolts of white lightning on the ocean, the one to starboard glowing angrily and belching earsplitting thunderous noises. The storm ahead thundered in answer. The cloud mass to starboard spit yellow-white bolts of lightning, one after the other. On shore we could see ugly grey-yellow clouds, funneling their energy in bolts of lightning that shot down to the land.

All through the voyage the crew especially enjoyed Phil Frank's Farley cartoons run in the *San Francisco Chronicle*. In the series, Bruce the Raven joined the ship in Panama outbound and made the entire trip with us. Someone suggested we paint Bruce's image on the crow's nest, and what better place for a raven. Phil Frank generously gave copyright permission.

At noon, Friday, September 9, word went around the ship, "The Raven has landed." On the front of the crow's nest was a full-color painting of Bruce, his wing draped protectively over a keg of brandy.

"The Raven has landed." Bruce makes his appearance on the crow's nest as official mascot.
Alex Hochstraser.

30

HOME FROM THE SEA

The *Jeremiah O'Brien* took arrival .8 miles off the San Francisco Light Buoy at 0530, September 23, 1994. Shortly after 0600 the pilot boarded, along with members of the press. Ahead was a large flotilla of boats coming out the Gate — President Roosevelt's yacht, the *Potomac*, fireboats from San Francisco, Oakland and other ports in the Bay, the historic hay scow *Alma*, the steam tug *Hercules*, the *Hawaiian Chieftain*, a replica square-rigger that had come from Hawaii for the event, and hundreds of motorboats, yachts, tugs and excursion boats.

On the way up from Panama, we stopped at San Diego and Long Beach, spending a few days at each port. The *Lane Victory*[1] sailed with us from Long Beach and was following.

---

[1] The *Lane Victory* was to be part of The Last Convoy. She got as far as Acapulco but had to return home due to boiler problems, much to the disappointment of her crew.

Left to right, Pat Burke, Carol Fisch and Alex Hochstraser help ready our largest American flag as we enter the Golden Gate. Bob Black.

As the ship approached the Golden Gate Bridge the boats surrounded her, the fireboats shooting foaming sprays of water in giant arcs. The bridge walkway was lined with spectators looking down at the ship, waving and cheering. American flags and welcome home banners hung from the railings. The square-rigger fired her antique brass cannons, the *Lane Victory* answered with her ship's guns and then we shot ours.

The *Jeremiah O'Brien* passed under the Golden Gate Bridge at 0804, after five and-a-half months, fifteen ports and more than

In the crow's nest Bruce had a spectacular view, but his lady friend flew the coop. Phil Frank and *San Francisco Chronicle*.

At Last — Our Ship Comes In

Mike Martino (left) and Jim Anderson waved flags as the O'Brien passed under the Golden Gate Bridge

Rowers tipped their hats to the O'Brien as a tugboat pushed it toward its berth at Pier 27

PHOTOS BY MICHAEL MALONEY/THE CHRONICLE

Crowds, Boats and Parade Hail Historic Voyage

Our home town paper gave us grand coverage on our return, capturing the spirit of the occasion. San Francisco Chronicle.

17,000 miles. Capt. Jahn said, "Give 'em the whistle." The response to our deep, bellowing foghorn was a deafening cacophony of toots, honks, blasts, squeals and peeps from the fleet surrounding us. Thousands of red carnations rained down on us from the bridge. Thousands of people lined the shore.

We steamed toward the San Francisco waterfront amidst a thousand rainbows of spray from the fireboats' nozzles. The *Jeremiah O'Brien* could hardly be seen, sometimes, through the

The billboard to beat all billboards marked the end of one of the piers on the San Francisco waterfront. Jean Yates.

rainbows. Soldiers at the Presidio fired a nineteen gun salute. The *O'Brien* rode slowly past the Embarcadero and slid into her berth.

Slowly and deliberately, Capt. Jahn said, "Ring her off." I walked over to the telegraph and swung the handle from full ahead to full astern four times, then stopped in the final position. We both watched the engine room answer. The pointer came to rest. "Finished With Engines."

Finished with engines. George Bonawit.

The engine room revolution counter at the end of the voyage showed more than 8,600,000 revolutions since it went past 99,999,999. Author's collection.

The SS Jeremiah O'Brien *passing under the Oakland-Bay Bridge.* National Liberty Ship Memorial.

Today (2004), the *Jeremiah O'Brien* is berthed at Pier 45 in San Francisco. Open to the public every day (unless she is cruising), the third weekend of each month continues as the traditional "Steaming Weekend." Day cruises continue on the Maritime Day weekend in May and during Fleet Week in October. With the coming of the twenty-first century, annual cruises to Stockton and Sacramento were added.

The S.S. *Jeremiah O'Brien* is berthed at Pier 45, San Francisco, in the heart of Fisherman's Wharf. The ship is open daily from 10:00 A.M. TO 4 P.M. Day cruises occur on the weekend closest to Maritime Day (May 21) and the weekend of Fleet Week (early October). Ticket prices and additional information is available by writing:

S.S. *Jeremiah O'Brien*
Pier 23
San Francisco, CA 94111
Tel: 415-544-0100
Fax: 415-544-9890
Internet: www.ssjeremiahobrien.com

APPENDIX A
STATISTICS

Name: *SS Jeremiah O'Brien.*

Keel Laid: May 6, 1943.

Launched June 19, 1943.

Builder's dock trial: June 26, 1943.

Official Dock Trial: June 29, 1943.

Delivered: June 30, 1943.

Type: Steam screw.

Hull: Steel

Built for: The United States of America represented by the United
            States Maritime Commission.

Decks: 2

Masts: 3

Stem: Raked

Stern: Cruiser-elliptical.

Length between perpendiculars: 416' 0".

Length overall: 441' 6"

Beam molded: 56' 10 3/4"

Breadth: 57'

Depth molded to upper deck: 37' 4"

Depth: 34' 8.5/10

Draft, keel loaded: 27' 6 7/8"

Displacement tonnage, at loaded draft: 14,245.

Cargo and fuel tonnage: 9,146.

Gross Tonnage: 7176.49

Net Tonnage: 4380.41

Deadweight tonnage: 10,735.

Engine: Reciprocating (triple expansion), built at Hamilton, Ohio
    by General Machinery Corp., Steam powered.

Fuel consumption: 170 barrels per day at 11 knots giving a range
    of 19,000 nautical miles.

Normal IHP: 2,500.

MCE Hull No. 806

Yard Hull # 230.

CAPACITIES

CARGO

Compartment	Grain Cap. Cu. Ft.	Bale Cap. Cu. Ft.
No. 1 Hold	41,257	36,083
Tween Decks	42,924	39,322
No. 2 Hold	98,860	92,008
Tween Decks	46,744	42,630
No. 3 Hold	68,459	59,793
Tween Decks	27,970	23,904
No. 4 Hold	58,620	51,571
Tween Decks	34,570	30,864
No. 1 Deep Tank, Port	3,639	2,729
" " Stbd.	3,639	3,004
No. 2 Deep Tank, Port	7,473	5,294
" " Stbd.	7,473	5,578
No. 3 Deep Tank, Port	13,674	12,506
" " Stbd.	13,188	12,024
Total	562,608	499,573

WATER BALLAST

Tank	Cu. Ft.	Tons at 35 Cu. Ft.
Fore Peak	4,845	138

No. 1 Water Ballast		5,045	144
No. 2 Water Ballast,	Port	6,041	173
" "	Stbd.	6,041	173
No. 3 " "	Port	4,453	127
" "	Stbd.	4,453	127
No. 5 " "	Port	4,485	128
" "	Stbd.	4,485	128
No. 6 " "		4,191	120
After Peak Culinary Water		5,318	152
No. 1 Deep Tank, Port		3,983	114
" "	Stbd.	3,983	114
No. 2 " "	Port	7,427	212
" "	Stbd.	7,427	212
No. 3 " "	Port	13,583	388
" "	Stbd.	13,101	374
	Total	98,861	2,824

Fresh Water

No. 4 Reserve Feed, Port		18,042	67
" " Stbd.		18,042	67
Fresh Water, Fr. 108-113, Port		7,387	27
" " " Stbd.		7,387	27
	Total	50,858	188

Fuel Oil

Tank	Gals.	Tons at 37.23 cu. ft.
No. 1 Fuel Oil Tank	37,038	133
No. 2 Fuel Oil Tank, Port	44,278	159
" " " Stbd.	44,278	159

No. 3 Fuel Oil Tank, Port	32,582	117
" " " Stbd.	32,582	117
No. 5 Fuel Oil Tank, Port	32,861	118
" " " Stbd.	32,861	118
No. 6 Fuel Oil Tank	30,633	110
Total	287,113	1,031
F.O. Settling Tank Fr. 88-96 Port	13,924	50
F.O. Settling Tank Fr. 88-96 Stbd.	13,924	50
Total	27,848	100

Cargo Oil or Fuel Oil

No. 3 Deep Tank, Port	99,696	358
" " Stbd.	96,076	345
Total	195,733	703
Total (all F.O.)	510,733	1,834

STORE ROOMS

Space	Cu.Ft.
Bos'n stores on 2nd deck F.P. to Fr. 12	3,034
Bos'n stores on flat bet. 2nd & upper decks	3,492
Cabin Stores 2nd deck (Frs. 88-106)	4,329
Linen Locker	585
Bonded Stores	186

Refrigerated Stores:	Gross Cu. Ft.	Net Cu. Ft.
Meat	801	628
Fish	173	128
Vegetables	768	765
Dairy	176	154

Appendix B

Plans and Drawings

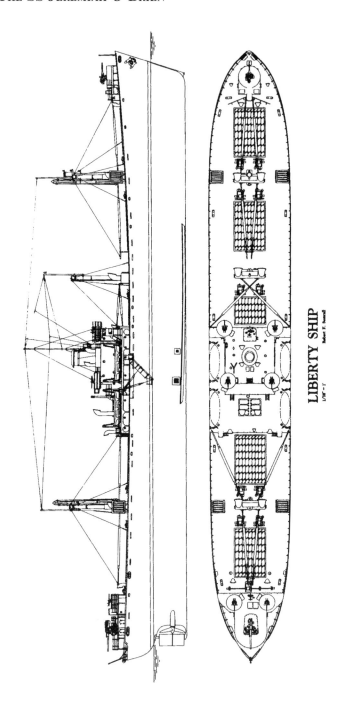

LIBERTY SHIP

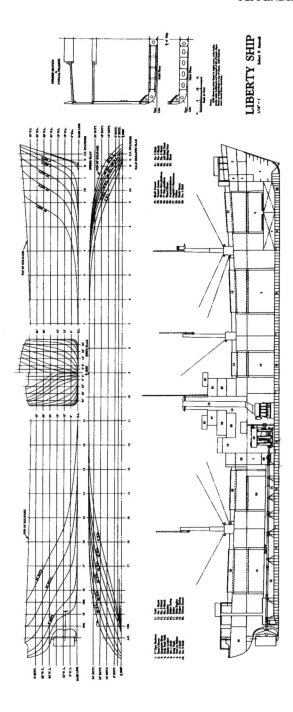

LIBERTY SHIP

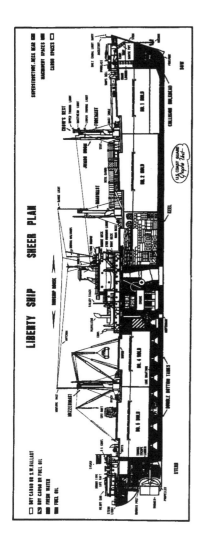

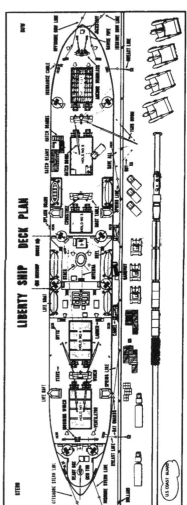

World War II sheer and deck plans. Note the military cargo, including the disassembled P-38s.

APPENDIX C
THE WORLD WAR II VOYAGES
OF THE *SS JEREMIAH O'BRIEN*
AND CREW LISTS

Voyage 1 — July 10, 1943 to September 11, 1943

Ports of Call:

Portland, Maine
Boston, Massachusetts
Halifax, Nova Scotia
Aultbea, Loch Ewe, Scotland
Methil, Firth of Forth, Scotland
London, England
Southend, England
Methil, Firth of Forth, Scotland
Aultbea, Loch Ewe, Scotland
Gourock, Firth of Clyde, Scotland
New York, New York

Crew:[1]

Oscar Southerland	Master
Charles A. Christenson	Chief Officer
Frank Pellegrino	Second Officer
Oliver Morgan	Third Officer
Robert C. Morgan	Radio Operator
Thomas J. Ender	Senior Purser
Theodore Samaras	Carpenter
John C. Gird	Boatswain (Bosun)
Mario Di Lorenzo	AB (Able-Bodied seaman)
Leo Doyle	AB
Charles McCarthy	AB

---

[1] Because the ship made a coastwise voyage and then signed foreign articles there are additional crew listed, *i.e.* two chief stewards, two chief cooks and so on. This reflects changes in crew after the ship reached Boston.

William Fallon	AB
Manuel Dias, Jr.	AB
Thomas Sullivan	AB
Sebastian De Manuel	OS (Ordinary Seaman)
Donald Corbett	OS
Sigmund Rudnitsky	AB
Coleman Schneider	Deck Cadet
Richardson Montgomery	Chief Engineer
William J. Shields	First Asssistant Engineer
Donald Morrison	Second Assistant Engineer
Leo G. Halpin	Third Assistant Engineer
Thomas J. Gill	Junior Engineer
Herman C. Bryce	Oiler
Frank Smith	Oiler
William J. McCarthy	Oiler
Lester C. Card	FWT (Fireman WaterTender)
Timothy E. Harrington	FWT
Joseph E. Charleton	FWT
Tom C. Hall	Wiper
Richard Lannan	Wiper
James D'Andrea	Engine Cadet
William C. Austin	Oiler
Ricardo Briones Zapata	Chief Steward
L. F. Fillmore	Chief Cook
Ormon T. Bibbs	Second Cook
Donald T. Vaughan	Third Cook
Vincenzo Carista	Messman
Nicholas Carista	Messman
Rosario Carista	Crew Messman
Francis McCormick	OS
Lam Spark	Chief Cook
Tee Kai	Second Cook
Ow Tong Gee	Third Cook
Lee Ah Nyok	Utility
Albert K. Bernardo	Chief Steward
Edmond Botelho	Utility
Joseph J. Brown	Utility
Louis Lambert	Utility
Vincenzo Patrinzi	AB
Joseph Cadogan	AB
Frederick C. Warren	FWT
John Float	Wiper

Armed Guard:

Charles L. Foote	Ensign
Robert Nelson Caron	Seaman 1/c
Herbert Emmett Landrum	Coxswain
James Francis Godsell	Gunner's Mate 3/c
Morgan Casto Williams	Gunner's Mate 3/c
Charles Robert Garbett	Seaman 3/c
Harmon Eugene Morick	Radioman 3/c
Lewis Edwin Hudson	Radioman 3/c
Howard Leon Campbell	Seaman 1/c
William James Chisolm	Seaman 1/c
Armando Frank Felci	Seaman 1/c
Philip Frederick Gould	Seaman 1/c
Thomas W. Hodgson, Jr.	Seaman 1/c
Kenneth Lloyd Holsapple	Seaman 1/c
John Joseph Hunt	Seaman 1/c
Henry Douglas Pinkerton	Seaman 1/c
Georges Jack Serra	Seaman 1/c
Jerome Edgar Shaw	Seaman 1/c
Edward Jardine Smedley, Jr.	Seaman 1/c
Raymond Smith	Seaman 1/c
Ludwig Joseph Stojek	Seaman 1/c
Alvis Franklin Straughan	Seaman 1/c
Gildo Ralph Surdi	Seaman 1/c
Clarence Swisher	Seaman 1/c
Edward Anthony Sznukowski	Seaman 1/c
Charles Talyai	Seaman 1/c
James Carwile Thomas	Seaman 1/c
Herbert Leslie Tyler	Seaman 1/c

Voyage 2 — September 11, 1943 to November 3, 1943

Ports of Call:	New York, New York
	Jersey City, New Jersey
	Liverpool, England
	New York, New York

Crew:[2]

Oscar Southerland	Master

---

[2] Because the official log for voyage No. 2 is not available there is no source of merchant crew names for voyage No. 2. The names listed are those who made voyages No. 1 and No. 3 and logically would have been on voyage No. 2.

Charles Christenson	Chief Officer
Frank Pellegrino	Second Officer
Oliver Morgan	Third Officer
Thomas J. Ender	Purser
Theodore Samaras	Carpenter
Donald Corbett	AB
Joseph Cadogen	AB
Donald L. Moors?	AB
Francis McCormick	OS
Coleman Schneider	Deck Cadet
Richardson Montgomery	Chief Engineer
James D'Andrea	Engine Cadet
Lee Ah Yok	Third Cook

Armed Guard:

Charles L. Foote	Ensign
Herbert Emmett Landrum	Coxswain
James Francis Goodsell	Gunner's Mate 3/c
Morgan Casto Williams	Gunner's Mate 3/c
Charles Robert Garbett	Seaman 3/c
Harmon Eugene Morick	Radioman 3/c
Lewis Edwin Hudson	Radioman 3/c
Howard Leon Campbell	Seaman 1/c
William James Chisolm	Seaman 1/c
Armando Frank Felci	Seaman 1/c
Philip Frederick Gould	Seaman 1/c
Thomas W. Hodgson, Jr.	Seaman 1/c
Kenneth Lloyd Holsapple	Seaman 1/c
John Joseph Hunt	Seaman 1/c
Georges Jack Serra	Seaman 1/c
Jerome Edgar Shaw	Seaman 1/c
Edward Jardine Smedley, Jr.	Seaman 1/c
Raymond Smith	Seaman 1/c
Ludwig Joseph Stojek	Seaman 1/c
Alvis Franklin Straughan	Seaman 1/c
Gildo Ralph Surdi	Seaman 1/c
Clarence Swisher	Seaman 1/c
Edward Anthony Sznukowski	Seaman 1/c
Charles Talyai	Seaman 1/c
James Carwile Thomas	Seaman 1/c
Herbert Leslie Tyler	Seaman 1/c
Robert Nelson Caron	Seaman 1/c

Joined in New York on September 13, 1943:
William James Rose   Seaman 1/c
Robert Martin Howell   Seaman 1/c

Voyage 3 — November 19, 1943 to March 24, 1944

Ports of Call: New York, New York
                                  Loch Ewe, Scotland
                                  Methil, Firth of Forth, Scotland
                                  Immingham, England
                                  Methil, Firth of Forth, Scotland
                                  Loch Ewe, Scotland
                                  St. John, New Brunswick
                                  Halifax, Nova Scotia
                                  Oban, Scotland
                                  Leith, Scotland
                                  Loch Ewe, Scotland
                                  New York, New York

Crew:
Oscar Southerland   Master
Charles Christenson   Chief Officer
Frank Pellegrino   Second Officer
Oliver Morgan   Third Officer
Robert Milby   Radio Officer
Louis Harris   Purser
Theodore Samaras   Carpenter
Alton Cook   Boatswain (Bosun)
Terry Trendell   AB (Able-Bodied Seaman)
Walter Weingaertner   AB
Sherman Valentine   AB
Donald Corbett   AB
Daniel Bron   AB
Joseph Cadogan   AB
Joseph Cioffi   OS (Ordinary Seaman)
Sebastian DeManuel   OS
Francis McCormick   OS
Coleman Schneider   Deck Cadet
Richardson Montgomery   Chief Engineer
Donald Morrison   First Assistant Engineer
Walter Whitney   Second Assistant Engineer

William Watson	Third Assistant Engineer
Carlos Pinheiro	Junior Engineer
Tom Hall	Oiler
Michael Wasko	Oiler
Clarence Bonem	Oiler
Vernon Joell	FWT (Fireman/Watertender)
Henry Ruppert	FWT
Martin Twiggs	FWT
Isaac Cuevas	Wiper
Jose Tiban	Wiper
James D'Andrea	Engine Cadet
Percy Martin	Chief Steward
Ming Wee Sung	Chief Cook
Yeu Wee Hie	Second Cook
Lee Ah Yok	Third Cook
George Quistgaard	Utility
Francis Start	Saloon Messman
Noel Cramer	Messman
Jose Dias	Utility
Dong Ah Wee	Utility
Yeo Sung Hai	Utility
Albert E. Haas	Purser
Russell J. Smith	Third Officer

Armed Guard:

Charles L. Foote	Ensign
Robert Nelson Caron	Seaman 1/c
Herbert Emmett Landrum	Coxswain
Morgan Casto Williams	Gunner's Mate 3/c
Charles Robert Garbett	Seaman 3/c
Harmon Eugene Morick	Radioman 3/c
Lewis Edwin Hudson	Radioman 3/c
Howard Leon Campbell	Seaman 1/c
William James Chisolm	Seaman 1/c
Armando Frank Felci	Seaman 1/c
Philip Frederick Gould	Seaman 1/c
Thomas W. Hodgson, Jr.	Seaman 1/c
Kenneth Lloyd Holsapple	Seaman 1/c
John Joseph Hunt	Seaman 1/c
William J. Rose	Seaman 1/c
Georges Jack Serra	Seaman 1/c
Jerome Edgar Shaw	Seaman 1/c

Edward Jardine Smedley, Jr.   Seaman 1/c
Raymond Smith   Seaman 1/c
Ludwig Joseph Stojek   Seaman 1/c
Alvis Franklin Straughan   Seaman 1/c
Gildo Ralph Surdi   Seaman 1/c
Clarence Swisher   Seaman 1/c
Charles Talyai   Seaman 1/c
James Carwile Thomas   Seaman 1/c
Herbert Leslie Tyler   Seaman 1/c

Joined in New York on November 8, 1943:
Buford Veitch Mitchell   Seaman 1/c
Edwin Lewis Williams   Seaman 1/c
Jack William Roberts   Radioman 3/c
Daniel Glendyn Bandy   Seaman 1/c
Robert Noble Mason   Seaman 1/c

Joined Halifax on January 27, 1944:
Allen R. Memhard, Jr.   Lieutenant
Alfonse Adolph De Smedt   Master

Joined in Halifax on February 6, 1944:
Joe Emmett Morris   Seaman 1/c

Voyage 4 — March 25, 1944 to October 12, 1944.

Ports of call:		New York, New York
		Brooklyn, New York
		Newport, Wales
		Gourock-the-Clyde, Scotland
		Southampton, England
	1	Omaha Beachhead, Normandy
		Southampton, England
	2	Omaha Beachhead, Normandy
		Southampton, England
		Belfast, Ireland
	3	Utah Beachhead, Normandy
		Southampton, England
	4	Utah Beachhead, Normandy,
		Southampton, England
	5	Omaha, Beachhead, Normandy
		Southampton, England

6	Omaha Beachhead, Normandy
	Southampton, England
7	Utah Beachhead, Normandy
	Southampton, England
8	Utah Beachhead, Normandy
	Southampton, England
9	Utah Beachhead, Normandy
	Southampton, England
10	Utah Beachhead, Normandy
	Southampton, England
11	Utah Beachhead, Normandy
	Cherbourg, France
	Mumbles Point, Swansea, England
	Milford Haven, England
	New York, New York

Crew:

A. A. DeSmedt	Master
Frank Pellegrino	Chief Officer
Oliver Morgan	Second Officer
Edward Seymour	Third Officer
Robert A. Milby	First Radio
Gerrit deWaard	Second Radio
Albert E. Haas	Purser
Thomas McGeehan	Cadet
Henry Kusel	Cadet
Theodore Samaras	Carpenter
Alton Cook	Boatswain (Bosun)
Trendell L. Terry	AB (Able-Bodied seaman)
Sherman A. Valentine	AB
Daniel Bron	AB
Donald H. Corbett	AB
Henry Klittsgaard	AB
James Rudesill	AB
Louis S. Garcia	OS (Ordinary Seaman)
Osborne P. Jones	OS
Emil Bennes	OS
Richardson Montgomery	Chief Engineer
Ludvig Lauritsen	First Assistant Engineer
Walter C. Whitney	Second Assistant Engineer
William L. Watson	Third Assistant Engineer
Harris Wentworth	Junior Engineer

Vernon R. Joell	Oiler
Francis E. Erdmann	Oiler
Herman H. Kuber	Oiler
Martin J. Twiggs	FWT (Fireman WaterTender)
Ernest A. Ooghe	FWT
Jose C. Tibau	FWT
Hubert Miller	Wiper
Olaf M. Saxvik	Wiper
Lo Kite	Steward
Ming Wee Sung	Chief Cook
Geo Wee Hie	Second Cook
Foo Hee Song	Third Cook
Noel Cramer	Messman
John Yacynik	Messman
George M. Wray	Messman
Jose N. Dias	Utility
Dong Ah Wee	Utility
Yeo Sung Hai	Utility
Herbert Doyle	AB

Armed Guard:

Allen R. Memhard, Jr.	Lieutenant
Daniel Glendyn Bandy	Coxswain
Robert Noble Mason	Seaman 3/c
James Jones	Gunner's Mate 3/c
James Davis Potts	Gunner's Mate 3/c
Morgan Casto Williams	Gunner's Mate 3/c
Wallace James Hardin	Seaman 3/c
Joseph William Bires	Seaman 1/c
Samuel Clifton Christian	Seaman 1/c
Luther Wetzel Counts	Seaman 1/c
Stanley Morrell Cunningham	Seaman 1/c
Fred Dennison	Seaman 1/c
Alvin Leroy Huffstetler	Seaman 1/c
William Robert Gorman	Seaman 1/c
Albert Frederick Helbling	Seaman 1/c
James Lamonica	Seaman 1/c
John Thomas Murphy	Seaman 1/c
Robert Roy Pilcher	Seaman 1/c
John Paul Planeta	Seaman 1/c
Robert Jerome Robichaud	Seaman 1/c
Melvin David Rubin	Seaman 1/c

Richard Paul Savering	Seaman 1/c
Elbert Ray Sharpe	Seaman 1/c
John Edwin Sirrine	Seaman 1/c
Donald Harvey Slaight	Seaman 1/c
Clarence Alvin Swanson	Seaman 1/c
Donald Oirse Weeks	Seaman 1/c

Voyage 5 — October 14, 1944 to December 15, 1944

Ports of call:

Hoboken, New Jersey
Cristobal, Canal Zone
Antofagasta, Chile
Callao, Peru
Balboa, Canal Zone
West Wego, Louisiana
New Orleans, Louisiana

Crew:

Arthur J. Gunderson	Master
R. H. Scott	Chief Officer
R. N. Cruickshanks	Second Officer
W. J. Ganley	Third Officer
G. J. de Waard	Radio Operator
Joao Thiago	Bosun
T. Samaras	Carpenter
Arthur Graham	AB (Able-Bodied seaman)
Trendell Terry	AB
Louis Salas	AB
Manuel Lopez	AB
Angel Targa	AB
William Roper	AB
Robert W. Glasgow	OS (Ordinary Seaman)
Cornelius Duffy	OS
Louis Larouche	OS
R. Montgomery	Chief Engineer
W. Wallace	First Assistant Engineer
Ralph Prado	Second Assistant engineer
Carl A. Scharpf	Third Assistant Engineer
Joseph Leifken	Jr. Enginer
Richard Bush	Oiler
Paul Kemper	Oiler
V. Joell	Oiler

M. Twiggs	FWT (Fireman WaterTender)
J. Tiban	FWT
E. Ondesko	Wiper
R. Camelo	Wiper
J. H. Zoetjes	Wiper
Philip Hegarty	Ch. Steward
Tela Owens	Second Cook
Low Bow Eng	2nd Cook
Jose Dias	3rd Cook
David C. Smith	Messman
D.D. Magers	Messman
J. Esposito	Messman
Redames Arias, Jr.	Utility
W. S. Halliday	Utility
H. Wentworth	Oiler
E. A. Haney	Purser

Armed Guard:

Norman Evans Robinson	Ensign
James Joseph Doyle	Coxswain
Robert Arthur Crocker	Gunner's mate 3/c
Henry Walter Morieko	Gunner's mate 3/c
Louis Bator	Seaman 1/c
LeRoy George Bartels	Seaman 1/c
Clarence Earle Barnett	Seaman 1/c
Earl Roy Carver	Seaman 1/c
James Daniel Casey	Seaman 1/c
Charles Grant Conklin	Seaman 1/c
Orval Franklin Crumley	Seaman 1/c
Johnny McDonald Curtis	Seaman 1/c
John Wesley Davis	Seaman 1/c
Marion LaVerne Henzen	Seaman 1/c
Cleveland Joseph Hassler	Seaman 1/c
David Bicking Kennedy	Seaman 1/c
Charles Edgar Lewis	Seaman 1/c
Theodore S. Martin	Seaman 1/c
Albert Joseph Ogonowski	Seaman 1/c
George Joseph Poskie	Seaman 1/c
Joseph Peter Salandino	Seaman 1/c
Robert James Swan	Seaman 1/c
Vernon Earl Williams	Seaman 1/c
Robert Lee Wilson	Seaman 1/c

Kermit Lee Roy	Seaman 1/c
William Clayton Kuhlman	Seaman 1/c
Joseph Walker	Seaman 1/c
John R. Andrews	Seaman 1/c
Wesley R. Armour	Seaman 1/c
Louis Elmer Veatch	Seaman 1/c

Voyage 6 — December 16, 1944 to July 10, 1945

Ports of call:
New Orleans, Louisiana
Houston, Texas
Balboa, Canal Zone
Manus, Admiralty Islands
    (Seeadler Harbor)
Hollandia, New Guinea
Tacloban, Philippine Islands
San Jose, Philippine Islands
Subic Bay, Philippine Islands
Hollandia, New Guinea
Oro Bay, New Guinea
Hollandia, New Guinea
Subic Bay, Philippine Islands
San Fernando, Philippine Islands
San Francisco, California

Crew:

Oscar J. Gunderson	Master
Arthur Antony	Chief Mate (Acting)
William Ganley	Second Mate (Acting)
John Crosby	Third Mate
Edwin Haney	Purser
Gerritt de Waard	Chief Radio Operator
John Callahan	Second Radio Operator
Merill Hubbard	Third Radio Operator
Theodore Samaras	Carpenter
William Sterling	Boatswain (Bosun)
Louis Salas	AB (Able Seaman)
Manuel Lopez	AB
Paul Stallings	AB
Spellman Patterson	AB
Vincent Sunday	AB (Acting)
Max Carman	AB (Acting)

Paul Kinesiak	OS (Ordinary Seaman)
David Daly	OS
Carroll Douglas	OS
Richardson Montgomery	Chief Engineer
John Tagert	First Assistant Engineer
John E. Torppa	Second Assistant Engineer
Roy E. Simpson	Third Assistant Engineer
Harris Wentworth	Junior Engineer
Paul Kemfer	Oiler
Clinton Lanier	Oiler
Melton Brooks	Oiler
John Wright	Oiler
Harold Anderson	FWT (Fireman WaterTender)
Louis Ordonez	FWT
Wilbert Morris	FWT/Wiper
Malcolm Louney	FWT
Jose Tiban	FWT
Billie Hemphill	Wiper
Stanislaus Wajdo	Wiper
Howard Edwards	Steward
Philip Hegarty	Chief Cook
Edward Denny	Second Cook
Charles Mestoyen	Assistant Cook
Jose Dias	Utility
John Louse	Utility
Ivan Vozquez	Utility
Carlos Mora	Utility
Emmette Thomas	Messman
Robert Surmall	Messman
Jeff Fragler	Messman
Don Vaughn	Messman
Joseph Martin	OS
Thomas Carter	Boatswain

Armed Guard:

Norman Evans Robinson	Ensign
Robert Arthur Crocker	Gunner's mate 3/c
Henry Walter Morieko	Gunner's mate 3/c
Louis Bator	Seaman 1/c
LeRoy George Bartels	Seaman 1/c
Clarence Earle Barnett	Seaman 1/c
Earl Roy Carver	Seaman 1/c

James Daniel Casey	Seaman 1/c
Orval Franklin Crumley	Seaman 1/c
Johnny McDonald Curtis	Seaman 1/c
Marion LaVerne Henzen	Seaman 1/c
Cleveland Joseph Hassler	Seaman 1/c
David Bicking Kennedy	Seaman 1/c
Theodore S. Martin	Seaman 1/c
Albert Joseph Ogonowski	Seaman 1/c
George Joseph Poskie	Seaman 1/c
Joseph Peter Salandino	Seaman 1/c
Robert James Swan	Seaman 1/c
Vernon Earl Williams	Seaman 1/c
Robert Lee Wilson	Seaman 1/c
Kermit Lee Roy	Seaman 1/c
William Clayton Kuhlman	Seaman 1/c
John R. Andrews	Seaman 1/c
Louis Elmer Veatch	Seaman 1/c

Joined May 18, 1945 at Hollandia.

Ballard Lee Howell, Sr.	Gunner's Mate 3/c
Henry H. Dent, Jr.	Seaman 1/c
Eryl B. Dickinson	Seaman 1/c

Voyage 7 — July 11 1945 to January 17, 1946

Ports of call:
San Francisco, California
San Pedro, California
Port Darwin, Australia
Calcutta, India
Shanghai, China
Manila, Philippine Islands
Fremantle, Australia
San Francisco, California

Crew:

George Gerdes	Master
Martin C. Moen	Chief Mate
David Holmes	Second Mate
Charles R. Kent	Third Mate
Roy E. Petherbridge	Chief Radio Operator
Edward L. Hanyak	Second Radio Operator
Bruce S. Meador	Purser/Pharmacist

Robert Gallagher	Boatswain (Bosun)
Carlos Q. Kellner	Carpenter
Frank Novick	AB (Able Bodied Seaman)
Phillip J. Brox	AB
Robert J. Pardy	AB
George Cicic	AB
William C. Coats	AB (Acting)
Roy Anderson	AB (Acting)
Pedro A. Delgado	OS (Ordinary Seaman)
Layton E. Branson	OS
Oscar D. Pearson	OS
Carl B. Weyls	Chief Engineer
George A. Swanson	First Assistant Engineer
Donald E. Kranich	Second Assistant Engineer
Charles N. McGrinty	Third Assistant Engineer
Theodore J. Pennington	Deck Engineer
Thomas L. Schinskey	Oiler
Robert H. Anderson	Oiler
Harold W. Wolfe	Oiler
Manuel Taibo	FWT (Fireman WaterTender)
Charles E Hord	FWT
Howard W. Fogle	FWT
Albert Giaccki, Jr.	Wiper
Edward A. Burtch	Wiper
Juanito P. Lazano	Steward
Joseph Candias	Chief Cook
Robert C. Flowers	Second Cook and Baker
Jose D. N. Dias	Third Cook
Aloys F. La Gates	Utility Messman
Morris Shaw	Utility Messman
Richard C. Tozer, Jr.	Utility Messman
George E. Ward, Jr.	Utility Messman
Joseph T. Sizemore	Utility Messman
Roy O. Mason	Utility Messman
Francis D. Porter	Utility Messman
Rafael Santos	Oiler
Eimar Argerup	Chief Mate
J. Clarke	Galleyman
Kennedy Watt	AB

Armed Guard:

Ambrose Patrick McGowan	Lieutenant

John R. Andrews	Signalman 3/c
Louis Bator	Gunner's Mate 3/c
Robert Arthur Crocker	Gunner's mate 3/c
James Joseph Doyle	Coxswain
Ballard Lee Howell, Sr.	Gunner's Mate 3/c
William Clayton Kuhlman	Signalman 3/c
Theodore S. Martin	Coxswain
Henry Walter Morieko	Gunner's mate 3/c
George Joseph Poskie	Gunner's Mate 3/c
Robert Lee Wilson	Coxswain
LeRoy George Bartels	Seaman 1/c
Clarence Earle Barnett	Seaman 1/c
Earl Roy Carver	Seaman 1/c
James Daniel Casey	Seaman 1/c
Orval Franklin Crumley	Seaman 1/c
Johnny McDonald Curtis	Seaman 1/c
Henry H. Dent, Jr.	Seaman 1/c
Eryl Dickinson	Seaman 1/c
Marion LaVerne Henzen	Seaman 1/c
David Bicking Kennedy	Seaman 1/c
Albert Joseph Ogonowski	Seaman 1/c
Joseph Peter Salandino	Seaman 1/c
Robert James Swan	Seaman 1/c
Louis Elmer Veatch	Seaman 1/c
Vernon Earl Williams	Seaman 1/c

Joined July 16, 1945 in San Francisco

Bert Erwin, Jr.	Gunner's Mate 3/c

Joined July 23, 1945 in San Francisco

Ambrose Patrick McGowan	Lieutenant

Joined July 28, 1945 in San Francisco

Ira Jim Cook	Seaman 1/c
Clifford Francis Bartel	Seaman 2/c
Charles Thomas Cunningham	Seaman 1/c
Joseph Sherlock Davey	Seaman 1/c
Leon Flores	Seaman 1/c
Paul Peter Lafave	Seaman 1/c
Thomas Frederick Kelly	Seaman 1/c
George A. Toalson	Seaman 1/c

| Casey Lonzo Walker | Seaman 1/c |
| Frankie Lee Lucas | Seaman 1/c |

Armed Guard on board after Manila
Theodore S. Martin, Coxswain
R. J. Swan, Seaman 1/c

Passengers boarded in Fremantle.
Arthur, Catherine Lilliam
Arthur, Maria Florence (daughter) age 6 months
Benesh, Edith Florence
Benesh, Robert Antone (son) age 2 years, 2 months
Czatynski, Doris Lesley
Dexter, Grace
Guillemette, Dorothy Leslie
Konkel, Doreen
Konkel, Elsworth Leroy (son) age 8 months
Marks, Patricia
Yocum, Brenda Kathleen
Quackenbush, Thora Venetia

APPENDIX D
THE 1994 NORMANDY
VOYAGE CREW

Name	Position	Voyage Leg
Ahlgren, Ralph	Oiler	Le Havre-San Francisco
Alexander, Tom	Oiler	Panama-London
Anderson, Gene	Oiler	San Francisco-Le Havre
Anderson, Nils	Wiper	Rouen-San Francisco
Arellano, Rudolph	Messman	San Francisco-London
Aris, David	FWT	Le Havre-San Francisco
Bara, Stanley	3rd Asst. Eng.	Jacksonville-San Francisco
Beckwith, Susannah	Storekeeper	Cherbourg-Rouen
Bennett, William	AB	ALL
Black, Robert	Deck Utility/OS	Rouen-San Francisco
Borowiec, John	Messman	Portland-Jacksonville
Bosch, Maria	Wiper	London-Le Havre
Brannon, Richard	Chief Engineer	ALL
Burke, Norman	Oiler	San Francisco-Panama
Burke, Patrick	Deck Utility	Jacksonville-San Francisco
Burnett, Robert	Carpenter	ALL
Callahan, Joseph	Deck Utility	San Francisco-Portsmouth
Cannady, William	Oiler	Le Havre-Baltimore
Caron, Jean-Paul	Wiper	Panama-San Francisco
Carraher, John	Messman/Gunner	ALL
Casaletto, Louis	Messman	Rouen-San Francisco
Concannon, William	Oiler	San Francisco-Portsmouth
Conrady, Monica	Storekeeper	Portsmouth-Le Havre
Conrady, Raymond	Second Mate	ALL
Conwell, James	AB	San Francisco-Le Havre
Crocker, Robert	Messman	Portland-Jacksonville
Cumming, John	Engine Utility	Jacksonville-San Francisco
Currie, Richard	FWT	San Francisco-London; Baltimore-San Francisco

Dewing, Fred	2nd Asst. Eng.	Portsmouth-London
Dickerson, William	Third Mate	Portsmouth-London
Dow, Gary	Engine Utility	Portland-Baltimore
Duncan, William	Deck Engineer, 3rd Asst. Eng.	ALL
Duncan, Dorothea	Storekeeper/ Messman	Portsmouth-London; Portland-San Francisco
Emery , Michael	OS	San Francisco-Cherbourg
Fairfield, William	AB	Le Havre-San Francisco
Farras, James	Second Cook	ALL
Fenton, William	OS	Jacksonville-San Francisco
Fitzgerald, John	AB	Jacksonville-San Francisco
Franklin, Wallace	3rd Asst. Eng.	Kings Point-Baltimore
Geronimo, Lou	Third Mate	Le Havre-Portland
Gillis, James	3rd Asst. Eng.	San Francisco-Panama
	2nd Asst. Eng.	Panama-Portsmouth
Gisslow, Robert	Radio Operator	ALL
Goldman, Brian	FWT	Rouen-San Francisco
Goldwaithe, Lawrence	Oiler	Le Havre-Baltimore
Gregory, Alvin	Storekeeper	Cherbourg-Rouen
Guzzetta, Joe	Messman	Portland-San Francisco
Haslam, Kenneth	Doctor	ALL
Hill, Richard	Oiler	San Francisco-Le Havre; Baltimore-San Francisco
Hobbs, George	2nd Asst. Eng.	London-Le Havre
Hochstraser, Alex	FWT	ALL
Hook, Clifford	OS/AB	Le Havre-San Francisco
Hooper, Marci	Business Manager	Portsmouth-Cherbourg
Jaffee, Walter	Chief Mate	ALL
Jahn, George	Master	ALL
Jellinek, Arlene	Storekeeper	Cherbourg-Le Havre
Jellinek, Steve	FWT	London-Le Havre
Jennings, Charles	Messman	London-Portland
Keinanen, Sven	Third Mate	London-Le Havre
Kaplan, Maxine	Storekeeper	Portland-Jacksonville; Long Beach-San Francisco
Kilduff, Kevin	2nd Asst. Eng.	Le Havre-San Francisco
Kinsella, Tim	Asst. Radio Op.	Southampton-Le Havre
Kreidler, Carl	Gunner	San Francisco-Le Havre
Lawrence, Jo	Storekeeper	Portsmouth-London
Le Pendu, François	Engine Utility	San Francisco-Le Havre
Linderman, John	AB	Rouen-Portland

Lingenfield, Edgar	FWT	ALL
Londos, Erika	Storekeeper	Portsmouth-London
Lyse, Peter	Third Mate	San Francisco-Portsmouth
Martino, Allen	Chief Cook	ALL
Masterson, Wes	AB	London-Le Havre
Malls, William	3rd Asst. Eng.	Panama-Le Havre
McCafferty, Patrick	Messman/Utility	ALL
McMurtry, Bruce	OS	San Francisco-Portsmouth
Miller, Hans	3rd Asst. Eng.	San Francisco-Panama
Miller, James	AB	ALL
Mosholder, Russell	Chief Steward	ALL
Mooney, Charlie	Wiper	London-Le Havre
Mooney, George	Oiler	London-Le Havre
Noiseux, Robert	FWT	San Francisco-London
Nolte, Carl	Deck Utility/OS	San Francisco-London; Panama-San Francisco
Otterberg, Carl	Staff Captain	European ports
Otterberg, Nell	Storekeeper	European ports
Palange, Tim	2nd Asst. Eng. 1st Asst. Eng.	ALL
Patterson, Ann	Storekeeper	Portsmouth-Le Havre
Patterson, Thomas J.	Commodore	ALL
Phelps, Otis	Third Mate	Portland-San Francisco
Pubill, Eduardo	Third Cook	ALL
Radovich, Raymond	OS	London-Le Havre
Rapp, Tony	Deck Utility	Jacksonville-San Francisco
Reed, Richard	Boatswain	San Francisco-Le Havre
Reidy, Edward	Wiper	Le Havre-Panama
Rivers, John	Storekeeper	Portsmouth-London
Robson, Ron	Store Manager	Portsmouth-Le Havre
Robson, Ruth	Storekeeper/ Messman	Portsmouth-San Francisco
Rodd, Denis	Oiler	Panama-Chatham
Rowlands, William	AB	ALL
Schneider, Coleman	Messman/Utility	San Francisco-Panama
Sears, Arnold	Wiper	San Francisco-London
Shields, Martin	OS	ALL
Sinnott, Philip	AB	San Francisco-Le Havre
Smith, Edward	Deck Engineer	San Francisco-Chatham; Rouen-San Francisco
Smith, Michael	Deck Utility	Portsmouth-London
Smith, Ronald	Messman/Gunner	ALL

Sommerauer, Otto	Gunners Mate	San Francisco-Le Havre
Speight, Jeff	2nd Asst. Eng.	Le Havre-Baltimore
Speight, Barbara	Storekeeper	Cherbourg-Le Havre; Portland-Baltimore
Steenburn, Kenneth	Oiler	Jacksonville-San Francisco
Steinberg, Mary	Wiper	San Francisco-Chatham
Taber, Arthur	Storekeeper	Portsmouth-Le Havre
Taylor, Nathan	Deck Cadet	San Francisco-Rouen
Vincenzo, Frank	Oiler	Le Havre-Baltimore
Von der Porten, Edward	Storekeeper	Portsmouth-London
Von der Porten, Saryl	Storekeeper	Portsmouth-London
Wade, James	Purser	ALL
Warren, Dirk	Engine Cadet	San Francisco-Rouen
Wefald, Martin	AB/Bosun	ALL
Williams, Greg	Messman/Utility	ALL
Williams, Bill	Oiler	Portsmouth-Le Havre
Wood, Samuel	OS/AB	ALL
Worthy, Stephan	1st Asst. Eng.	San Francisco-Panama
Yates, Jean	OS	San Francisco-Le Havre

DOCENT VOLUNTEERS IN EUROPE:
Addie, Ted
Banks, Arnold
Cole, Pierre
Curtis, Darwin
Dallas, Charles
Egan, Michael
Fawcett, Bernard J .
Guikink, Hans
Hook, Jean
Tofield, Robert
Turner, Ron
Wartenberg, Charles

BIBLIOGRAPHY

Anderson, Robert Earle. *The Merchant Marine & World Frontiers*.

Blackburn, Graham. *Overlook Dictionary of Nautical Terms*. Woodstock, N.Y.: The Overlook Press, 1981.

Brouwer, Norman J. *International Register of Historic Ships*. Annapolis, Maryland: Naval Institute Press, 1985.

Bunker, John Gorley. *Liberty Ships, The Ugly Ducklings of World War II*. Annapolis: U.S. Naval Institute, 1972.

Cohen, Susan. *Historic Preservation*. "World War II Ugly Duckling Comes Home." March-April 1980.

Hahn, Herbert Paul. *American Mariner, A Documentary Biography*. Kings Point, New York: American Merchant Marine Museum Foundation, 1990.

Haws, Duncan and Alex Hurst. *The Maritime History of the World - 2*. Brighton, Sussex: Teredo Books, Ltd. 1985.

Hughes, Terry and John Costello. *Battle of the Atlantic, The*. New York: The Dial Press/James Wade, 1977.

Jones, Herbert G. *Portland Ships Are Good Ships*. Portland, Maine: Machigonne Press, 1945.

Kooiman, William. *The Grace Ships, 1869-1968*. Point Reyes, California: Komar Publishing, 1990.

Kortum, Karl and Adm. Thomas J. Patterson. "How We Saved the *Jeremiah O'Brien*." *Sea History*. Winter 1988-89.

Ladd, J. D. *Assault From the Sea 1939-45*. New York City: Hippocrene Books, Inc., 1976

Levingston, Steven E. *Historic Ships of San Francisco*. San Francisco: Chronicle Books, 1984.

Maclay, Edgar S. *History of American Privateers, A*. 1899.

Mangone, Gerard J. *Marine Policy For America, The United States At Sea*. Lexington: D.C. Heath and Company, 1977.

Matloff, Maurice. Editor. *World War II, A Concise Military History of America's All-Out, Two-Front War*. New York City: Galahad Books, 1982.

Medway News. Friday, 25 March 1994. Medway Dockyard Supplement.

Mitchell, C. Bradford. *Every Kind of Shipwork.* New York: 1981

Morison, Samuel Eliot. *Invasion of France and Germany, 1944-1945, The.* Boston: Little, Brown and Company, 1957.

Palmer, M.B. *We fight With Merchant Ships.* Indianapolis: Bobbs Merrill Co.

Pitt, Barrie and the editors of Time-Life Books, *Battle of the Atlantic, The.* Vol. 5 of the series World War II. Alexandria, Virginia: 1977.

Rubin, Hal. "The Last of the 'Libertys'." *Oceans.* March 1979.

Ryan, Cornelius. *Longest Day, June 6, 1944, The.* New York: Simon and Schuster, 1959.

Sawyer, L.A. and W. H. Mitchell. *The Liberty Ships*, Second Edition. London: Lloyd's of London Press Ltd., 1985.

Schofield, William G. *Eastward the Convoys.* Chicago: Rand McNally & Company, 1965.

Sherman, Rev. Andrew M. *Life of Jeremiah O'Brien.* Morristown, N. J.: Jerseyman Office, 1902.

Steinberg, Rafael and the editors of Time-Life Books. *Island Fighting.* Vol. 10 of the series World War II. Alexandria, Virginia: 1977.

Taylor, J. E. *Last Passage, The.* London: George Allen & Unwin Ltd., 1946.

United States Advisory Committee on the Merchant Marine. *Report Of The President's Advisory Committee On The Merchant Marine.* Washington: GPO, 1947.

Wall, Robert. *Ocean Liners.* Secaucus, New Jersey: Chartwell Books, Inc. 1977.

Zich, Arthur and the editors of Time-Life Books. *The Rising Sun.* Vol. 4 of the series World War II. Alexandria, Virginia: 1977.

INDEX